LEGENDA

European Humanities Research Centre

University of Oxford

ASSUMING THE LIGHT
THE PARISIAN LITERARY APPRENTICESHIP
OF MIGUEL ANGEL ASTURIAS

THE EUROPEAN HUMANITIES RESEARCH CENTRE

UNIVERSITY OF OXFORD

The European Humanities Research Centre of the University of Oxford organizes a range of academic activities, including conferences and workshops, and publishes scholarly works under its own imprint, LEGENDA. Within Oxford, the EHRC bridges, at the research level, the main humanities faculties: Modern Languages, English, Modern History, Literae Humaniores, Music and Theology. The Centre stimulates interdisciplinary research collaboration throughout these subject areas and provides an Oxford base for advanced researchers in the humanities.

The Centre's publications programme focuses on making available the results of advanced research in medieval and modern languages and related interdisciplinary areas. An Editorial Board, whose members are drawn from across the British university system, covers the principal European languages. Titles include works on French, German, Italian, Portuguese, Russian and Spanish literature. In addition, the EHRC co-publishes with the Society for French Studies, the British Comparative Literature Association and the Modern Humanities Research Association. The Centre also publishes *Oxford German Studies* and *Film Studies*, and has launched a Special Lecture Series under the LEGENDA imprint.

Enquiries about the Centre's publishing activities should be addressed to:
Professor Malcolm Bowie, Director

Further information:
Kareni Bannister, Senior Publications Officer
European Humanities Research Centre
University of Oxford
47 Wellington Square, Oxford OX1 2JF
enquiries@ehrc.ox.ac.uk
www.ehrc.ox.ac.uk

Assuming the Light
The Parisian Literary Apprenticeship of Miguel Angel Asturias

❖

STEPHEN HENIGHAN

LEGENDA

European Humanities Research Centre
University of Oxford
1999

Published by the
European Humanities Research Centre
of the University of Oxford
47 Wellington Square
Oxford OX1 2JF

LEGENDA is the publications imprint of the
European Humanities Research Centre

ISBN 1 900755 19 X

First published 1999

British Library Cataloguing in Publication Data
A CIP catalogue record for this book is available from the British Library

© European Humanities Research Centre of the University of Oxford 1999

LEGENDA series designed by Cox Design Partnership, Witney, Oxon
Printed in Great Britain by
Information Press
Eynsham
Oxford OX8 1JJ

Chief Copy-Editor: Genevieve Hawkins

1002672405

CONTENTS

ACKNOWLEDGEMENTS

I would like to thank Robin Fiddian for his support on various fronts of my academic career over a number of years. I am grateful to Clive Griffin for his meticulous reading of an earlier version, to Mark Millington for suggestions on the overall form, to Ian Michael and John Rutherford for useful comments on the first three chapters, and to Jeremy Ahearne and Ramona Fotiade for help with, respectively, Julia Kristeva and Surrealism.

My research was facilitated by the courteous co-operation I received from the staffs of several libraries: Taylorian Institution (Oxford), Modern Languages Faculty Library (Oxford), Maison Française (Oxford), Salle des manuscrits, Bibliothèque nationale (Paris) and Centro de Investigaciones Regionales Meso-Americanas (CIRMA) (Antigua, Guatemala).

I was able to undertake this project thanks to a Doctoral Fellowship from the Social Sciences and Humanities Research Council of Canada and an Overseas Research Students Award from the Committee of Vice-Chancellors and Principals of the Universities of the United Kingdom. Grants from the Pollard Fund, Wadham College, and the Interfaculty Committee on Latin American Studies, University of Oxford, assisted me with my research travel.

Versions of parts of this book have been published in *The Modern Language Review, Comparative Literature Studies, Hispamérica, Journal of Hispanic Research, Romance Studies* and *Tesserae*.

ABBREVIATIONS

BP	M. A. Asturias, 'La barba provisional', in *Novelas y cuentos de juventud*, ed. Claude Couffon (Paris: Centre de Recherches de l'Institut d'Etudes Hispaniques, 1971)
EA	M. A. Asturias, *El Alhajadito* (Buenos Aires: Goyanarte, 1961)
HM	M. A. Asturias, *Hombres de maíz* (1949; Nanterre: Centre de Recherches Latino-Américaines, 1992)
LA	Robert Desnos, *La liberté ou l'amour! suivi de Deuil pour Deuil* (Paris: Gallimard, 1962)
LG	M. A. Asturias, *Leyendas de Guatemala* (1930; Buenos Aires: Editorial Losada, 1957)
NC	M. A. Asturias, *Novelas y cuentos de juventud*, ed. Claude Couffon (Paris: Centre de Recherches de l'Institut d'Etudes Hispaniques, 1971)
SP	M. A. Asturias, *El señor presidente* (1946; Buenos Aires: Losada, 1991)

INTRODUCTION

'Would you like to go to South America, Jake?' he asked.
'No.'
'Why not?'
'I don't know. I never wanted to go. Too expensive. You can see
  all the South Americans you want in Paris anyway.'
'They're not the real South Americans.'
'They look awfully real to me.'

ERNEST HEMINGWAY, *The Sun Also Rises*[1]

'I am Mexican by will and by imagination', Carlos Fuentes has
written.[2] He was not the first Spanish American writer to discover
that a cultural identity is created, through experience, determination
and self-consciousness, rather than inherited. For many years Paris was
the central star in the constellation of Spanish American literature: it
was to Paris that young writers came to discover themselves as writers
and, increasingly, as Spanish Americans. Angel Rama argues that the
centrality of Paris to Spanish American literature

nace del esfuerzo por la independencia cultural que las antiguas colonias de
España y Portugal desarrollaron desde la época de la Independencia,
buscando en Francia—que ya era la capital de la modernidad—una nutrición
espiritual acorde con los tiempos. Desde el viaje de Esteban Echeverría, en
1825, hasta el viaje de Julio Cortázar en 1953 [*sic*], no hay interrupción en el
fluir de escritores latinoamericanos que van a París, aunque ese movimiento
admite algunas fechas óptimas en este siglo, como 1900, 1925, 1950, que
corresponden a otros tantos epicentros del proceso cultural francés.[3]

The generation of young Spanish American writers who arrived in
Paris around 1925 is of particular interest. Actively courted by their
French contemporaries, they interacted more closely with French
writers of their day (in this case primarily the Surrealists) than any
generation before or since. In terms of Spanish American literary

history, they are a transitional generation. Miguel Angel Asturias defined them as 'esta generación mía de escritores latinoamericanos, que pudiéramos llamar la "generación del veinte", en que estaban Alejo Carpentier, Arturo Uslar Pietri, el cholo Vallejo y Pablo Neruda'.[4] The two leading prose writers among this group, Asturias himself and Alejo Carpentier, would go on, in their middle years, to write novels that would bridge the gap between the *regionalismo* of the early twentieth century and the 'Boom' novels of the 1960s and 1970s. The writers of Asturias and Carpentier's generation were at once closer to France and more assertive of their Spanish American particularity than previous generations. By tracing the process through which one of these writers elaborated his cultural identity during his years in Paris, this study tries to shine light on patterns imprinted on the bedrock of the contemporary Spanish American novel. Asturias, far more rooted in a particular Spanish American society than the eternal immigrant Carpentier, also left behind, in his journalism and his early fiction, a legible record of his constitution of his cultural identity in the Paris of the 1920s and 1930s. The chameleonic Carpentier, bilingual to the point of being able to pass for a native speaker (and writer) of French, wrote little fiction during this period; his journalism is elegant but opaque, his real views almost impossible to decipher. It was Asturias who grappled most obviously and candidly with problems of literary language, French cultural influence and Latin American identity. By analysing Asturias's early writing in light of the French literary and cultural formations to which he had been exposed, this study assesses the ideological stances implicit in his struggle simultaneously to infuse the Spanish American novel with the literary forms of international modernity and to enhance its ability to speak in a distinctively Spanish American voice.

In assuming his right to universalize his own experience, rather than acquiescing to the claims to universality of European cultural productions, Asturias made assumptions and adopted roles whose origins lay in the internal historical evolution of Europe. When Asturias repudiated European tradition, he did so largely within a space carved out for him by contemporary artistic creeds, notably Surrealism. Detailed scrutiny of Asturias's Parisian writings makes possible the evaluation of this paradox of a turning away from Europe largely promoted by European historical imperatives.

Culture, Carpentier wrote in an article sent back to Cuba from Paris, consisted of 'el acopio de conocimientos que permiten a un hombre establecer relaciones, por encima del tiempo y del espacio, entre dos realidades semejantes o análogas, explicando una en función de sus similitudes con otra que puede haberse producido muchos siglos atrás'.[5] It was by establishing links, making comparisons, drawing connections between French and Spanish American realities—were they analogous? if so, how? if not, how not?—that Asturias began to define his own cultural identity. Contrary to Carpentier's assertion, the analogies that permitted Asturias to forge a sense of his Guatemalan and Spanish American identities were strictly subordinated to time and place: the intellectual currents prevalent in Paris in the 1920s were crucial to his election of the Maya as the dominant symbol of Guatemalan identity. This study assumes that culture, for Asturias and his generation, meant a syncretic cultural tradition, defined primarily in terms of the artistic forms of 'high' culture (literature, painting, classical music) and its concomitant institutions (vibrant universities and newspapers, for example), but also admitting the importance of experimental art, or cultural forms originating outside Europe: these would include Surrealist films and photography, Afro-Cuban music, Amerindian sculpture and Mayan narrative.

This book concentrates on Asturias's Paris years, though it is primarily the achievements of his later life which make his literary development worthy of study.[6] The son of a judge on the Guatemalan Supreme Court and a mother who was noticeably darker than her husband, Asturias was born in 1899. During his infancy, as a result of a dispute between his father and the dictator Estrada Cabrera, the family endured four years' 'internal exile' in the ranching region of Baja Verapaz, where Asturias came into contact for the first time with the country's native population.

Asturias's university years were tumultuous. He changed careers from medicine to law, led a student strike against the dictatorship, published his first short stories in student magazines and wrote a positivist-influenced thesis which, though naïve, presaged his later interest in the problems of Guatemala's Mayan majority. In 1924, shortly after graduating as a lawyer, he left for London, later moving to Paris.

The work of Asturias's Paris years, discussed in later chapters of this book, included the pivotal short story collection *Leyendas de Guatemala* (1930) and the novel *El señor presidente* (completed in 1932, published in 1946). In 1933 economic circumstances forced him to return to Guatemala. Living under a dictatorship once again and deprived of the stimulating environment of Paris (including the company of his companion of four years, Andrée Brossut), Asturias crumpled into inactivity. Prevented by the iron rule of the new dictator, Jorge Ubico, from publishing *El señor presidente*, he wrote only a handful of poems during the next dozen years. His personal life, damaged by his professional frustrations and by alcoholism, included a short-lived marriage which produced two sons; the elder, Rodrigo, became a well-known guerrilla leader whose career spanned the period from the 1960s to the late 1990s.[7] During the Ubico years, Asturias held positions on a variety of newspapers and radio stations under constant threat of closure by the dictatorship. In 1942, demoralized, Asturias finally compromised with the dictatorship by accepting a seat in Ubico's puppet legislature.

When Ubico was overthrown in 1944 by a revolution led by liberal military officers and nationalist middle-class professionals, Asturias found himself regarded as a collaborator by a government whose political convictions he shared. He was forced to go into exile in Mexico. The intervention of the Chilean poet Pablo Neruda, whom Asturias had met during his Paris years, persuaded the new president, Juan José Arévalo, of Asturias's trustworthiness. During the two 'October Revolution' governments of presidents Arévalo and Arbenz (1944–54), Asturias became a valued diplomatic representative, serving as Guatemala's cultural attaché in Mexico (1946), cultural attaché in Argentina (1947–52), diplomatic adviser in Paris (1952) and ambassador to El Salvador (1953–4).

The October Revolution years also saw Asturias establish himself as an important literary figure in Spanish America. *El señor presidente*, published privately in Mexico in 1946, was relaunched by Editorial Losada of Buenos Aires in 1948 and found a large readership. In 1949 Losada published *Hombres de maíz*, a novel regarded today as Asturias's most important work, though it received a mixed reception at the time. In 1950 Asturias published *Viento fuerte*, the first novel in *La trilogía bananera* (the other volumes are *El Papa verde* (1954) and *Los ojos de los enterrados* (1960)). These novels, popular in their day though little read since the 1960s, cemented Asturias's reputation as champion of the downtrodden of Central America. The rise in Asturias's literary and political fortunes during the October Revolution years coincided with renewed personal happiness, as he married the Argentine critic Blanca Mora y Araujo in 1950.

In 1954 Guatemala was invaded by an army trained, supplied and supported (both from the air and from its embassy in Guatemala City) by the United States. The democratically elected government of Jacobo Arbenz was overthrown and replaced with a pro-US dictatorship. Asturias went into exile in Argentina, where he published an angry fictionalized account of the invasion, the short story sequence, *Week-End en Guatemala* (1956). In 1962, in the aftermath of a military coup in Argentina, Asturias, at this time seriously ill, was gaoled, apparently by mistake. Offered political asylum and medical treatment by Romania, he spent several months in that country, during which time he appears to have completed his last major novel, *Mulata de tal* (1963). He also wrote a travel book about Romania, *Rumania, su nueva imagen* (1964), which will be discussed in the Conclusion.

For most of the rest of his life, Asturias lived in Paris, spending short periods in Italy and Spain and travelling widely. In 1966 he became president of the French PEN Club. Later that year he was awarded the Lenin Prize by the government of the Soviet Union, and, as a result of a change of government in Guatemala, was named Guatemalan Ambassador to France, a post he was widely criticized for accepting from a president whose democratic credentials remained tarnished. In 1967 Asturias became the first Spanish American prose writer to be awarded the Nobel Prize for literature. The attention generated by the prize resulted in many invitations to travel and lecture. Asturias's final works included the autobiographical novel *Viernes de Dolores* (1972) and the artistic testament *Tres de cuatro soles* (1977), originally published in French in Geneva in 1971. Asturias died in Madrid in 1974 and was buried in the Père Lachaise cemetery in Paris. His career during the 1950s and 1960s—ambassador, political exile, bestselling denouncer of dictatorial regimes—made him an internationally recognized figure, yet in artistic terms his contribution to Spanish American literature stemmed from his domestication of French influences, his efforts to integrate the pre-Columbian past, his quest for a language capable of dramatizing life in countries where large segments of the population perceived reality through an animist prism. The evolution charted by *Leyendas de Guatemala*, *El señor presidente* and *Hombres de maíz* constitutes a vital legacy to later generations of Spanish American novelists.

It is important, though, in a study such as this one to guard against a teleological triumphalism suggesting a rising curve of Spanish

American cultural autonomy and creative prowess. Asturias's definition of his cultural identity was a fraught, flawed success. He did not slay the dragon-shadow of Paris for all future Spanish American novelists. Mario Vargas Llosa, one of the central figures of the Boom, reports having suffered in his youth from anxieties not dissimilar to those of earlier generations:

Esa ansiedad por saber francés y por irme a vivir un día a Francia, país que fue, durante todo mi adolescencia, el anhelo más codiciado, un país que se asociaba en mis fantasías y deseos con todo aquello que me hubiera gustado que fuera la vida: belleza, aventura, audacia, generosidad, elegancia, pasiones ardientes, sentimentalismo crudo, gestos desmesurados.[8]

Peripheral literatures will always have to define themselves by hewing out new spaces within and against metropolitan traditions. To some extent, the process is recapitulated in each generation, though the identity of the metropoles and the content of their claims to centrality may change over time. Similarly, peripheral writers' strategies will change, often overleaping stages or tactics judged to have been exhausted by earlier generations. One of the many reasons that the fiction of Mario Vargas Llosa differs in tone, technique and use of language from the novels of Asturias (or Carpentier) is that Vargas Llosa was able to read and contemplate the earlier writers' works during or prior to his own Parisian apprenticeship. Seen in this light, Asturias's wrestling with his identity through his Paris years becomes not only a key to understanding his later fiction, but also part of the literary heritage of all subsequent generations of Spanish American writers.

Notes to Introduction

1. Ernest Hemingway, *The Sun Also Rises* (1926; London: Arrow Books, 1994), 8.
2. Carlos Fuentes, *Myself With Others: Selected Essays* (London: André Deutsch, 1988), 4.
3. Angel Rama, *La novela en América Latina: Panoramas, 1920–1980* (Bogotá: Procultura/Instituto Colombiano de Cultura, 1982), 107. Cortázar arrived in Paris in 1951.
4. Luis López Alvarez, *Conversaciones con Miguel Angel Asturias* (Madrid: Editorial Magisterio Español, 1974), 174.
5. Alejo Carpentier, *La novela latinoamericana en vísperas de un nuevo siglo* (Mexico, D.F.: Siglo Veintiuno Editores, 1981), 17.
6. The account of Asturias's life which follows draws on the chronology established by Gerald Martin in his critical edition of *Hombres de maíz*. See Miguel Angel Asturias, *Hombres de maíz*, ed. Gerald Martin (1949; Nanterre: Centre de

Recherches Latino-Américaines, 1992), 461–7. This has been supplemented by sources such as Luis Cardoza y Aragón, *Miguel Angel Asturias: casi novela* (Mexico: Ediciones Era, 1991); Luis Harss, *Los nuestros* (Buenos Aires, Editorial Sudamericana, 1973); López Alvarez, *Conversaciones*; René Prieto, *Miguel Angel Asturias's Archeology of Return* (Cambridge: Cambridge University Press, 1993); Jimena Sáenz, *Genio y figura de Miguel Angel Asturias* (Buenos Aires: Editorial Universitaria de Buenos Aires, 1974); Stephen Schlesinger and Stephen Kinzer, *Bitter Fruit: The Untold Story of the American Coup in Guatemala* (Garden City, New York: Doubleday, 1982).

7. See M.D.A., 'Rodrigo Asturias: "No Debemos Pasarnos las Facturas"', *Cambio 16* (3 Nov. 1997), 49.

8. Mario Vargas Llosa, *El pez en el agua* (Barcelona: Seix Barral, 1993), 116.

CHAPTER 1

Asturias in Guatemala

The principal imaginative tension shaping Miguel Angel Asturias's childhood and youth lay in the competing and ultimately contradictory claims of the Roman Catholic church and the liberal ideals deriving from French political and intellectual culture. Catechism classes at La Merced church, which Asturias attended from the age of 8, deepened the already powerful faith instilled in him by his parents. As Gerald Martin has noted: 'La familia de Asturias en Guatemala es conocida como una de las más tradicionalistas y devotas, y él nunca se apartó del todo de las influencias católicas de su infancia.'[1] Asturias's early religious schooling left an enduring mark on his intellectual and emotional personality. Noting the contradiction generated by the co-existence of Asturias's faith with his progressive and even revolutionary allegiances, in an era preceding the advent of liberation theology, his compatriot and near-contemporary Luis Cardoza y Aragón has written: 'El catolicismo lo impregnó en la infancia definitivamente. Le daba seguridad, consuelo. Esta Iglesia [en Guatemala] casi siempre ha estado coludida con los opresores.'[2]

The lasting impact of Asturias's youthful religious education was such, Cardoza y Aragón argues, that 'no debemos sorprendernos en manera alguna de que Miguel Angel a los 47 años continuara participando como "cucurucho" (nazareno) en la Semana Santa, cargando a Cristo hacia el Calvario' (*Asturias*, 206). The Venezuelan novelist Miguel Otero Silva reported having encountered Asturias, by then winner of the Lenin Prize, in an Italian church 'de rodillas, con los brazos abiertos, rezando en voz alta' (Cardoza y Aragón, *Asturias*, 201).

The young Asturias also began to be exposed to the stimulating enticements of cosmopolitan culture. In turn-of-the-century Guatemala, this took the form of a romanticized devotion to the ideals of the French Enlightenment. Asturias's secondary education at the

Instituto Nacional Central de Varones, whose curriculum reflected the anti-clerical reformism of the nineteenth-century Mexican president Benito Juárez, countered his conservative religious faith with a French-influenced zeal for social progress. The outbreak of the First World War in 1914 gave the 15-year-old Asturias his first taste of political activism.

Nos dimos cuenta de que el dictador era no un poco germanófilo, sino mucho, y a nosotros los estudios que habíamos hecho nos hacían ser aliadófilos, sobre todo por lo que Francia significaba como bandera de libertad. Empezamos, pues, a agitarnos, lo que era muy raro, pero no podía la dictadura suprimir algunas de nuestras manifestaciones hacia la Legación de Francia. Llegábamos cantando la Marsellesa, con la bandera francesa, y así íbamos entrando en la vida política.[3]

As Asturias makes clear, his initial revolt against the Estrada Cabrera dictatorship (1898–1920) was inspired by a desire to rally around the French cause in the First World War. Over the years, his concerns would shift. Guatemala's social misery would become his abiding obsession; the cultural wealth of its trampled indigenous peoples would grow into the core of his imaginative universe. Yet his debt to French political idealism left him prey to an enduring paradox. No matter how intensely Guatemalan his preoccupations became during his decades of expatriation and exile, European—and particularly French—culture remained, sometimes covertly but almost always perceptibly, his source of ultimate authority and legitimation. In Paris, his Guatemalan identity would be forged in a European crucible. The mature Asturias was the most pungently Latin American of writers. Despite the modernity of his innovations in language and form, his work revealed less of an obvious debt to foreign models and themes than that of almost any of his contemporaries. But the fact that his intellectual personality had been constituted under the sway of visions of a distant, mythologized France, and later in France itself, generated a tension that he never entirely succeeded in resolving. This tension is inextricably bound up in his literary development. Not surprisingly, his first taste of great literature is also linked to his secondary-school adulation of France. 'Durante la guerra, en el Instituto Nacional llega a formarse una especie de célula de gente pro-Francia. Empezamos a cambiar ideas, a leer a Víctor Hugo, a Zola....Así llegué a bachiller' (López Alvarez, *Conversaciones*, 57).
    These enthusiasms were common ones for young bourgeois

intellectuals of Asturias's generation. His literary vision began to acquire an original cast that demanded creative expression only after the social and psychological upheaval of the 1917 earthquakes.

The succession of earthquakes that levelled Guatemala City on 25 December 1917 appears to have shattered Asturias's faith in the social order represented by his *ladino* privileges and the morality of the Catholic church. In old age, he returned frequently to the subject of the earthquake. 'En mi vida causa una ruptura el terremoto de mil novecientos diecisiete', he told Luis López Alvarez in his final extended series of interviews (López Alvarez, *Conversaciones*, 62). In his introductory comments to Claude Couffon's anthology of his early, uncollected stories, published three years before his death, Asturias noted that the 1917 earthquake and its aftershocks marked the beginning of his career as a writer of fiction. Identifying the unpublished short novel *Un par de invierno* as his first attempt at fiction, he wrote:

La novela fue escrita de diciembre 1917 a marzo 1918, bajo una carpa, porque fue el momento del gran terremoto y fuimos a vivir fuera de las casas que estaban cayendo. Entonces, por hacer algo, me puse a escribir esa novela [...]. Fue mi primer ejercicio largo. Hasta entonces yo había escrito pequeños poemas, pequeñas semblanzas de la gente que huía del terremoto, sacando sus pobres trapos.[4]

From young adulthood on, Asturias presented 1917 as the moment when Guatemala's traditionalist social values crumbled.[5] The earthquakes appear to have had the long-term effect of snapping the dynamic tension that had kept Catholic obedience and French-inspired defiance in a fine balance throughout his youth. The smashing of the social institutions buttressing the conservative *ladino* order deprived Asturias of one of the two intellectual and moral poles of his existence.[6] He came to depend more and more on the ethos of his French heroes. The themes and imagery of his fiction continued to betray his Catholic training, and his *ladino* biases remained starkly in evidence in his law thesis, but these traits were challenged ever more powerfully by his energetic pursuit of the Parisian ideals of liberty, social justice and individual creative prowess.

Asturias's youthful creative work exhibits the defects of most novice work: imprecisely evoked backgrounds and characters, an uneasy grasp of form and a failure to match literary language to the material being treated. Many of the weaknesses of his youthful writings stem from his lack of understanding of his own society. Given his position in the *ladino* bourgeoisie and his foreign-dominated literary and cultural enthusiasms, he needed to develop ideologically, not just literarily, in order to overcome his artistic deficiencies. *Un par de invierno* makes this clear. Pablo and Raquel, the star-crossed lovers of the text, are poor. But their poverty is not the ugly, hunger-inducing deprivation inflicted by Guatemala's racial and economic cleavages. Pablo and Raquel are poor in the way that displaced characters in the novels of European Romanticism are poor: they do not enjoy the privileges of the landed gentry; their poverty is really a form of shared Romantic alienation. The lovers are emotional outcasts rather than people whose economic position places them at the bottom of the country's social structure. Pablo's plans for the future take for granted a degree of upward mobility that Guatemala's rigidly stratified social castes have never permitted.

Cuando mejoraran de posición a fuerza de economías y ya pudieran vivir en una casita más confortable, en un barrio mejor visto y de mejor calibre él cuidaría de las flores, cuchillo en mano sembraría, trasplantando cuando fuera necesario y haciendo prodigios para que su casa fuera un jardín y ya en una casa más grande tendrían algunas jaulas para que el trino de los pájaros rodara líquido sobre la beatitud de los corredores. (*NC*, 33)

Romantic commonplaces, such as the adoration of nature, coexist in this passage with a deeply bourgeois conception of happiness as the inexorable progression through a succession of houses, each one larger than the last. While Asturias's doomed protagonists might have been plucked from the pages of Victor Hugo, his underlying ethos remains that of a privileged, culturally alienated *ladino*. Where, in these pages, is Guatemala? Descriptions of the poorer quarters of the city are cursory and impressionistic; evocation of detail dissolves into pathetic fallacy: 'La casa acurrucada a uno de los muros desmantelados del cementerio mantenía una cara triste, un gesto lóbrego' (*NC*, 73). The wealthy Doña Clara, the pivot of the creaky plot which enables Asturias to separate Pablo and Raquel, does charity work. But her forays into the poor districts of the city are described mainly in terms of the inconvenience they cause her coachman:

largos ratos la esperaba el carruaje a la puerta de casuchas de mal aspecto, allí donde anidaba el dolor, allí donde sufrían, allí donde renegaban la vida, donde había una niñita de quince años, pálida y demacrada por el hambre, allí estaba ella. (*NC*, 90)

The absence of telling detail in this passage is striking.[7] The rhetorical structure based on the repetition of 'allí' enables the narrator to reel off a succession of abstractions—'el dolor', 'la vida', 'el hambre'—which hold the gritty details of life in the slums at a safe distance. The description spares both narrator and reader the ordeal of contemplating human misery.

Through a Romantic inversion that is both stereotypical and revealing of the specific tensions animating Asturias's early fiction, it is wealth, not poverty, that *Un par de invierno* portrays as a prison. 'Bah! nacieron ricos pero quizás no son felices', Raquel proclaims (*NC*, 96). This Romantic cliché acquires greater resonance once Raquel, having assumed her secret identity as Doña Clara's long-lost daughter, is absorbed into the world of privilege, where she is sequestered behind the grating ('rejas') of Doña Clara's garden. She accedes to the garden that she and Pablo have dreamt of cultivating together, at the cost of sacrificing her love. Locked out of this world, Pablo disappears. Raquel's final lament—'¡Pablo, qué feliz era pobre!' (*NC*, 114)—issues from behind the bars of privilege that have prised them apart. Membership of the bourgeoisie is revealed as a barrier to understanding the poor—incarnated by Pablo—and thus to personal fulfilment.[8] The conclusion not only exposes Asturias's alienation from Guatemalan social reality; it also expresses the crusading young student's yearning for a more intimate acquaintance with his less privileged compatriots.

Pablo, the core of the opening sections, fades steadily from centre stage as the novella advances. Asturias does not know the poor well enough to sustain his description of an indigent character. Doña Clara and Raquel, both of whom eventually inhabit the world Asturias understands, are obliged to take over the story. The narrative's gradual suppression of Pablo reveals that while French Romanticism has infused Asturias with the desire for a more just society, its methods have failed to offer him a means of entering and dramatizing the world of the downtrodden majority. It may also suggest that despite its progressive veneer, Asturias's political awareness has not yet evolved to the point where he can, without feeling threatened, make a poor or marginalized character the central dramatic focus of his art.

The two remaining pieces of fiction that Asturias is known to have written as a student show him, unable to resolve the problems raised by *Un par de invierno*, reining in his narrative ambition. He retreats into the complacent religious orthodoxy in which he was brought up. 'El toque de ánimas', which Asturias identified as 'mi primer cuento publicado' (NC, 21) appeared in the January–March 1922 issue of the student magazine *Studium*. It was intended to be the first chapter of a novel; the second chapter, 'La hora del repaso', was written but remained unpublished. Closer to sketches than full-fledged short stories, these two pieces lack the complexity of the illuminating, if deeply flawed, *Un par de invierno*. Their brevity enables Asturias to keep them under tight ideological control. 'El toque de ánimas' shows religious faith soothing the pain of poverty. It concludes with a celebratory shout: '¡Gloria...! Gloria, porque ya son ricos los pobres, los desheredados, los rotos' (NC, 122). The imagery of the story corroborates its insistently devotional message: 'Venían bullanqueros como los fariseos y charlatanes que ofrecen su mercancía bajo las bóvedas de un templo' (NC, 119). 'La hora del repaso', a less polished and even shorter piece, presents a dewy-eyed memoir of Easter choir practices.

The most telling point about these fragments is that Asturias proved incapable of completing *El acólito Cristo*, the projected novel of which they were to form part. The stories lack drama because they summon up a world in which religious dogma explains everything; they fail to give adequate expression to the tensions prevalent in the author's psyche. The stories represent the youthful Asturias's final attempt to take refuge in the Catholic certitudes which, since the 1917 earthquakes, he had ceased to trust as a system for understanding and acting to improve Guatemalan society. Yet, as *Un par de invierno* had demonstrated, the mere desire to emulate French masters did not in itself furnish a method of inquiry, a means for entering into and bringing to life the daily existence of people belonging to social classes removed from his own. Religious credos and foreign Romantic clichés both fostered a tendency to skim over the specifics of Guatemalan life in grandiloquent phrases. In 'Por esos caminos de Dios', his first article for *El Imparcial*, the newspaper to which he would contribute on a regular basis during his years in Paris, the two forces combine to blind Asturias to the existence of his own society. This long nature sketch, relating a trip through rural Guatemala, is remarkable for its near-obliviousness to the presence of human life. The lyrically overblown descriptive passages are permeated with religious and Romantic banalities:

Guatemala se alza en el medio día, con la frescura de una ropa limpia, revive en el paisaje la emoción de las ciudades evangélicas, y el menos imaginativo la llama: desposada... niña inocente... barca tranquila... ¡Oh! (*París 1924–1933*, 504)

Nearly 2000 words into the article, human beings make their appearance. They are presented in a generalized, collective and blandly universalizing way:

Los arrieros se indignan con voces terribles. En la calina del medio día, nada y se cuaja esta vida magnífica del trópico; las sombras de los árboles se acuestan sobre el polvo vivo; se oyen sudar los hombres y caer sobre la tierra venerable y sufrida, las palabras del *Eclesiastés*: ¡nada nuevo debajo del sol! (*París 1924–1933*, 504)

The muleteers are not people, but features of the landscape. Asturias's paean of praise to 'esta magnífica vida del trópico' imitates European romanticizations of nature. The description evinces a yearning to live up to foreign visions of exotic tropical paradises; at the same time, the quotation from Ecclesiastes serves to reassure both author and reader that Guatemala's exoticism need not be construed as shameful or freakish, since human nature, which is everywhere the same, makes all decent people equals. The article suppresses Guatemala's cultural particularities. In addition, it ignores the fact that most Guatemalan country people are members of indigenous communities. 'Por esos caminos de Dios' is ultimately an exercise in urban *ladino* self-congratulation. The only rustic mentioned by name, a certain Don Pablo, is introduced solely to be mocked for the quaint way in which he says *Comonó*.

'Por esos caminos de Dios' was published on 30 March 1924. The article's date of composition is unclear, but it stands as a graphic illustration of the gaping hole at the core of Asturias's early prose. In order to lend his writing authenticity, Asturias desperately needed an angle, a voice, a method. His most sustained attempt at imposing this sort of consistency on his approach to the world around him, prior to his departure from Guatemala, was his law thesis, *El problema social del indio*.

In 1921 Asturias had travelled to Mexico as one of three Guatemalan delegates to the first Congreso Internacional de Estudiantes. Having revered the French Revolution since his early teens,[9] he now had the opportunity to visit a country in which a revolutionary government had taken power. The progressive social legislation promulgated in Mexico renewed his desire to see similar advances occur in Guatemala. These yearnings were galvanized by his meeting with José Vasconcelos, to whom he outlined his project of embarking on a scientific study of the role of the Indian in Guatemalan society. According to Claude Couffon, 'El gran intelectual mejicano lo había animado a proseguir su empresa, que debía esclarecer nuevos aspectos de la realidad guatemalteca'.[10] The influence of Vasconcelos's thought, especially his reliance on the concept of the 'alma nacional', is implicit in Couffon's words: Asturias started his research with the assumption that there was, or should be, a single, unified 'realidad guatemalteca'. This approach, reinforcing the dominant liberal positivist emphasis on 'progress', from which he had not yet begun to emancipate himself, led Asturias to the conclusion (in later years a source of embarrassment both to himself and to his supporters) that the solution to Guatemala's social ills lay in systematic assimilation of the Maya. As Arturo Taracena Arriola has written: 'Sin la integración del indígena, la formación del "alma nacional" propuesta por Vasconcelos no tenía sentido'.[11]

The 'alma nacional' furnished Asturias with a goal. His method, though, appears to have been adopted wholesale from the prevailing prejudices of his milieu. The 'alma nacional', in Asturias's formulation, is to become the vehicle for making Guatemala into a modern nation. This will be achieved, Asturias contends (faithfully reflecting the deepest insecurities of the *ladino* bourgeoisie), by 'improving the race', making Guatemala's population whiter and more European. The Indian, clearly inferior, must be eliminated by planned *mestizaje*. Asturias's recommendations reflect the liberal positivist ideology prevalent at the time among the Spanish American bourgeoisie. Edwin Williamson writes:

This new version of liberal ideology was derived from the positivism of the French philosopher Auguste Comte. It regarded scientific method as the only means to truth: by observation and experiment it was possible to arrive at a knowledge of facts and the basic laws of nature and society. Because only an enlightened minority was capable of acquiring this scientific outlook, the business of government should be conducted by an élite prepared to undertake the measures necessary to modernize backward countries where 'the people' had been vitiated by superstition and unproductive habits.

In republics with large non-white populations, this kind of 'scientific politics' came very close to an officially sanctioned racism—Indians, mestizos and blacks tended to be regarded as irredeemably unskilled, indeed as obstacles to the nation's progress.[12]

The notion that Asturias, the 'Gran Lengua', voice of the indigenous peoples of the Americas and tireless revitalizer of Mayan mythology, initiated his literary career by denouncing as degenerate the cultures he would later champion, makes many critics uneasy. This is especially true of European and US critics. Giuseppe Bellini, Richard Callan, Marc Cheymol, Claude Couffon, Gerald Martin and René Prieto, the six most assiduous Western Asturias scholars, all play down the importance of *El problema social del indio*, summarizing its contents in ways that blunt Asturias's unpalatable message.

In his generally reliable study *La narrativa di Miguel Angel Asturias*, Bellini skims over *El problema social del indio* as a 'dura denuncia delle ingiustizie da lui [Asturias] direttamente comprovate nel lungo contatto con gli indios del suo paese'.[13] Neither Bellini's characterization of the book as a 'dura denuncia' nor his claim that Asturias wrote out of 'lungo contatto' with the Indians withstands scrutiny. It is difficult to believe that Bellini had read *El problema social del indio* at the time of writing his book.[14]

Callan accords the thesis equally perfunctory treatment. His book-length study of Asturias's work merely notes that 'Asturias obtained his law degree in 1923 with a thesis on Indian problems, for which he received the Gálvez Prize'.[15]

Prieto, distinguishing himself from most other critics by acknowledging Asturias's early racism, none the less presents his outlook as a passing phase. 'Merely four years later', he writes, 'this attitude had evolved full circle' (*Archeology of Return*, 243). While superficially accurate, this judgement obscures the fact that the definitions and vocabulary underlying Asturias's racism continued to guide his work in later years.

Cheymol's analysis of the thesis attributes Asturias's emphasis on the Indians as a degenerate race to a broadly Marxist class analysis which the thesis does not undertake: 'Pour Asturias, les Indiens sont des paysans attachés à des moyens de production qui ne leur appartiennent pas, et donc une race dégénerée'.[16]

Couffon, in his summary, substitutes geographical isolation and political neglect for the racial criteria to which Asturias ascribes Indian degeneracy: 'El aislamiento en el que la civilización occidental, traída por el conquistador español, había dejado al indio, tras haber destruido su civilización, estaba a la base de la "degeneración"'.[17]

Martin, for his part, reverses Asturias's emphasis by portraying the main thrust of the thesis as an attack on social injustice, when in fact

Asturias's references to the mistreatment of the Indians are far outnumbered by his allusions to their status as a decadent race: 'Su tesis había sido ambigua: él veía por todas partes la injusticia de la condición indígena, pero también pensaba que se trataba de una raza vencida y agotada'.[18]

If there were any doubt that *El problema social del indio* expressed the alienation and insecurity of Guatemala's *ladino* bourgeoisie, Asturias soon lays such questions to rest. By its second paragraph, the thesis has turned its gaze anxiously towards Europe. Referring to earlier writings on the indigenous civilizations of the Americas, Asturias comments: 'No alcanzarían muchos meses para hojear los volúmenes escritos, los más de los cuales de oídas sabemos que existen en museos y bibliotecas de las ciudades europeas' (*El problema*, 31–2). The act of writing—even writing about Guatemala—cannot be purged of fears that Guatemalan backwardness will condemn to inferiority the cultural productions of even a privileged *ladino*. The status of *ladino*, in the harsh racial dichotomy of Guatemalan society, was equivalent to that of a representative of European culture—even though most of the caste's members remained anxiously aware of their own mixed blood. Cardoza y Aragón elaborates: 'Cabe explicar que llamamos ladino a quien no consideramos indio; poco se habla de mestizo. Hay indios y hay ladinos' (*Asturias*, 116). The desire to stamp out Guatemalan backwardness—including the *ladino*'s fears of his own inferiority to European culture—by extirpating from the social fabric the Indians who retard the nation's progress is the source of Asturias's recourse to positivist formulas.[19] These, as noted earlier, combine with notions of the assumed desirability of a unified 'alma nacional,' initially derived from Vasconcelos. Asturias writes: 'El estudio de nuestras sociedades ha de ponernos en posibilidad de hacer de Guatemala una nación racial, cultural, lingüística y económicamente idéntica' (*El problema*, 34).

This goal taints the thesis's second chapter, in which Asturias summarizes the fate of the Guatemalan Indian since the conquest. Asturias the Enlightenment-influenced rebel gives an outraged account of the treatment meted out to the Indian during the colonial period. He blames the breakdown of the Indian family (one of his recurring proofs of Indian degeneracy) on the conquistadors, who 'mientras [el indio] laboraba la tierra de su señor [...] iba y abusaba de la mujer y sus hijas' (*El problema*, 48). His view of Guatemalan independence is boldly dismissive: 'Para el indio la independencia representa un cambio de amo; y nada más' (*El problema*, 52). But when he turns to describing the nature and condition of the Indian, especially in the later chapters, his positivist faith crushes his Romantic instincts. Ironically—if inevitably—both sides of his intellectual scales originate in France. *El problema social del indio*, one of the first sociology theses in Latin America, is drenched in the influence of Auguste Comte. Asturias's attempt to approach sociology 'scientifically' and his emphasis on family structure as an indicator of social health both derive from Comte. His efforts to work back from a desired—in this case uniformly *mestizo*—future to prescriptions for present policies reflect Comte's recommended procedure:

Au lieu de dire: le passé, le présent, et l'avenir, il faut dire: le passé, l'avenir et le présent. Ce n'est, en effet, que lorsque, par le passé, on a conçu l'avenir, qu'on peut revenir utilement sur le présent, qui n'est qu'un point, de façon à saisir son véritable caractère.[20]

It cannot be proved that Asturias had read Comte at this time; but he had read Comte's follower Gustave Le Bon. In the final chapter of his thesis, arguing for large-scale European immigration as the cure to Guatemala's ills, Asturias makes an undocumented reference to the 'tres condiciones [que] formula Le Bon para lograr un buen resultado' (*El problema*, 108). The conditions he cites correspond to those listed by Le Bon in his *Les Lois psychologiques de l'évolution des peuples* (1894), where he argues: 'Plusieurs conditions sont nécessaires pour que des races arrivent à se fusionner et à former une race nouvelle plus ou moins homogène'.[21] It seems clear that Asturias absorbed a substantial portion of his intellectual approach, including his particular interpretation of the 'alma nacional', through his study of Le Bon.

While Vasconcelos introduced Asturias to the terminology of the 'national soul', Le Bon's writing provided him with a theory of the concept's implications and importance. In Le Bon's formulation the national soul became a defining trait of the modern nation-state:

Restreinte d'abord à la famille et graduellement propagée au village, à la cité, à la province, l'âme collective ne s'est étendue à tous les habitants d'un pays qu'à une époque assez moderne. C'est alors seulement qu'est née la notion de patrie telle que nous la comprenons aujourd'hui. Elle n'est possible que lorsqu'une âme nationale est formée. (*Lois psychologiques*, 17)

Dependent upon the fusion of populations 'pas trop dissemblables' (*Lois psychologiques*, 18) the national soul served as the litmus test of a nation's having attained a high degree of civilization. In his conclusions, Le Bon states: 'L'acquisition d'une âme collective solidement constituée marque pour un peuple l'apogée de sa grandeur. La dissociation de cette âme marque toujours l'heure de sa décadence' (*Lois psychologiques*, 169). Asturias applies the second part of this axiom in his critique of Guatemalan Indian populations as 'degenerate'. Even in the second chapter, where Asturias condemns his society's treatment of its native inhabitants, the Indian is portrayed not as someone oppressed by laws and power-structures susceptible to reform, but as a being whose nature has been organically weakened by a succession of calamities. Asturias assumes that this enfeeblement is irrevocable. He attributes the failure of the 1893 reform law (forbidding the sale of each community's tract of common land) to improve the Indian's living conditions, not to political or even cultural obstacles, but to the irreversible degradation of the indigenous peoples: 'cansado en el tiempo y en el dolor que lleva de ser bestia de carga, [el indio] no da muestras de vida ni se aprovecha de estas leyes' (*El problema*, 53). Asturias depicts this torpor as the outcome of a long-term decline whose origins lie in the immediate aftermath of the conquest: 'El período colonial, representa para el indio el desgaste de sus fuerzas materiales' (*El problema*, 51).

Asturias's descriptions of the Indian in the later chapters of the thesis employ a language which aspires to the scientific objectivity endorsed by positivism. Yet the very coolness of Asturias's phrasing contributes to his relentless distancing of Indian reality from that of himself and his implied readers. He summarizes the Indian's psychology:

Sentimiento moral, utilitarista; mentalidad relativamente escasa y voluntad nula.

Es cruel en sus relaciones familiares; silencioso, calculador, no se deja arrebatar por la pasión ni el entusiasmo; ríe con una mueca terrible, es huraño y ve con los ojos helados de malicia. [...]

[...] Es notable su facilidad para imitar (cualidad de las razas inferiores) gracias a esta facilidad es hábil para la arquitectura y el dibujo; pero es incapaz de crear. (*El problema*, 57)

Similarly, Asturias's sketch of the Indian's physical characteristics conjures up a portrait of a being irredeemably removed from civilized *ladino* existence: 'Necesidades energéticas muy inferiores a las de las razas europeas y muy semejantes a las de los habitantes del Congo' (*El problema*, 81). This sentence underlines Asturias's construction of the

Indian as the Other, the outsider whose obdurate difference stymies the realization of the Guatemalan national soul. The sentence sets up a dichotomy in which the Indian is equated with 'los habitantes del Congo', while the *ladino* implicitly slips into the role of 'las razas europeas'. The correspondence constitutes a form of *ladino* wish-fulfilment, in which bourgeois racial insecurities dissolve. By virtue of his superiority to the Indian, the mixed-race urban *ladino* becomes a European. His elevated status authorizes him to regard the Indian with disdain: 'el prototipo del hombre anti-higiénico' (*El problema*, 100). By condemning the Indian as suffering from 'enfermedades sociales tan arraigadas [que] no se curan con leyes ni con discursos' (*El problema*, 61), he frees himself—despite the fact that he is writing his thesis for the law faculty!—to suggest answers to the 'problema del indio' which transcend purely legislative remedies. The most soothing solution—the only one which meets the varied demands of *ladino* alienation, positivist faith in progress, the touted 'alma nacional' and, in dubiously distorted form, a neo-Hugoesque impulse to reform society—is to bid the Indian to join the *ladino* in the counterfeit Europeanness of *mestizaje*. Asturias's recommendation of enforced intermarriage contains a telling reference to Europe:

La mestización, es indudable que hubiera proporcionado al indígena una puerta ancha para pasar de su primitivo estado social al estado social que la civilización europea dejó en estos suelos. (*El problema*, 101)

The forward-looking *ladino*, in this view, inhabits a vestigial European civilization impeded from realizing its full potential by the backwardness of the Indian. Asturias has opted for the most reassuring conclusion any researcher can reach: that the problems he is investigating will be solved if everyone can become like him. His analysis consecrates his own deeply problematic *ladino* condition as an untroubled extension of European culture onto American soil. At the same time, by blaming the Indian for the failings of the society presided over by his own race and class, Asturias furnishes himself with a covert defence against Le Bon's bleak description of Spanish American societies as sinking beneath the 'decadence' induced by racial inferiority, which Asturias appears to have internalized. Le Bon argues:

Par ce seul fait que la race est différente et manque des qualités fondamentales que possède celle qui peuple les Etats-Unis, toutes ces républiques, sans une seule exception, sont perpétuellement en proie à la plus sanglante anarchie

[…]. L'absence de moralité, surtout, dépasse tout ce que nous connaissons de pire en Europe. […]
Ce n'est pas seulement en politique, naturellement, que se manifeste la décadence de la race latine qui peuple le sud de l'Amérique mais bien dans tous les éléments de la civilisation. Réduites à elles-mêmes, ces malheureuses républiques retourneraient à la pure barbarie. […]
Cette effroyable décadence de la race latine, abandonnée à elle-même […] est une des plus sombres, des plus tristes et en même temps, des plus instructives expériences que l'on puisse citer. (*Lois psychologiques*, 59, 67–8)

Having adopted Le Bon's racial framework for the analysis of nations, Asturias confronts the need to explain away Le Bon's vision of his own 'race' as 'decadent' and unable to manage its own affairs. He does this by isolating the Indians as the source of degeneracy within Guatemalan society. It is this need to locate the origin of the 'decadence' criticized by Le Bon which lies at the source of the contradictory tendency in Asturias's argument to present the Indians both as 'naturally' inferior and, at the same time, as belonging to a race which has collapsed into 'degeneracy' (implying that their current state was preceded by something better and is therefore not 'natural'). Having internalized Le Bon's critique of Latin American society as 'decadent', Asturias must identify the origin of this decadence; at the same time, his need to distinguish his own class from that responsible for diminishing his nation and besmirching the Guatemalan 'national soul' leads him to portray Indians as inherently (that is, 'naturally') different from people of his own background. The *ladino*, the wounds of his identity crisis annealed, becomes the answer to a problem rather than a site of conflict. But this assessment begs further questions—primarily that of how such degeneracy is to be cured. Asturias presents his prescription of immigration from selected areas of Europe as the alternative to a more insidious process already underway: immigration from Asia. His absorption of Le Bon's racial hierarchies is so thorough that even the tiny community of Chinese shopkeepers in Guatemala City becomes magnified into a major threat to the 'purity' of the *ladino* élite.

Los chinos han venido a dar el tiro de gracia a nuestros valores de vida. Raza degenerada y viciosa cuya existencia mueve a bascas y cuyas aspiraciones son risibles […]. ¿Cómo se va a contrapesar el germen degenerativo que la sangre china ha dejado en nuestras venas, sino con sangre nueva y vigorosa?
La degeneración cierra nuestros pasos. En la vena exhausta del indio deja caer el chino sus vicios y deficiencias raciales. (*El problema*, 108)

When Asturias writes of 'el germen degenerativo [...] en *nuestras venas*' (emphasis added), he inadvertently demolishes his own ideological apparatus. The racial dialectic he has established between the *ladino* as the inheritor of European culture and the Indian as inferior, non-European degenerate is unmasked as the product of *ladino* self-hatred. The real anxiety animating *El problema social del indio*, the reader perceives, is not the status of the Indian but the status of the *ladino*. The Indian's primeval traditions and economic misery expose the backwardness which superficial imitation of European customs has not sufficed to expel from the life of the Guatemalan bourgeoisie. The Indian is a social problem because he embarrasses the *ladino* by laying bare the *ladino*'s kinship with the primitive.

Asturias's solution to the identity crisis racking his class and nation is to ally Guatemala more closely with Europe. He recommends that the Indian highlands be opened to European immigration. Intermarriage between Indians and immigrants will improve the race. But this must be done scientifically. Not all Europeans are suited to life in the tropics; not all possess the racial characteristics necessary to enhance the stock of the Guatemalan Indian. The Europeans whom Guatemala seeks to attract must display specific physical traits:

Recordando los signos degenerativos del indio...se han de traer, las siguientes cualidades, sobre otras, para contrapesar sus deficiencias y defectos: talla y peso superiores; ochenta y dos grados de ángulo facial, aproximadamente; raza blanca, sanguíneo-nerviosa (temperamento propio para las alturas y zonas tórridas). (*El problema*, 109)

In order to combat the disintegration of the Indian family, the immigrants must bring with them 'una sólida base moral en sus afectos familiares' (*El problema*, 109). They must exhibit high moral standards, a strong work ethic and an attachment to rural life. Asturias concludes: 'En Suiza, Bélgica, Holanda, Baviera, Wutemberg [*sic*] y el Tirol, pueden encontrarse ejemplares que reúnen las condiciones mencionadas' (*El problema*, 110).

Asturias's pseudo-scientific prescriptions underline the intellectual poverty, profound insecurities and ingrained racism of the bourgeois *ladino* milieu of Guatemala City in the 1920s. An understanding of these attitudes, as they pertain both to Indians and, more generally, to the question of Guatemalan identity, for which the Indian problem came to serve Asturias as a kind of code, is essential to grasping the traumatic intensity of the change that was forced upon him in Paris.

It also alerts the reader of his work to important continuities chafing against the shifts in his mentality and imposing limits on his self-awareness. Asturias's instinctive privileging of French cultural precepts over those developed by representatives of his own culture, already in evidence in *El problema social del indio*, became a crucial factor in his construction of his own identity in the Paris of the 1920s. Asturias, after all, *chose* to accept Gustave Le Bon's racial framework, with its disparaging view of Latin American societies; other models were available to him. The anti-imperialist Argentine writer and politician Manuel Ugarte, whom Asturias also read while researching his thesis, expressed a far more sanguine view of the impact of the Indian on the Latin American 'race'. In *El porvenir de la América Latina* (1910), whose passages on the influence of Spanish immigration Asturias cites with approval in his thesis (*El problema*, 110), Ugarte contends:

> La alianza con el primer ocupante, lejos de ser nociva, es útil, no sólo porque nos hace, por así decirlo, herederos de los primeros propietarios de la tierra, sino porque tiene que rejuvenecer la estirpe, infundiéndole algo de la firmeza, la salud y la sinceridad de Moctezuma o Guatemozín, de quienes nadie puede avergonzarse.[22]

Despite his affirmative view of the Indian, Ugarte accepted the positivist dictum that 'lo que fortifica a las naciones es la unidad de la raza' (*El Porvenir*, 74–5). In this sense, Ugarte's work did not provide Asturias with a full-fledged defence against Le Bon's assault on Latin American 'decadence'. Yet Asturias could have accepted the need for greater national unity without projecting the accusation of 'decadence' onto his Indian compatriots. The fact that he elected to do this reveals both his conditioned *ladino* racism and his related tendency to bow to the decrees of Parisian prophets.

None the less, Cheymol, Couffon and Martin all do Asturias a disservice by obscuring the full racist thrust of *El problema social del indio*. Despite the traceable continuities in his intellectual make-up, the gap between the student who wrote the law thesis and the mature novelist of *Hombres de maíz* (1949) is wider than their various analyses will admit; Asturias deserves immense credit for crossing this gulf. At the same time, as this study will argue, even the later Asturias, the revered spokesman of Latin America's most oppressed peoples, conceives his crusading role within the assumed context of *ladino* superiority in Guatemala and Parisian cultural hegemony in the wider world. By portraying Asturias as always having been drastically estranged from the values of his class, his latent revolutionary consciousness requiring no more than the prod of an inexorable (and implicitly inevitable) maturation, Cheymol, Couffon and Martin efface this contradictory, more problematic dimension of Asturias's *obra*. The result is to diminish the psychological complexity of his creative struggle. Both Cheymol's reading of the thesis as attributing the Indians' 'degeneracy' to their status as peasants shackled to feudal means of production which they do not control, and Couffon's contention that Asturias blames isolation and the destruction of native culture for 'la degeneración', extrapolate back from the public image of the Asturias of the 1950s and early 1960s—the poet of revolution and Marxist fellow traveller—rather than accurately reflecting the writings of the *ladino* student of the 1920s. These explanations fail to mesh with Asturias's insistence throughout the thesis that 'El estancamiento en que se encuentra la raza indígena [...] [tiene] origen en la falta de corrientes sanguíneas que la impulsen con vigoroso anhelo hacia el progreso' (*El problema*, 106). Martin's assertion that Asturias's primary concern is the social injustice to which the Indian was subjected and that this outlook is merely rendered 'ambiguous' by his perception of the indigenous people as an exhausted race, is only valid for the thesis's second chapter; the remaining seven chapters are charged with positivist fervour and thin on social protest.

Latin American critics have been more unflinching in their discussions of Asturias's youthful racism. The Peruvian-born sociologist Braulio Muñoz writes: 'Asturias took a clearly racist attitude to the problem and recommended eliminating the Indian through planned mestizaje'.[23] But he also gives Asturias credit for having evolved over the course of his career. By the time Asturias writes *Hombres de maíz*, Muñoz argues, his narrative world is one in which 'the mestizo can no longer wish the Indian away' (*Sons of the Wind*, 259).

The approach of Guatemalan critics has been somewhat less unforgiving than that of Muñoz. Arturo Taracena Arriola praises Asturias's prescience in having hit upon the central contradiction of Guatemalan society and had the courage to write about it, but notes that 'sus posiciones apenas escapaban a las formulaciones hechas por el positivismo liberal'.[24] Manuel José Arce writes: '*El problema social del indio* es un trabajo de juventud que revela la carencia de información y la estrechez ideológica de la universidad guatemalteca de esa época'.[25] Arce also makes the important point that, outlandish as

Asturias's views on the Indians may seem in light of his later identification with Mayan culture, his mere choice of subject for his law thesis gave evidence of an original and inquiring mind and hinted at his future course.

El hecho en sí de que un joven estudiante de Derecho de entonces abordara el tema del *indio* guatemalteco como un *problema social*, lleva a detectar en él una preocupación clave para la comprensión de su obra. (*París 1924–1933*, 892)

Asturias's thesis, which was published and awarded a prize shortly after its presentation to the law faculty of the Universidad Nacional, caused 'cierta agitación en el medio conservador y racista de la capital'[26] merely by virtue of its subject. Once his thesis had been accepted, Asturias sailed for England. He later moved to France. Despite his youthful vow not to abandon his country, like 'la mayoría de los virtuosos',[27] his journey was an almost inevitable part of his apprenticeship. What was less than inevitable, though, was his decision to live in Europe for nearly a decade. Even more particular, personal and unpredictable was the impact Paris would have upon his creative intelligence. Asturias arrived in the French capital as a Catholic bourgeois *ladino* whose law thesis had resounded with an aching need to consolidate his pseudo-European identity through closer contact with the French culture that had served him as a beacon throughout his adolescence and young adulthood. By crossing the Atlantic, he was following his own recommendations in *El problema social del indio*: he was improving himself by mingling with Europe. But the Paris which had gripped him—the capital of Enlightenment liberation, the home of Victor Hugo and Remy de Gourmont—no longer existed. The Paris of 1924 would offer Asturias a different vision of the world and of his potential roles within it.

Notes to Chapter 1

1. Gerald Martin, 'Asturias y *El Imparcial*: Pensamiento y creación literaria', in Asturias, *París 1924–1933*. *Periodismo y creación literaria*, ed. Amos Segala (Nanterre: Centre de Recherches Latino-américaines, 1988), 824.

2. Luis Cardoza y Aragón, *Miguel Angel Asturias: casi novela* (Mexico, D.F.: Ediciones Era, 1991), 144.

3. López Alvarez, *Conversaciones*, 56.

4. Miguel Angel Asturias, *Novelas y cuentos de juventud*, ed. Claude Couffon (Paris: Centre de Recherches de l'Institut d'Etudes Hispaniques, 1971), 20–1: henceforth *NC*. Asturias makes even more explicit the earthquake's role as the

catalyst of his creative career in his posthumous artistic testament: 'Lo que salvé de mi casa, destruida por el terremoto, fue mi sabiduría poética' (*Tres de cuatro soles* (Paris–Mexico: Editions Klincksieck/Fondo de Cultura Económica, 1977), 29).

5. In 'El amor, la mujer y el niño', the long concluding lecture in the book that grew out of his 1928 speaking tour of Guatemala, Asturias went so far as to blame the 1917 earthquake for destroying the traditional sexual continence of the *ladino* bourgeoisie. See *La arquitectura de la vida nueva* (Guatemala: Editores Goubaud & Cia., 1928), 71–124. The 20-page description of an earthquake which destroys the social order, killing most of the major characters, at the close of his bleak late novel *Mulata de tal* (1963), demonstrates the seemingly indelible imprint of this image of dissolution on Asturias's imagination.

6. The conflict between conservative religious beliefs and political activism forms the core of Asturias's autobiographical novel *Viernes de Dolores* (1972), in which two bourgeois students agree to participate in a strike and protest march timed to coincide with Holy Week. Troyano Montemayor y Gual's decision to ride on a cart proclaiming 'los horrores del cristianismo' confirms his political commitment. His devout sister berates him: 'Tú, educado en colegios religiosos, de buena familia, con un apellido [...]. Ah, pero tus ideas... tus ideas...' (*Viernes de Dolores* (Buenos Aires: Editorial Losada, 1972), 87).

7. The mature Asturias would evoke the poor neighbourhoods of 1920s Guatemala City with far greater precision: 'Se metió entre casas viejas, medio derruidas unas, otras recién pintadas, o edificadas con los adobes o ladrillos de sus paredes, aún sin repellar. Perros, niños entre los perros, aguas sucias, excrementos. A lo lejos, sobre tejados y techos de cinc, grupos de araucarias altísimas. Cada vez más lejano el estruendo de las bocinas de los automóviles' (*Viernes de Dolores*, 113).

8. 'Ese confuso malestar que lo acompañaba siempre, disgusto por lo que más de cerca, en su casa, le rodeaba, no conseguía borrarlo, admirando, sometiéndose, aceptando servilmente la forma de vivir, de pensar, de sentir, de la gente de Ana Julia, a quien acompañaba a la iglesia', Asturias writes of Ricardo Tantanis, one of the student protagonists of *Viernes de Dolores* (p. 109).

9. In *Viernes de Dolores*, Asturias underlines the extent to which his generation of students venerated the French Revolution as an ideal of progressive action. Ricardo, in a moment of disillusionment, thinks: 'Es la farsa de un mundo muerto. El cobarde escribe sobre el héroe. El retrógrado prepara su tesis sobre la Revolución Francesa' (pp. 133–4).

10. Claude Couffon, 'Introducción', in Asturias, *El problema social*, 10.

11. Arturo Taracena Arriola, 'Miguel Angel Asturias y la búsqueda del "alma nacional" guatemalteca. Itinerario político, 1920–1933', in Asturias, *París, 1924–1933*, 685.

12. Edwin Williamson, *The Penguin History of Latin America* (Harmondsworth: Penguin, 1992), 298–9.

13. Giuseppe Bellini, *La narrativa di Miguel Angel Asturias* (Milano: Istituto Editoriale Cisalpino, 1966), 14.

14. This suspicion is reinforced by Bellini's later article, 'Dimensión mítica en la narrativa de Miguel Angel Asturias', *Studi di Letteratura Ispano-Americana*, 22 (1991), 35–44, in which he discusses *El problema social del indio* as though he has just discovered it. Bellini writes: 'Parece como si el novelista se hubiese

convencido de que no hay solidaridad posible, en lo concreto, hacia el indígena' (p. 37).

15. Richard Callan, *Miguel Angel Asturias* (New York: Twayne Publishers, 1970), 11.
16. Marc Cheymol, *Miguel Angel Asturias dans le Paris des années folles* (Grenoble: Presses Universitaires de Grenoble, 1987), 142.
17. Couffon, 'Introducción', in Asturias, *El problema social*, 11.
18. Gerald Martin, 'Asturias y *El Imparcial:*', in Asturias, *París 1924–1933*, 824.
19. Asturias was conversant with such ideas from childhood. Cheymol notes that Asturias grew up in 'un hogar cristiano, impregnado a la vez de positivismo' (Marc Cheymol, 'Miguel Angel Asturias entre latinidad e indigenismo: Los viajes de Prensa Latina y los seminarios de cultura maya en la Sorbona', in Asturias, *París 1924–1933*, 846).
20. Pierre Arnaud (ed.), *Politique d'Auguste Comte: Textes choisis* (Paris: Armand Colin, 1965), 90.
21. Gustave Le Bon, *Les Lois psychologiques de l'évolution des peuples* (Paris: Félix Alcan, 1894), 46. The three conditions mentioned by Le Bon and repeated by Asturias are: that the races being 'crossed' should not be greatly unequal in number; that their racial characteristics should not differ too dramatically; and that should they cohabit in similar social circumstances over an extended period of time.
22. Manuel Ugarte, *El porvenir de la América Latina* (Valencia: F. Sempere y Compañía, 1910), 72–3.
23. Braulio Muñoz, *Sons of the Wind: The Search for Identity in Spanish-American Indian Literature*. (New Brunswick, New Jersey: Rutgers University Press, 1982) 163.
24. Taracena Arriola, 'Miguel Angel Asturias y la búsqueda del "alma nacional" guatemalteca. Itinerario político, 1920–1933', in Asturias, *París 1924–1933*, 686.
25. Manuel José Arce, 'Guatemala versus Miguel Angel Asturias. Breve relato de un conflicto', in Asturias, *París, 1924–1933*, 892.
26. Amos Segala, 'Introducción del Coordinador', in Asturias, *París 1924–1933*, p. xxiii.
27. Cited by Jack Himelblau in 'Love, Self and Cosmos in the Early Works of Miguel Angel Asturias', *Kentucky Romance Quarterly*, 18/3 (1971), 256.

CHAPTER 2

❖

The Parisian Background and the Choice of an Identity

The formation of Asturias's literary and cultural persona in the Paris of the 1920s grew out of a rich soil of assumptions, obsessions and illusions generated by more than a century's interaction between Parisian fashions and Latin American intellectual hunger. Only within this historical context, and particularly in light of the experiences of the *modernistas* who directly preceded the generation of the 1920s, can Asturias's evolution be understood.

   The origins of the Spanish American intellectual's subservience to French literary and political fashion lie in the Enlightenment. From the 1770s, Edwin Williamson writes, 'France increasingly became the beacon of civilization, since the Enlightenment in the Iberian world was but an extension of French ideas'.[1] Williamson overplays the centrality of French culture to the Spanish Enlightenment, where German and English influences also exercised significant authority, but his comment accurately summarizes the overwhelming importance accorded to French models in Spanish and Portuguese America. The wars of independence consolidated this tendency. As a result of the French training received by its intellectuals, Spanish America approached self-government through the prism of French Enlightenment ideals. As Carlos Fuentes has observed:

We enter this modern world with independence—we have to choose what is deemed to be the modern time, which is the time of the eighteenth century, the Enlightenment, a linear, progressive time which will take us again to happiness and progress and the perfectibility of human nature and human institutions [...]. But this is a denial of half our being, of our past, a denial of many things that define us as a polycultural and multiracial society in Latin America.[2]

   For most of the nineteenth century, Latin American writers lacked the cultural self-confidence to break down this denial. The intelligentsia of the new national bourgeoisies imported intellectual fashions wholesale. France established itself in Latin American eyes not merely as the source of the world's most vital and prestigious cultural developments, but also as the principal conduit for the achievements of other European cultures. Latin Americans read *Faust* in Gérard de Nerval's translation, Byron translated by Amédée Pichot, Poe by Baudelaire and Walt Whitman by Bazalgette.[3] The French language acquired such prestige among educated Latin Americans that by 1850 Rafael-M. Baralt had published in Venezuela his *Diccionario de galicismos*.[4] The ideals of the Enlightenment proved to be the first in a succession of intellectual systems whose imposition filled the moral and intellectual vacuum left by the revolutionary rupture with Spain:

L'esprit des Lumières, puis le positivisme, les écoles littéraires européennes du XIXe siècle (romantisme, naturalisme, symbolisme, etc.) avaient en effet remplacé, sous l'égide française, la monarchie espagnole d'inspiration catholique dans son rôle de modèle culturel et fourni à une Amérique qui se considérait volontiers elle-même comme 'primitive' une vision du monde et une esthétique.[5]

Yet the Catholicism associated with the Spanish Crown had not vanished. Asturias, growing up in Guatemala in the years before the First World War, had found himself torn between the competing imperatives of liberal French ideas and conservative Catholic demands. During the last two decades of the nineteenth century, the increasing prosperity of the Spanish American bourgeoisie had enabled numerous Spanish American writers to test their spiritual longing for French culture against the yardstick of a period of residence in Paris. At the turn of the century, the tension with which Asturias would later wrestle crystallized in the emergence of the *afrancesado*, or Frenchified Spanish American.

One of the first effects of this prosperity was to encourage the buying of more European prestige art products—paintings, European-designed houses and public buildings, imported books and furniture. Here, France was the important source of supply, partly because French civilization was generally regarded as setting the highest standard of elegance, and also because a large number of Latin Americans lived in Paris for shorter or longer periods and hence adopted French values.[6]

As the century drew to a close, the adoption of French models became a standard trait of cultured, literate Latin American families.

Describing his own upbringing in a *familia afrancesada*, Octavio Paz has written:

Basta con leer a nuestros historiadores, novelistas y pensadores para comprobar que, desde fines del siglo XVIII, se comenzó a llamar 'afrancesados' a los partidarios de la Ilustración y, un poco después, a los que simpatizaban con la Revolución francesa. La palabra se siguió empleando a lo largo del siglo XIX para designar a los liberales [...]. Al final del siglo el vocablo adquirió una coloración estética y ser 'afrancesado' significó ser simbolista o 'decadente,' adorador de Flaubert o de Zola y, en fin, como dice Rubén Darío, ser 'con Hugo fuerte y Verlaine ambiguo'.[7]

The final stage mentioned by Paz in the evolution of the *afrancesado* coincided with the rise of *modernismo*. One of the defining characteristics of this movement lay in its elaboration and embellishment of the 'myth of Paris'. Sylvia Molloy has written that with the advent of *modernismo*

[l]es écrivains hispano-américains ne se contentent plus de recevoir les livres et revues français, il leur faut désormais aller toucher d'eux-mêmes aux sources de cette culture qu'ils réclament [...]. C'est cette période d'or où les Hispano-Américains passent la moitié de l'année à Paris et l'autre moitié à Buenos Aires ou à Caracas, où des maisonnées entières déménagent, accompagnées parfois d'une vache chargée d'assurer le lait aux enfants pendant la longue traversée. (*La Diffusion*, 18–20)

The glorification of France entailed a neglect, sometimes amounting to denigration, of Spain. 'France indeed supplied all that Spain lacked', Jean Franco observes (*The Modern Culture*, 17). Among its advantages, France counted an enticingly different culture, a more supple and refined literary language and an ambience favourable to intellectual and artistic ferment. The *modernistas* elevated the 'myth of Paris' to a veritable religion. Rubén Darío wrote: 'Yo soñaba con París desde niño, a punto que cuando hacía mis oraciones, rogaba a Dios que no me dejase morir sin conocer a París. París era para mí como un paraíso en donde se respirase la esencia de la felicidad sobre la tierra.'[8]

While the poet Darío remained the pre-eminent voice among the *modernistas*, the movement's leading prose stylist was the Guatemalan writer of novels and sketches, Enrique Gómez Carrillo. Owing to their shared nationality and Parisian residence, Gómez Carrillo served Asturias first as an inspiration and influence and later as a deficient model whose example he must reject and surpass in order to forge an original language in which to dramatize Spanish American realities.

Gómez Carrillo, who settled in Paris in 1891 and lived there until his death in 1927, elevated the 'myth of Paris' to unprecedented rhetorical heights. The opening pages of his picaresque auto-biographical novel, *En plena bohemia* (1920), describe the city in ludicrously rhapsodic terms:

París, para los que lo conocemos en toda su suavidad y lo amamos en todo su esplendor, es algo más que un nido, algo más que un refugio: es un santuario, es la fuente milagrosa de las nobles inspiraciones, es la ciudad santa del mundo moderno.

[...] esta ciudad, en la cual hay más mujeres que se suicidan por amor que en el resto del universo, en la cual los extranjeros perseguidos encuentran una nueva patria, en la cual al artista no se le pregunta nunca de dónde viene.[9]

The novel's loose, episodic structure follows a nameless Guatemalan narrator who arrives in Paris drenched in French *lectures*. He is at first disappointed by the city's apparent failure to live up to his romantic reveries. Alice, the French wife of his Guatemalan contact Dr Garay, reinvigorates him with her assurances that the Paris of his illusions remains intact: 'París es hoy lo que era ayer, lo que será siempre' (*En plena bohemia*, 24). The narrator falls in love with Alice and steals her from Dr Garay, appropriating Paris in emblematic form. The lovers devote themselves to a mythologized universe of Parisian bohemia:

Vivíamos tranquilos, sin pensar en nada que no fuese arte, belleza, amor, entusiasmo, fantasía, ideal [...]. Yo escribía a su lado páginas muy frívolas en las cuales trataba de destilar algunas gotas de la esencia de la galantería parisiense. (*En plena bohemia*, 133)

The novel serves as both a blatant advertisement for Gómez Carrillo's extravagant public persona—he plants in the text an ostentatious denial of one of the most famous exploits attributed to him, that of having been Mata Hari's lover (*En plena bohemia*, 157)—and, on an emblematic level, as an allegory of his rejection of his origins. The Gómez-like narrator betrays Guatemala in the form of his compatriot, Dr Garay. After the early pages the Guatemalan characters disappear, leaving the narrator fully immersed in a French bohemian ambience. He has realized the adolescent fantasy of every young Spanish American intellectual smitten with French literature: he has become French, assuming the life of one of his literary heroes; his nebulous, stigmatized Central American-ness is erased.

Gómez Carrillo's lifelong effort to assimilate into an idealized Paris sprang from a deep discomfort with his Guatemalan roots. In a rare moment of self-doubt—significantly preceding the restorative balm of his liaison with Alice—the narrator of *En plena bohemia* confesses:

Había en mi alma una herida que me hacía sufrir, y que es la misma de que han sufrido todos los hispanoamericanos en Europa. 'De Guatemala... de Venezuela... del Uruguay... de Bolivia' [...]. Son palabras que un francés o un inglés pronuncia con el mismo acento con que el personaje famoso de Montesquieu decía: '¿cómo puede uno ser persa?' No se concibe ni en Picadilly ni en el Bulevar, en efecto, que un caballero que habla bien, que viste bien y que no tiene cara de mono pueda ser de esas comarcas exóticas. (*En plena bohemia*, 30)

The narrator resolves to answer all future enquiries about his origins by presenting himself as a Greek from Athens. Rejecting the exoticism which threatens to exclude him from Parisian artistic life, he identifies himself with the cradle of Western civilization. The strategy echoes Gómez Carrillo's own total identification with Paris. Unlike Asturias, who would eventually make his way in France by cultivating the 'primitive', non-European aspects of Guatemalan culture, Gómez Carrillo fled the suggestion of any link with a nation whose inhabitants 'tiene[n] cara de mono'. For most of his life he denied his Guatemalan nationality: 'No soy americano, sino español. No hay literatura americana. Porque en realidad no la hay. Es más: no hay América' (Molloy, *La Difusión*, 62). Gómez Carrillo parlayed self-denial into a portmanteau identity, more Spanish than Spanish American: that of the dashing, witty man-about-town, the debonair Latin lover, the composer of charming, trivial sketches. The glamorized 'myth of Paris' demanded a correspondingly sanitized 'myth of Spanish America'.

Tant en France qu'en Amérique, [Gómez Carrillo] servit surtout à affermir des mythes. A Paris, il dut certainement contribuer à cette image de l'homme de lettres hispano-américain dont les Français auraient quelque mal à se débarrasser: l'esprit superficiel et brillant, le diseur de bons mots, le rastaquouère intelligent qui amuse mais qu'on ne prend pas toujours au sérieux [...].
    Aux yeux des Hispano-Américains, par contre, Gómez Carrillo incarna le mythe de Paris: ses livres auront été, pour plus d'un de ses lecteurs, la façon de satisfaire par voie indirecte, la nostalgie de luxe, de beauté, d'aventures faciles, d'exotisme, de tout ce que Paris pouvait représenter en Amérique hispanique. (Molloy, *La Difusión*, 27–8)

Gómez Carrillo's huge reputation has proved to be ephemeral. A few years after his death, his work was virtually forgotten, while that of Darío—whom the French ignored and failed to translate even while he lived among them—has continued to grow in stature. Yet Gómez Carrillo's polished prose remains readable today, and the long shadow he cast over writers of the generation succeeding his must be carefully weighed in any evaluation of Asturias's response to Paris. In *El recurso del método* (1974), one of the elements in Alejo Carpentier's critique of what Williamson has termed the dictatorial Primer Magistrado's 'excessive reverence for European civilization which provides him with a pretext for tyranny',[10] consists of a virtual parody of passages of *En plena bohemia*. For the Primer Magistrado (and by extension for the entire generation of Spanish Americans preceding that of Asturias and Carpentier), Paris is

Tierra de Jauja y Tierra Promisión, Santo Lugar de la Inteligencia, Metrópoli del Saber Vivir, Fuente de Toda Cultura que, año tras año, en diarios, periódicos, revistas, libros, alababan—luego de colmar una suprema ambición de vivir *aquí*—los Rubén Darío, Gómez Carrillo, Amado Nervo, y tantos otros latinoamericanos que de la Ciudad Mayor habían hecho, cada cual a su manera, una suerte de Ciudad de Dios [...][11]

Behind the frivolousness of Gómez Carrillo's persona, as young writers such as Asturias were well aware, lay the exacting labour of a skilled craftsman. Gómez Carrillo's example of self-deformation as a defence against ridicule, leading to servile conformity to European cultural practices, came wrapped in an elegant *modernista* prose style that any young writer would wish to emulate.

La misma levedad, al parecer sencilla y natural, de su prosa, era el difícil fruto de su esfuerzo paciente por producir una impresión de ligereza, capaz de atraer y mantener viva la atención del lector. A lo largo de sus crónicas hay un vasto acopio de lecturas y conocimientos, que se mencionan sin alarde, casi de pasada, como quien da a entender que, si algo sabe, lo debe más a la casualidad que al estudio [...].
Gómez Carrillo no cae jamás en el mal gusto de la llamada *prosa poética*. Cuida, por el contrario, de mantener el ritmo natural de la prosa.[12]

Yet despite his abstinence from the worst excesses of *modernista* artificiality, Gómez Carrillo remained one of the key protagonists in a literary movement whose quest for a certain mannered elegance remained inextricably bound to an *afrancesado* outlook. As Henríquez Ureña goes on to suggest: 'Al amaneramiento en el decir se acoplaba en los muchachos de la nueva hora el amor por los temas exóticos y el ansia de vivir una vida artificial con los ojos de la imaginación vueltos hacia París' (*Breve historia*, 161). Edwin Williamson argues that Gómez Carrillo's *crónicas* played an important role in initiating the Spanish American bourgeoisie into a knowledge of the outside world;[13] his effect on younger writers, though, was to instill an attitude of paralysed awe towards European culture and its products. Gómez Carrillo's unquestioning acceptance of the centrality of Paris and the innate superiority of Parisian artistic fashion, reinforced by his investment in promoting a highly romanticized image of the city in whose name he had abandoned his homeland and identity, nullified any talent he might have possessed for subverting these assumptions. For all his personal suavity and stylistic brio, by the 1920s Gómez Carrillo represented an outmoded vision of Spanish American identity.

The need to develop a style and language different from those of Gómez Carrillo was particularly pressing for Asturias since he would write in the same form. During his entire residence in Paris, Asturias served as free-ranging correspondent for the Guatemalan newspaper *El Imparcial*. If his fiction stands as the most enduring portion of his Paris *obra*, the journalism—far greater in bulk and written with more disciplined regularity at an earlier stage of his career—remains his true apprenticeship. Like Gómez Carrillo, Asturias became a *cronista*; he turned to journalism, on an almost daily basis, to work out his emerging style, vision and sense of cultural identity. But it was impossible for him to assume this role without grappling, albeit in disguised form, with the shadow of Gómez Carrillo. Despite the divergence of their respective conceptions of Guatemalan identity, Asturias could not help but admire the older writer's achievement. He once stated that Gómez Carrillo 'modificó la frase en prosa como Rubén Darío lo había hecho con el verso';[14] in an interview in later life Asturias gave this description of the period of his arrival in Paris: 'Era la época en que soñaba con ser corresponsal y poder emular a don Enrique Gómez Carrillo, que es el gran periodista de Guatemala, porque nació periodista, fue periodista y murió periodista.'[15]

These assessments are surprisingly generous in light of Asturias's apparent reluctance to acknowledge his predecessor's existence in his work. His journalism makes scant mention of Gómez Carrillo, whose name appears only six times in the 440 dispatches Asturias contributed to *El Imparcial* between 1924 and 1933. The originality of stance for which Asturias strove depended on his conceiving his Parisian vantage point differently than had Gómez Carrillo. By virtue of his almost unnatural absence from the pages of Asturias's journalism (otherwise strikingly attentive to the Spanish American intellectual community in Paris),[16] Gómez Carrillo becomes the sublimated force whose existence generates Asturias's emerging vision. In *The Anxiety of Influence*, Harold Bloom quotes André Malraux on the relationship of young prose writers with their predecessors:

'Every young man's heart,' Malraux says, 'is a graveyard in which are inscribed the names of a thousand dead artists but whose only actual denizens are a few mighty, often antagonistic ghosts.' […] As his main concerns are visual and narrative, Malraux arrives at the formula: 'from pastiche to style.'[17]

As one of Asturias's 'mighty, often antagonistic ghosts', Gómez Carrillo is rarely visible, even though, as Gerald Martin argues, one senses 'su presencia fantasmal por dondequiera en las primeras crónicas de Asturias en París'.[18] Gómez Carrillo's infrequent appearances are charged with significance. The first mention of his name comes in the first article Asturias contributed to *El Imparcial* from Paris, an interview with Miguel de Unamuno. Asturias writes:

El maestro se desampara un momento; su recuerdo vuelve con nostalgia hacia sus familiares y discípulos. Después nos habla de Guatemala, la tierra de Carrillo y la de un señor que conoció hace mucho tiempo. Se interesa por los problemas de América y se duele de que nos conozcamos tan poco. (*París 1924–1933*, 4)

Asturias's imaginative point of departure is clear: Guatemala, in European eyes, is 'la tierra de Carrillo'; as a result of Gómez Carrillo's failure to take advantage of his privileged position to divulge the nature of his homeland to his European readership, one of the problems dividing Europeans and Spanish Americans is that 'nos [conocemos] tan poco'. Gómez Carrillo is the first Spanish American writer mentioned by name in Asturias's journalism. His provocative example provides at least part of the impetus for Asturias's obsessive working-through of Guatemala's problems in his articles over the next ten years. The tension created by Gómez Carrillo's refusal to propagandize in France on Guatemala's behalf is also one of the sources of Asturias's indefatigable literary and political campaign, especially evident in his later years, to bring Guatemalan social injustice to the attention of French readers.

Asturias's later references to Gómez Carrillo are equally revealing. The second mention occurs in another article on Unamuno where, seeking a means of expressing the vividness of Unamuno's verbal description of the charms of Greece, Asturias writes: 'pues inmediatamente me inquieto y quisiera ir a Grecia, oír el tiempo que no pasa y ver el espacio inmóvil en el sagrado templo de la Diosa de los ojos verdes, que dice Gómez Carrillo' (*París 1924–1933*, 32). The allusion is remarkable in that Asturias not only defers to Gómez Carrillo's cultural influence, but acknowledges that he has read and absorbed the older writer's work. The choice of subject matter, though, slots Gómez Carrillo as an artist whose preoccupations expose his alienation from Asturias's Guatemalan readership: Gómez Carrillo is cited as an authority on Europe, not on Spanish America. Concentrating ever more firmly on moving the eccentric, marginalized concerns of Guatemala to the centre of his work, Asturias marginalizes the centralist concerns of his predecessor.

Asturias's third and fourth references to Gómez Carrillo appear in his interview with the Costa Rican writer León Pacheco (*París 1924–1933*, 59–61), at that time Gómez Carrillo's protegé. The bulk of the article is printed in question-and-answer format; Pacheco's appreciative recognition of Gómez Carrillo's assistance is quoted without comment. Yet despite Asturias's approving comments on Pacheco's approach to Parisian literary life, the implicit contrast between the two young writers is unmistakable: Pacheco, three years Asturias's junior, is Gómez Carrillo's follower; Asturias himself is not.

The final two references to Gómez Carrillo are harsher, dwelling on Asturias's hardening disagreement with his compatriot's cultural and political views respectively. His whimsical description of a gathering of expatriate poets pokes fun at Gómez Carrillo's facile exoticism:

Al pie de los faroles la evocación encuentra a Rubén Darío y lo seduce con la seda de sus medias, como en las crónicas de Gómez Carrillo seducen las mujeres del bulevar a los tropicales que vienen en busca de complicaciònes amorosas. (*París 1924–1933*, 151)

Asturias's final mention of Gómez Carrillo, written in 1928, the year after the older writer's death, is more acrimonious and unveils a hitherto concealed source of enmity towards Gómez Carrillo.

De México y de Rusia corren noticias abracadabrantes que los diplomáticos se apresuran a rectificar día a día. Esto nos trae a la memoria la buena época en que el genial escritor Gómez Carrillo defendía a diario la fama y nombre del genial estadista Estrada Cabrera. (*París 1924–1933*, 293)

Gómez Carrillo, in Asturias's eyes, is twice a traitor: he betrayed Guatemala by denying his origins and he betrayed the Guatemalan people by acting as an apologist for the Estrada Cabrera dictatorship which ruined Asturias's youth. His double treachery breeds a disturbing contradiction. Where Asturias, as described in the previous chapter, buttressed his opposition to the dictatorship with French literature and slogans from the French Revolution, Gómez Carrillo, the most *afrancesado* of all Spanish American writers, supported the dictatorship's primitive brutality. One bitter lesson of Gómez Carrillo's example was that cosmopolitanism was not *de facto* a progressive force. Commitment to Guatemalan reality must precede other doctrines; Asturias's gleanings from Parisian art, culture and experience would be put to the service of this primordial interest. Gómez Carrillo had conceived of Paris in terms of myth; Asturias, at least at a conscious level, saw the city as a repository of stimulating information capable of better equipping him to fulfil his obligation towards Guatemala. It is here that the two writers' paths diverge. One of the most conspicuous gaps in Asturias's coverage of Spanish American life in Paris is the silence with which he greeted Gómez Carrillo's death in 1927—despite apparently having attended his lavish funeral.[19] The lapse is both significant and ironic: in 1974 Asturias would be buried almost by Gómez Carrillo's side in the Père Lachaise cemetery.

Defining himself against Gómez Carrillo was an integral part of Asturias's larger task of elaborating his identity as a Spanish American writer in Paris. The *modernistas'* approach to Paris had been conditioned by a profound cultural insecurity. Manuel Ugarte, who counted himself, alongside writers such as Darío and Gómez Carrillo, as a member of the so-called 'Generación de 1900', recalled:

Hablábamos fuerte, exagerábamos las propinas, empujábamos a los transeúntes, reíamos a destiempo, cuidábamos demasiado el traje, porque carecíamos, en los gestos, en los pensamientos y en las palabras, de medida, porque obrábamos, en suma, como primitivos, frente a una civilización milenaria que había limado los ángulos salientes para dar en todo la nota precisa y cabal.[20]

By the 1920s the position and attitudes of Spanish American writers in Europe had changed substantially. Part of this change, Marc Cheymol proposes, stemmed from the successes of *modernismo*.

Le modernisme avait représenté à la fois une grande libération et un enrichissement qui avait dépassé les limites de l'Amérique latine, pour atteindre l'Espagne; pour la première fois le sens de l'influence s'était inversé [...]. Mais une fois le modernisme épuisé, comment donner à cette jeune littérature un avenir digne d'elle? Comment résoudre le problème de l'originalité spécifique de l'Amérique latine, et de l'européanisation de ses principaux écrivains? (*Années folles*, 39)

This was a more subtly challenging, but less immediately daunting mission than that which had confronted the *modernistas*. *Modernismo*'s infatuation with the myth of Paris had blunted its ability to express Spanish American subject matter; yet the movement had entered the European consciousness *as a movement*, accustoming French and Spanish writers and critics to thinking of Spanish American literature as an entity possessing a discrete history rather than as a random scattering of curiosities. The increased French receptiveness to Spanish American writing facilitated intellectual exchange between French and Spanish American writers and critics. Molloy writes: 'Entre 1920 et 1940 les contacts entre les écrivains hispano-américains et les écrivains français semblent moins livrés au hasard qu'auparavant' (*La Diffusion*, 95). French literary journals grew more willing to publish, in translation, the work of young Spanish American writers resident in Paris; books published in French translation began to be reviewed rather than ignored. The young Spanish American writers of the 1920s aided their cause by approaching French culture with a less reverential attitude than the preceding generation. The First World War had tarnished the 'myth of Paris'.

By 1918 [...] belief in the superiority of European cultural and social systems was shattered. The spectacle of the great powers dedicating the resources of science and industry to exterminating one another seemed a mockery to those Latin Americans for whom Europe had been equated with the highest human values. (Franco, *The Modern Culture*, 69)

The narrator of Alejo Carpentier's novel, *El recurso del método*, set during this period, comments: 'El Viejo Continente había fallado en lo de ofrecerse como un ejemplo de cordura' (Carpentier, *El recurso*, 167). Paris remained a beacon, a nucleus of cultural ferment; but, through a Spanish American optic, the city's absolute centrality had yielded to a revised status as an important point—perhaps still the most important point—in a multipolar cultural network.

Before each writer in the 1920s [...] lay the vision of New York, home of capitalist modernity; Moscow, home of socialist revolution; and above all, Paris, home of Latinity, high culture and the avant-garde, and unofficial capital in exile of a disunited American continent.[21]

One consequence of this new orientation was that Paris became ensconced in the Spanish American consciousness as the site of continental debate. Young intellectuals left for Paris in search not only of European culture but of other Spanish Americans. The city developed into the best place in the world for a Spanish American artist to feel out the contours of his identity, testing his experiences and intuitions against those of writers and intellectuals from fraternal countries. The emergence of this image helped to deflate the *afrancesado* myth. Many members of the Spanish American bourgeoisie, including a number of writers, continued to make the journey to Paris in order to *afrancesarse*. Armando Godoy, the Cuban poet who served as his nation's minister in Paris, dropped the 'o' from his first name, Frenchified the pronunciation of his surname and began writing in French; the Peruvian César Moro, who 'abrazó el surrealismo no como influencia sino como patria',[22] also wrote in French; the Chilean poet Vicente Huidobro used both languages. But *afrancesamiento* was no longer axiomatic. A stay in Paris came to be seen, among all who could afford it, as an indispensable part of any literary apprenticeship. The Parisian *séjour* changed in nature, evolving into a period of months or years spent reading, writing, discussing and accumulating experiences rather than a permanent renunciation of Spanish America. Unlike the previous generation, the writers of the 1920s took for granted that they would one day return to their countries of origin—and nearly all did return. The fact of living in Paris, therefore, came to seem less like a betrayal than it might have done to progressive intellectuals of the previous generation. The Argentine poet Raúl González Tuñón, who attributed his political radicalization to his Parisian conversations with other Spanish American expatriates, exhorted his contemporaries to overcome their fear of uprooting themselves: 'Es necesario no asustarse de partir y volver, camaradas. Estamos en una encrucijada de caminos que parten y caminos que vuelven'.[23]

The Spanish American intellectuals' adoption of Paris as the terrain of their internal debates coincided with a surge of French interest in non-European cultures and modes of thought. French writers and thinkers, like their Spanish American counterparts, had had their confidence in European rationalism rocked by the First World War. As Maurice Nadeau has written with regard to the founders of Surrealism:

Breton, Eluard, Aragon, Péret, Soupault ont été profondément marqués par la guerre. Ils l'ont faite sans joie. Ils en sortent dégoûtés; ils ne veulent plus rien avoir de commun avec une civilisation qui les écrase et les tue, et le nihilisme radical qui les anime ne s'étend pas seulement à l'art, mais à toutes les manifestations de cette civilisation.[24]

The Spanish American writers who arrived in Paris in the 1920s entered an ambience in which Europe itself was questioning the foundations of European culture; their debates about Spanish American identity arose in conjunction with, and arguably as an extension of, Europe's quest for more spontaneous, 'natural' forms of life and self-expression—embodied most dramatically in the rise of Surrealism. The contrast with the generation of Gómez Carrillo and his imitators is obvious. The shared European and Spanish American consciousness of a crisis in Western thought, leading to an intensified awareness of what belonged to each continent, set up the conditions for cultural exchange. Once European and Spanish American intellectuals had agreed that the metropolitan culture in which both had deposited their faith a generation earlier was in crisis, it became possible to imagine the Spanish Americans' encounter with Paris as a reciprocal learning process, based on an increased French valorization of Spanish American cultural realities, rather than as a period of pure tutelage. Alejo Carpentier, arriving in Paris in 1928, found the French public starved for news of the Americas:

Después de haber ignorado a América durante centenares de años, los galos comienzan a interesarse poderosamente por las cosas de nuestro joven continente [...]. Hasta hace poco, América sólo era conocida en París por el tango y la *Gomina* [...]. Ahora, la boga del arte negro está a punto de verse suplantado por la boga del arte precolombino. Las revistas se disputan documentos fotográficos suramericanos [...]. Continuamente, en las redacciones de revistas nuevas, se me dice: 'Traduzca cosas de Latinoamérica, revélenos sus valores, busque poesías populares indias, guajiras y negras; dénos grabados, háblenos de allá'.[25]

The principal agent of this intellectual exchange with societies untainted by the corrupt 'civilization' responsible for the First World War, Gerald Martin argues, was Surrealism:

Its emphasis upon the unconscious, and therefore the primitive, its insistence that there was a world more real than the visible 'reality' of commonsense and positivism, the idea that art is a journey of discovery involving free association and the liberation of the repressed, were all tailor-made for Third World interpretations and applications, and therefore for cementing the growing cultural relationship between France and Latin America [...]. Moreover, this relationship in which, instead of superordinate to subordinate, imperialist to colonial, France exchanged her civilization on equal terms (she had no colonial axe to grind in Latin America) with the New World's supposed instinctual barbarism, was ideally suited to the interests of both parties and has been fertile, fruitful and productive ever since. (*Journeys through the Labyrinth*, 142)

Martin's summary of the mutual appeal of the two intellectual cultures takes a sanguine view of their interaction, maintaining that it occurred 'on equal terms'. But his concession that the pre-condition for the exchange lay in 'the New World's supposed instinctual barbarism' undermines that contention, adumbrating the central paradox of the post-First World War generation's conception of its cultural identity: the new atmosphere enabled Spanish American writers to repudiate European tradition within an intellectual space carved out for them by European artistic creeds. As Edward Said has written:

To achieve recognition is to rechart and then occupy the place in imperial cultural forms reserved for subordination, to occupy it self-consciously, fighting for it on the very same territory once ruled by a consciousness that assumed the subordination of a designated inferior Other.[26]

France, while never a major colonial power in Latin America, did have a history of colonial endeavour impelled by the creed of *la mission civilisatrice*. French cultural discourse, even when gutted of confidence by post-First World War disillusionment, reserved a place in its structures for the exotic, savage Other. It was this niche which it fell upon Spanish American writers of the 1920s to occupy, enlarge and alter. This turning-away from European culture itself partly promoted by European imperatives, while far more subtly coercive than the pressures exerted on Gómez Carrillo, none the less encouraged a role-playing which contained a large measure of self-distortion. While the *modernista* had presented himself to Paris as the witty, superficial boulevardier, the writer of the 1920s adopted the guise of the shaman, intuitively in touch with the primitive sources of his own inspiration. This stance enabled him to explore and celebrate his Spanish American heritage in a way that had not been possible for his *modernista* predecessor. The writer of the 1920s took advantage of his Parisian apprenticeship to deepen his understanding of his Spanish American identity and to enlarge his grasp of how Spanish America's peculiar richness might fruitfully interact with other world cultures. But this knowledge was bought at a price. The Spanish American writer had to live up to France's image of America as the source of the mad, the bizarre and the marvellous. As Alfonso Reyes noted in his Paris diary during this period: 'aquí sólo piden al americano que sea pintoresco y exótico'.[27] André Breton's allusion to the Americas as a means of conjuring up an affirmative vision of anti-rationalism at the opening of the first *Manifeste du Surréalisme* (1924) illustrates the prevailing associations evoked by the word: 'Il fallut que Colomb partît avec des fous pour découvrir l'Amérique. Et voyez comme cette folie a pris corps, et duré.'[28] Angel Rama's summary of the period, more sceptical and nuanced than Martin's, captures the contradiction:

No hay uno que no lo diga, con unción y pasmo: lo que han recuperado en París es la originalidad de América Latina, su especifidad, su acento, su realidad única. De ahí que con ellos no vuelva a repetirse la alienación finisecular que llevó a los poetas a habitar dentro de un Versalles de chalafonía y a los narradores a recontar *La gloria de Don Ramiro* o *El embrujo de Sevilla*; por el contrario se consagrarán a una América Latina viviente y contemporánea, situada en una circunstancia política precisa [...]. Este reconocimiento de la América Latina no impedirá, sin embargo, otras y más sútiles alienaciones.[29]

This environment's effects upon Asturias were immediate and dramatic. His law thesis—completed only a few months prior to his arrival in Paris—had endorsed a vision of Guatemalan identity based on the cohesive, homogenizing model of Vasconcelos's 'alma nacional'. His bourgeois paradigm consecrated the *ladino* as the bearer of European culture in the hinterlands of the Americas. In voyaging towards Europe, Asturias, in terms of the argument he had put forth in his thesis, was returning to the sources of his intellectual being. The home of Hugo, Comte and Remy de Gourmont—in their various ways the intellectual authorities supporting his belief that Guatemala would realize its 'alma nacional' once miscegenation had converted the Indians into *ladino* vessels of European culture and bourgeois Guatemalan nationalism—was sure to welcome him as one of its own, confirming that his *ladino* identity was European at the core. But this was not what happened.

There is little doubt that Asturias arrived in Paris ready to *afrancesarse* as diligently as any writer of the preceding generation. His persistent mythologizing of his Parisian advent displays a worshipful yearning to identify himself with French culture. In old age he maintained that he had arrived in Paris (after a few miserable weeks or months in London) on Bastille Day 1924: 'El catorce de julio de mil novecientos veinticuatro me fui a París a ver como eran las fiestas'.[30] The echo of Hemingway's *A Moveable Feast* (1964) evokes a romanticized bohemian milieu. By insisting that his arrival took place on the anniversary of the French Revolution, Asturias claims parentage with the progressive, liberating strain of French history. In fact, it is unlikely that he did arrive in Paris on this date. Documentation relating to his movements during 1923–4 is scarce and contradictory; Asturias himself may have deliberately obscured the record.[31] He appears to have propagated the belief that his stay in London was much shorter than was actually the case. Cheymol writes: 'Ce qui est sûr, c'est que l'écrivain voulut toujours présenter ce séjour à Londres comme une sorte de purgatoire douloureux, *avant* le coup de théâtre de son arrivée lumineuse à Paris' (*Années folles*, 24).

According to both his own account and those of others, Asturias arrived in Paris expecting to savour French cosmopolitanism, not—as turned out to be the case—to reconceptualize his Guatemalan identity. The Guatemalan writer José Castañeda recalled: 'Cuando llegó Miguel Angel yo le pregunté ¿qué vienes a hacer? Pues, antes de todo a vivir en París—me dice—a saturarme de París; pero también, para darle gusto al viejo—viejo le decía él con cariño a su padre—me voy a inscribir en la Sorbona.'[32]

From this point on, all becomes legend. The contours of this legend are of vital importance since they represent Asturias's reconstruction of his own identity under the impact of his Parisian experiences. The facts of history are of secondary interest: Asturias's first fictional creation—the one whose successful elaboration rendered possible the invention of all the others—was himself.

Strolling the halls of the Sorbonne in search of a suitable programme in which to register, the legend dictates, Asturias encountered a poster announcing Professor Georges Raynaud's course in Mayan religions. Asturias and members of his circle have repeated many times what occurred when the young Guatemalan attended

Raynaud's first seminar. Asturias gave his fullest account of this pivotal moment in his life and career in the interviews with López Alvarez, conducted nine months before his death.

Cuando asistí a la primera clase del profesor Raynaud me senté en el aula y noté que, al mismo tiempo que explicaba, se me quedaba mirando. Yo me decía qué pasaría. Me preguntaba si no sería que estaba en el lugar que me correspondía. Hasta llegué a sacar el recibo de mi inscripción para asegurarme de que había pagado mi derecho a estar allí sentado. El profesor mientras tanto me miraba y me miraba. Nada más terminar la clase, se levantó y se vino hacia mí y me dijo: 'Vous êtes maya', y al confirmarle que procedía de Guatemala, el hombre se puso entusiasmadísimo. Me pidió que fuese con él. Yo vivía entonces en una pensioncita en la misma plaza de la Sorbona, frente a la estatua de Auguste Comte. Le dije, al ver que paraba un taxi: 'No se moleste profesor, porque yo vivo aquí mismo'. Insistió mucho en que fuese hasta su casa [...]. Al entrar en su apartamento, abrió la puerta y me tomó del brazo hasta la cocina, en donde estaba su señora cocinando y le dijo: 'He aquí un maya. ¡Y tú que dices que los mayas no existen!' (López Alvarez, *Conversaciones*, 75)

Whatever the literal truth of this incident may be, however embellished Asturias's accounts of it may have become over the years, its symbolic significance remains crucial. Asturias had discovered that what Paris demanded of him was not European sophistication but primitive mystery. *Vous êtes maya*: the declaration's psychological effect upon Asturias must have been shattering. Having devoted his law thesis to delineating the gulf dividing his culture from that of his nation's Indian communities, and recommending those communities' racial and ideological integration into the bourgeois nationalism of the 'alma nacional', he confronted, in the Sorbonne itself—the citadel of Parisian intellectual authority—the reality that the Guatemala that Europe valued was that of the Indian. Indeed, for Europe—for the scholars of the Sorbonne and the artists of Montparnasse—Guatemala *was* the Indian. While in the surrounding cafés a generation of Spanish American writers debated the nature and even the very existence of their national and continental identities, Asturias received a swift and definitive answer to his questions: Guatemala was the Maya. To become an authentic Guatemalan, within the terms of the Europe from which cultural authority emanated, he must become a Maya. This imperative, while turning many of his previous assumptions on their heads, had the advantage of resolving certain difficult issues facing Asturias. The elusive Guatemalan 'alma nacional' no longer lacked a definition. The categorization of Guatemala as the land of the Maya and of modern Guatemalans as the descendants of a noble, mysterious and defeated race also enabled Asturias to draw an unambiguous line between himself and Gómez Carrillo. It provided him with a programme for converting Guatemala, in European eyes, from the 'tierra de Carrillo' to the 'tierra de Asturias'—a very different place, inhabited by shamans and spirits rather than dapper, Europeanized boulevardiers. Mayan mythology took over the task of representing Guatemala and its national aspirations to the outside world. The rest of Asturias's literary career would be devoted to reconciling—and subordinating—Mayan Guatemala to the middle-class nationalism that remained the driving force behind his work.

Asturias spent his early years in Paris reconstructing himself as the voice of the Maya. His creative notebooks for these years open with four pages of meticulous notes on Mayan culture and Guatemalan history, which precede and prepare the ground for his attempts at fiction.[33] Asturias's success in reinventing himself was phenomenal. French—and even Spanish and Spanish American—accounts of his appearance and origins consistently exaggerate his Indian characteristics and grasp of Mayan culture. His turning away from *ladino* positivism—symbolized, in the anecdote of his first meeting with Raynaud, by his entering the taxi to drive away from the statue of Auguste Comte—was universally accepted; he slipped with utter conviction into his new role as the man destined to demonstrate to sceptical Parisians such as Madame Raynaud that Mayas did in fact exist. Asturias became Paris's representative Maya. He conditioned his Parisian acquaintances to think of him as a Maya. The French critic Claude Couffon begins his book on Asturias's work with a description of the man that recapitulates this vision.

C'est à l'ancêtre indien, au dignitaire des bas-reliefs et des poteries mayas que l'on songe en regardant cet homme impassible, massif, aux yeux obliques, aux paupières proéminentes, au nez busqué écrasant le croissant pulpeux des lèvres qui s'ouvrent parfois sous la cascade d'un rire inattendu.[34]

The description treats Asturias as he had treated the Indians in his thesis: it distances him from European culture, constructing him as an exotic Other. Couffon's portrait conveys a respect for and interest in Guatemalan Indian culture, but it also dehumanizes Asturias. He becomes an image glimpsed on a shard of pottery rather than a man. French commentators adopted this approach to Asturias from the beginning of his career. In an article published in *El Imparcial* in 1932, entitled 'Por qué traduje las *Leyendas de Guatemala*', Francis de Miomandre wrote:

conocí a Miguel Angel Asturias personalmente y recuerdo hasta qué punto me sorprendió la analogía de su cara y de toda su persona con su arte. Era así como yo me imaginaba a Asturias: ardiente, grave, como consumido por el fuego interior del lirismo e iluminado por no sé qué luz venida del fondo de las edades.[35]

Again, Asturias is linked not with the present, but with a semi-mythological past in which the European reader, harried and disillusioned by the demands of modern technological existence, may take imaginative refuge. This mythological past becomes a vehicle for infusing the banal modern world with 'el fuego interior del lirismo'. In a similar vein, Asturias's friend Robert Desnos described him in a 1933 article as 'barbado como un indio de antes de la conquista'.[36] Such panegyrics reached new heights after Asturias was awarded the Nobel Prize. In a speech delivered at a ceremony celebrating the award—held, significantly, at the Sorbonne—Marcel Bataillon said:

On imagine l'émoi de Raynaud quand il découvrit un beau jour parmi ses auditeurs un visage maya quiché […].

Bien des siècles après que se seront tus les échos de son élection [au Prix Nobel] et de nos hommages [Asturias] vivra, mythique à son tour, dans le monde des dieux, des héros et des hommes de l'ancien Guatemala.[37]

This is a highly unconventional critical homage to pay to a twentieth-century avant-garde novelist. Bataillon proceeds from an unquestioning identification of Asturias as a Maya to his implicit inscription within the mythologized past of a fallen empire. Asturias is seen not as a man of the present but as a vestige of 'l'ancien Guatemala'; it is as an inhabitant of the pre-Columbian past, not as a protagonist in the evolution of the modern Spanish American novel, Bataillon suggests, that Asturias will be remembered. Artur Lundkvist, the Nobel official responsible for Latin America and a man instrumental in Asturias's selection for the prize, betrays a similar romanticization in his entirely extra-literary appreciation: 'J'ai tout de suit reconnu en lui le chef maya, à la haute stature, au visage d'ange'.[38] Günter Lorenz, having it both ways, claims at the same time that Asturias was from 'einer der wenigen aristokratischen Familien seines Landes' and, in contradiction of the evidence, that Asturias had 'die rein indianische Mutter'.[39]

Asturias's conversion of himself from *ladino* to Maya took place initially within the context of the Spanish American expatriate community. Jimena Sáenz reports that

[s]us compañeros lo llamaban 'el ídolo maya' [...]. La misma nariz, que no se encuentra en ningún otro miembro de su familia, lo identifica a él, misteriosamente, como un descendiente directo de los primitivos habitantes de su tierra [...]. Nuestro escritor [...] es el mejor representante de aquellos poetas precolombinos que cantaron a los guerreros y a los jefes en la casa de los poetas del Petén o del Yucatán. (*Genio y figura*, 41–2)

Asturias's friends continued to propagate his image as a Maya idol long after they had all put their Parisian apprenticeships behind them. Arturo Uslar Pietri's recollections of the period are typical in their lyrical overkill:

Aquel mozo risueño y ausente, con cara de estela maya que se hubiera escapado de una galería del Museo del Hombre para asomarse extraviado a la acera de Montparnasse en las tardes de París [...] hablaba un castellano de Pedro de Alvarado o de Bartolomé de las Casas y se quedaba en silencio, con un silencio de brujo de Kopán que aguarda la vuelta de Quetzalcóatl.[40]

Despite his rhetorical excesses, Uslar Pietri's Asturias remains more authentic than the ghost invoked in other accounts. By mentioning both conquistadores and Mesoamericans in his evocation, Uslar Pietri recognizes Asturias's *mestizo* essence. He places Asturias, inappropriately, in a legendary past; but that past is shared, like Asturias's own history, between Spanish and Indian figures. Unfortunately, Uslar Pietri's description stops short of a full-fledged acknowledgement of Asturias's complexities. His characterization of Asturias as having escaped from the Musée de l'homme depicts the Indian pole as dominant in Asturias's make-up; while recognizing his friend's racial duality, Uslar Pietri cannot prevent himself from disseminating the myth of Asturias the Mayan shaman.

The critic who expresses the greatest awareness of Asturias's Parisian re-invention of himself is Marc Cheymol. Unlike other prominent writers on Asturias, Cheymol recognizes the mythologizing process in which the author is engaged.[41]

Tous les propos d'Asturias [...] tissent l'image mythique qu'il voulait qu'on eût de lui: porte-parole du peuple indien, sorte de chaman, intermédiaire entre le monde des hommes et celui des dieux; victime politique d'autre part, persécuté d'exil en exil par les circonstances et les dictatures. (*Années folles*, 11)

But even Cheymol buys into part of the Asturias myth. His otherwise scrupulously researched book perpetuates the canard that Asturias spoke Quiché, supposedly having learned the language during early childhood, when his parents were exiled to the countryside for three years: 'il y apprit en même temps à parler le quiché, comme sa langue maternelle' (*Années folles*, 16). In fact, Asturias knew only a few words of the language; these he had almost certainly acquired in Professor Raynaud's seminars at the Sorbonne. This did not prevent him from speaking in eloquent terms of the Mayan *nana*, or nanny, who had cared for him and, he sometimes claimed, taught him her language during his residence in the town of Salamá. (Contemporary Salamá, set among high hills in a prosperous ranching region in eastern Guatemala, far from the Mayan highlands in the north-west part of the country, is remarkable as one of the minority of towns in Guatemala where native dress is not seen and native languages are not spoken.) In his preface to the Italian edition of Léopold Sedar Senghor's poetry, Asturias referred to his Paris years as 'les années où j'étudiai et traduisis, des langues indigènes en espagnol, le *Popol-Vuh* et *Los Anales de los Xahil*'.[42] This is a blatant fabrication. The research task for which Raynaud engaged Asturias and the Spanish-born Mexican J. M. González de Mendoza was to translate into Spanish Raynaud's *French* translation of the Quiché text. Given Asturias's rudimentary grasp of French at the time (he never became fully at ease in the language), he likely contributed little to the translation itself, devoting his energy to polishing the final Spanish text while González de Mendoza, who spoke French fluently, did the actual translating.[43]

At no time in his life was Asturias capable of translating from Quiché. He would not have learned Quiché even if his *nana* had taught him her language, because the predominantly *mestizo* and Spanish-speaking village of Salamá belonged to traditional *pipil* territory: it had been an Aztec enclave in Mayan Guatemala. The minority of the population still communicating in Indian languages at the time of Asturias's residence there between 1904 and 1907 were speaking Aztec-descended languages; in all likelihood, almost no one in Salamá spoke Quiché.[44]

Cheymol rectifies his account of Asturias's linguistic background, while extending his critique of Asturias's invention of his Mayan persona, in an article published the year after his book.

Desde su llegada a París, el joven Asturias habrá experimentado, ahora desde un punto de vista francés, la impresión sensacional que causaba el contraste entre su nombre y su físico. Como buen actor, y no sin un dejo de coquetería, sabrá jugar con esta apariencia de príncipe maya [...] aunque era, en realidad, un buen burgués católico y criollo, un verdadero *ladino*.[45]

Cheymol appears to attribute his gaffe in his book to Asturias's adept campaign to propagate his Mayan image. He writes:

Pretendió haber aprendido allí [en Salamá], en un ambiente típicamente indio, el idioma quiché con sus compañeros—verdaderos hijos del campo— como si fuera su idioma materno (el de su madre, de la madre-tierra), al mismo tiempo, o quizá antes, del español. (Asturias, *París 1924–1933*, 846)

That such a lucid critic as Cheymol, writing more than a dozen years after Asturias's death, should retain a lingering attachment to the image of Asturias the Quiché-speaking interpreter of Indian reality underlines the myth's power. (Only later in his article does Cheymol unequivocally renounce the idea that Asturias spoke Quiché: 'Nunca supo aquel idioma' (Asturias, *París 1924–1933*, 857).) The myth answered (and arguably continues to answer) strong needs in the Parisian psyche: it supplied a tangible source of the 'primitive', spontaneous elements lacking from French culture; it offered an alternative to decadent refinement and the lethal 'civilization' whose failings had resulted in the destruction of the First World War. From the moment that Raynaud told him, 'Vous êtes maya', France cast Asturias in the image of its own intellectual and psychological needs. Asturias responded by playing the role to the hilt, 'exagerando incluso su interés por la erudición etnoantropológica, y construye su mito de "príncipe indio": véanse las poses que toma en casi todas las fotos de la época' (Asturias, *París 1924–1933*, 857).

Asturias, in short, liberated himself on another culture's terms. The contradictions of this position fall into relief in the summary of his apprenticeship that he prepared for his introduction to Senghor's poems.

En 1923 [*sic*] j'arrivai à Paris, tandis que chantaient encore en moi les langueurs euphoniques et ineffables du moderniste Rubén Darío que j'avais apprises dans mes fréquentations littéraires et universitaires du milieu hispanisant 'blanc' de Ciudad de Guatemala [...]. C'est précisément à Paris que mes penchants juvéniles et naturels vers le cosmopolitanisme se décantèrent peu à peu, puis s'évanouirent. Les souvenirs de ma terre guatemaltèque, mystérieusement habitée par l'ineffable splendeur maya à laquelle nous rendions un peu tous un hommage hybride et inavoué venaient assiéger mon esprit et ma nouvelle ferveur d'écrivain [...]. C'est à cette époque que j'entrepris, soutenu par la lumière de probité et d'universalité du monde universitaire français, d'étudier avidement, de confronter, de rappeler, de retrouver en moi-même, les 'disjecta membra' du grand Empire maya que, plus tard, Arnold Toynbee devait appeler la 'Grèce d'Amérique'. C'est dans ce climat de passion que j'écrivis mes *Leyendas de Guatemala* qui plurent tant à Paul Valéry. (*Préface*, 41–2)

In order to make his past mesh with his present, Asturias engages in certain distortions. He claims that the young Guatemalans of his generation 'rendions un peu tous un hommage hybride et inavoué' to the grandeur of the Mayan Empire. No evidence exists to support this assertion; as the first chapter argued, evidence does exist to support the contrary assertion that the Indian was rarely discussed in *ladino* society and was not an object of homage—even hybrid and unavowed homage—on the part of bourgeois youth. Luis Cardoza y Aragón portrays the young Asturias as barred by his social background from meaningful knowledge of Indian reality: 'Un hombre de la capital, con su formación conservadora ¿cómo podía llegar de verdad al indio? No había camino, posibilidad alguna' (*Asturias*, 51). Not surprisingly, *Viernes de Dolores*, Asturias's mature, politically aware novel about the bourgeois Guatemalan youth of his generation, contains no mention of either Indians or ineffable Mayan splendour.[46]

Asturias's heartfelt praise of the 'lumière' provided by the French university system reinforces the contradictions intrinsic to his experience. There is no doubt that Raynaud's seminars enlarged Asturias's perspective and opened his mind; there is no doubt that Asturias threw himself into the study of the Mayan past with enthusiasm—even if, as Cheymol suggests, his enthusiasm contained a significant strain of calculation. Yet as his allusions to Arnold Toynbee and Paul Valéry reveal, Asturias's liberation remained partial. Mayan splendour was not, in his view, sufficient unto itself; it required Toynbee's certification that the Mayan Empire was the 'Grèce d'Amérique', just as *Leyendas de Guatemala* gained the imprimatur of acceptability through Paul Valéry's praise. The fact that Asturias continued to feel the need to draw attention to Valéry's praise of his work more than thirty-five years later, after he had won the Nobel Prize, demonstrates his continuing dependence on Parisian approval of his cultural identity. In this vision, the attainments of the New World existed in a subordinate relationship to the cultural facts of the Old World. It is impossible, for example, to imagine Asturias characterizing Greece (or Athens, at least) as the 'Tikal of Europe'.

The reasons for Asturias's failure to overcome this complex are embedded in history; it is important to remember his pioneering role in confronting these issues. Even anti-imperialist thinkers of the 1920s took European cultural superiority to be axiomatic. In a passage as important for its assumptions as it is for its analysis, Antonio Gramsci (whose prison writings are contemporaneous with Asturias's early years in Paris) wrote:

Even if one admits that other cultures have had an importance and a significance in the process of 'hierarchical' unification of world civilization (and this should certainly be admitted without question), they have had a universal value only in so far as they have become constituent elements of European culture, which is the only historically and concretely universal culture—in so far, that is, as they have contributed to the process of European thought and been assimilated by it.[47]

Yet Gramsci possessed a refined critique of the problems of identity created by cultural domination and the assimilation of alien views of one's own society. Elsewhere he wrote: 'Japan is the Far East not only for Europe but also perhaps for the American from California and even for the Japanese himself, who, through English political culture, may then call Egypt the Near East' (Hoare and Nowell-Smith, *Selections*, 447).

Gramsci's analysis of the distortions imposed upon non-European identities by European dominance offers as its main conceptual tool the notion of hegemony. 'Critical understanding of self', he wrote, 'takes place [...] through a struggle of political "hegemonies" and of opposing directions, first in the ethical field and then in that of politics proper, in order to arrive at a higher level of one's consciousness' (Hoare and Nowell-Smith, *Selections*, 333). The complex of dominant myths and cultural practices comprising the idea of hegemony provides one of the clearest methods of discussing the problem of self-assertion before a culture towards which one's own culture has been historically subservient—precisely the dilemma which Spanish-American writers of Asturias's generation confronted in Paris. As Gramsci himself wrote:

America has not yet emerged from the economic-corporate phase which Europe passed through in the Middle Ages—in other words, has not yet created a conception of the world or a group of great intellectuals to lead the people within the ambit of civil societies. (Hoare and Nowell-Smith, *Selections*, 272)

The novels of writers such as Asturias were to further the task of generating and universalizing a distinctively Latin American conception of the world. The Paris experience, despite its many contradictions, fostered the formation of a more independent—if still alienated—intellectual class. Both the breakthroughs and the limitations inherent in this position were to resonate through Asturias's Parisian writing.

Notes to Chapter 2

1. Williamson, *Penguin History of Latin America*, 163.
2. John King, 'Carlos Fuentes: An Interview', in *Modern Latin American Fiction: A Survey* , ed. John King (London: Faber and Faber, 1987), 141.
3. Sylvia Molloy, *La Diffusion de la littérature hispano-américaine en France au XXe siècle* (Paris: Presses Universitaires de France, 1972), 15.
4. Karl-D. Uitti, 'Remy de Gourmont et le monde hispanique', *Romanische Forschungen* 72/1–2 (1960), 53.
5. Marc Cheymol, *Miguel Angel Asturias dans le Paris des années folles* (Grenoble: Presses Universitaires de Grenoble, 1987), 9.
6. Jean Franco, *The Modern Culture of Latin America* (London: Pall Mall Press, 1967), 11.
7. Cited by Alberto Ruy Sánchez, *Una introducción a Octavio Paz* (Mexico: Editorial Joaquín Moritz, 1990), 17–18.
8. Rubén Darío, *Obras completas* (Madrid: Afrodisio Aguado, 1950–5), i. 69, cited by Molloy, *La Diffusion*, 34. Molloy also notes the frustration engendered in Spanish intellectuals by the Latin American obsession with Paris. She quotes Miguel de Unamuno, in an exasperated letter to Darío, complaining: 'Debo decirle que no acabo de comprender del todo esa atracción que sobre ustedes ejerce París, ni ese anhelo de que sea precisamente París, y no Londres, o Berlín, o Viena, o Bruselas, o Estocolmo, o [...] Heidelberg' (*La Diffusion*, 18).
9. Enrique Gómez Carrillo, *En plena bohemia* (Buenos Aires: Casa Vaccaro, 1921), 10–11.
10. Edwin Williamson, 'Coming to Terms With Modernity: Magical Realism and the Historical Process in the Novels of Alejo Carpentier', in *Modern Latin American Fiction: A Survey*, ed. John King (London: Faber and Faber, 1987), 96.
11. Alejo Carpentier, *El recurso del método* (1974; Mexico: Siglo Veintiuno, 1988), 22.
12. Max Henríquez Ureña, *Breve historia del modernismo* (Mexico: Fondo de Cultura Económica, 1954), 393–4.
13. 'The master of the *crónica* was the Guatemalan, Enrique Gómez Carrillo, who for some thirty years wrote pieces from Paris that were syndicated in newspapers throughout the continent. Through the *crónica*, the middle classes in the cities of Latin America received news of the styles and inventions of the great cultural metropolises of Europe.' Williamson, *Penguin History of Latin America*, 304.
14. Sáenz, *Genio y figura de Miguel Angel Asturias*, 40.
15. Interview with Sara Monzón Basterrechea, cited by Gerald Martin, 'Asturias y *El Imparcial*.', in Asturias, *París 1924–1933*, 794.

16. The other significant omission from Asturias's *crónicas* is that of César Vallejo. Cardoza y Aragón writes: 'Para mí es sorprendente que en sus crónicas no se mencione siquiera al latinoamericano más notable en esos años en París y en los siguientes, César Vallejo'. Luis Cardoza y Aragón, *Miguel Angel Asturias: casi novela* (Mexico, D.F.: Ediciones Era, 1991), 178.

17. Harold Bloom, *The Anxiety of Influence: A Theory of Poetry* (London: Oxford University Press, 1973), 26.

18. Gerald Martin, 'Notas', in Asturias, *París 1924–1933*, 567.

19. Asturias is reputed to have discovered Gómez Carrillo's coffin draped in the Argentine flag; he may have argued unsuccessfully with the Argentine delegation to the funeral to have the flag replaced with the Guatemalan one. See Cardoza y Aragón, *Miguel Angel Asturias*, 186.

20. Manuel Ugarte, *Escritores iberoamericanos de 1900* (Santiago de Chile: Ediciones Orbe, 1943), 25.

21. Gerald Martin, *Journeys through the Labyrinth: Latin American Fiction in the Twentieth Century* (London and New York: Verso, 1989), 23.

22. Luis Cardoza y Aragón, *El Río: Novelas de caballería* (México: Fondo de Cultura Económica, 1986), 562.

23. Cited by Beatriz Sarlo, *Una modernidad periférica: Buenos Aires 1920 y 1930* (Buenos Aires: Ediciones Nueva Visión, 1988), 168.

24. Maurice Nadeau, *Histoire du Surréalisme* (Paris: Editions du Seuil, 1945), 25.

25. Alejo Carpentier, *Crónicas 2* (La Habana: Instituto Cubano del Libro, 1976), 89.

26. Edward W. Said, *Culture and Imperialism* (London: Chatto & Windus, 1993), 253.

27. Alfonso Reyes, *Diario 1911–1930*. Cited by Cardoza y Aragón, *Miguel Angel Asturias*, 71.

28. André Breton, *Manifestes du Surréalisme* (Paris: Jean-Jacques Pauvert, 1962), 18.

29. Rama, *La novela*, 108.

30. López Alvarez, *Conversaciones*, 73.

31. René Prieto contends that Asturias added nearly a year to his European sojourn: 'A recently discovered telegram sent from Puerto Barrios before boarding the ship to Europe is dated June 24, 1924 […]. We must conclude that [Asturias] left Guatemala almost a year later than he always claimed and, second, that he either spent a very short time in London or left that city merely in order to interview Miguel de Unamuno in Paris and then returned to the British capital. This last hypothesis is confirmed by the date of the London articles published in *El Imparcial*, between January and March 1925, months after the Paris interview with Unamuno took place' (*Archeology of Return*, 28).

32. Mario Alberto Carrera (ed.), *¿Cómo era Miguel Angel Asturias?* (Guatemala: Universidad de San Carlos, 1975), 52.

33. Le Fonds Asturias, Bibliothèque nationale, Paris. Carnet de travail numéro 1, 1–4.

34. Claude Couffon, *Miguel Angel Asturias* (Paris: Editions Seghers, 1970), 5.

35. Francis de Miomandre, 'Por qué traduje las *Leyendas de Guatemala*', in Asturias, *París 1924–1933*, 533–4.

36. Robert Desnos, 'Hombres y leyendas tropicales: M. A. Asturias', in Asturias, *París 1924–1933*, 534.

37. Marcel Bataillon, 'Miguel Angel Asturias et Bartolomé de las Casas', *Europe* 473 (Sept. 1968), 7–10.

38. Artur Lundkvist, 'De Miguel Angel Asturias', *Europe* 553–4 (May–June 1975), 8.
39. Günter W. Lorenz, *Miguel Angel Asturias: Porträt und Poesie* (Bonn: Luchterhand, 1968), 10. Photographs show Asturias's *mestiza* mother as having been darker than his father; but she was far from being a 'pure' Indian.
40. Arturo Uslar Pietri, *Fantasmas de dos mundos* (Barcelona: Seix Barral, 1979), 13.
41. This insight is given its most radically disenchanted expression in Horst Rogmann's scathing polemic, 'Miguel Angel Asturias, dios maya', *Escritura: Teoría y Crítica Literarias*, iii. 5–6 (Jan.–Dec. 1978), 11–24. Rogmann's article is cuttingly perceptive in its attacks on French romanticizations of Asturias's persona and offers a provocative commentary on the ways in which Asturias's portrayal of his art as the spontaneous eruption of primitive Mayan sources led him to undervalue his own literary accomplishments. But Rogmann does not provide a coherent account of how or why Asturias came to elaborate his 'Mayan' identity, and his application of his insights to Asturias's *obra* is sketchy and inconsistent. By contrast, René Prieto, who accepts at face value Asturias's claim to extraordinary learning in Mayan mythology and anthropology, attributes the young Guatemalan's identification with the Maya to his never having 'resolve[d] his oedipal attachment [...] the identification with the maternal image brings with it, in this specific instance, an identification with María Rosales's Indian heritage'. Prieto, *Archeology of Return*, 26.
42. Asturias, 'Préface à la poésie de Léopold Sedar Senghor', *Europe* 553–4 (May–June 1975), 42.
43. For Asturias's poor French, see Cheymol, *Années folles*, 143. For the division of translation labours, see Cheymol, 'Miguel Angel Asturias entre latinidad e indigenismo: los viajes de Prensa Latina y los seminarios de cultura maya en la Sorbona', in Asturias, *París 1924–1933*, 879. The account of the translation process presented by Cheymol has been contested, most forcefully by Luis Cardoza y Aragón, who cites the following from an interview with Francisco Monterde, former president of the Academia Mexicana de la Lengua, in the Mexican newspaper *El Día*: 'Según me contó el Abate [Mendoza] [...] Miguel Angel Asturias [...] obtuvo del Gobierno de Guatemala la subvención para imprimir la obra si figuraba su nombre con el de González de Mendoza como colaborador [...]. Para justificarlos, Asturias se encargó de traducir únicamente los pies de grabados de las ilustraciones del *Popol Vuh*' (*El Río: Novelas de caballería*, 207–8). Cardoza y Aragón repeats this charge in *Miguel Angel Asturias*, 15. Whatever the truth of Cardoza y Aragón's contention that González de Mendoza is solely responsible for the translation, Monterde's account cannot be reconciled with the first edition of the translation, which acknowledges the funding of the Guatemalan government, but credits the translation equally to González and Asturias as 'alumnos titulares' of Raynaud, 'quien lee correctamente el castellano' and is credited with revising the translation (p. ix). The illustrations consist of five pages of line drawings of stelae, etc. Asturias could not have translated the captions, as Monterde claims, because the only caption consists of the phrase, appearing at the bottom of each of the five pages, 'Véase pág. 141 la explicación de los dibujos'. These explanations (conceivably what Monterde intends by 'los pies de los grabados') are extremely scanty, amounting to a total of less than one generously spaced page.

See *Los Dioses, los Héroes y los Hombres de Guatemala Antigua, o El libro del consejo POPOL-VUH de los indios Quichés* (Paris: Editorial París-América, 1927).

44. Martin Lienhard, 'La legitimación indígena en dos novelas centroamericanas', *Cuadernos Hispanoamericanos*, 414 (Dec. 1984), 120 n. Lorenz commits the most serious exaggeration of Asturias's linguistic abilities, claiming, with reference to Raynaud's French translation of the *Popol-Vuh*: 'Asturias, der mehrere indianische Dialekte Guatemalas beherrscht, studierte die Übersetzungen Raynauds sehr sorgfältig' (*Miguel Angel Asturias: Porträt und Poesie*, 31). The myth of Asturias's 'fluency' in Quiché refuses to die. In one of the most recent and critically sophisticated studies of Asturias's work, Dorita Nouhaud writes: 'Sous la direction de son professeur [Asturias] avait traduit le *Popol Vuh (Livre du Conseil)* du maya-quiché au français puis du français à l'espagnol.' Nouhaud, *Miguel Angel Asturias, l'écriture antérieure* (Paris: L'Harmattan, 1991), 9. While Lienhard gives the dates of Asturias's childhood residence in Salamá as 1904–7, Gerald Martin claims that the Asturias family lived in the town from 1903 to 1908. See Asturias, *Hombres de maíz* (1949; Nanterre: Centre de recherches Latino-Américaines, 1992), ed. Gerald Martin, 461.

45. Marc Cheymol, 'Miguel Angel Asturias entre latinidad e indigenismo: Los viajes de Prensa Latina y los seminarios de cultura maya en la sorbona', in Asturias, *París 1924–1933*, 846.

46. Nor did the Guatemalan novelists active during Asturias's youth offer any access to such a consciousness. In her survey of the works of the four most prominent Guatemalan novelists of the *modernista* generation (Gómez Carrillo, César Brañas, Máximo Soto-Hall and Rafael Arévalo Martínez) Adelaida Lorand de Olazagasti concludes that the first two did not mention the Indian in their fiction while the latter two confined Indian characters to stereotyped minor roles and that their portrayals reveal that, in general, 'despreciaron al indio'. Lorand de Olazagasti, *El indio en la narrativa guatemalteca* (San Juan: Editorial Universitaria–Universidad de Puerto Rico, 1968), 39–40.

47. Quinton Hoare and Geoffrey Nowell-Smith (eds.), *Selections from the Prison Notebooks of Antonio Gramsci* (London: Lawrence and Wishart, 1971), 416.

CHAPTER 3

The Constitution of an Identity: Asturias's Parisian Journalism

Asturias's engagement with European hegemony first took shape in a literary context in his Parisian journalism. His journalism fortified his literary style and refined his point of view; the strengths and outlook evident in his growing mastery of the *crónica* were carried over into his creative work. Following Rubén Darío, Asturias knew that journalism 'no mata sino a los débiles. Un intelectual no encontrará en la tarea periodística sino una gimnasia que lo robustece.'[1] He produced a huge number of *crónicas* during his Parisian years. As a result of the volume of his work, the speed with which it was produced and the provisional, exploratory nature of his encounters with Paris and Europe, contradictions and inconsistencies of perspective abound. A careful reading of the *crónicas* shows many of these contradictions to be integral to the gradually hardening contours of Asturias's cultural self-definition.

The persona generated by Asturias in his *crónicas* came to underlie and focus the assumptions of his fiction. In this respect, as in many others, his stance can be seen as an intermediate posture between the assertions of *modernismo* and the authority accorded the writers of the Boom generation. José Martí, Rubén Darío and Enrique Gómez Carrillo produced their polished *crónicas* at the cost of suppressing the impulse towards eccentric self-expression they had inherited from the Romantics' definition of authorship. As Aníbal González writes, the *modernistas* discovered that 'journalism undermines the idea of the "author"—so vital to nineteenth century literature and philology—because what matters most in journalism is the information itself and not the individual who transmits it'.[2]

By the 1980s, as González goes on to point out, this situation had been turned on its head. When major Hispanic writers contributed columns or opinion pieces to newspapers they did so in the role of 'the intellectual celebrity-commentator, a cultural pundit whose insights are less important than the person from whom they emanate' (*Journalism*, 109). Asturias's journalism constitutes part of the process through which the Spanish American author came to develop and express a distinctive yet culturally representative individuality.

In Asturias's first articles, remnants of Gómez Carrillo's 'myth of Paris' obtrude. The city becomes exotic and unpredictable; he likens it to a capricious woman: 'París, es una mujer que se da cuando ama o cuando no ama y quiere darse'.[3] Yet the potency of the *modernista* myth is vitiated by another, competing theme which did not preoccupy Gómez Carrillo: the construction of a Guatemalan national identity. Exposure to the daunting cultural self-confidence of the French throws Asturias back on the inadequacies and self-denigration of the Guatemalan bourgeoisie. He laments, at regular intervals, the feebleness of the Guatemalan 'alma nacional'. His three-part series on 'Realidad social guatemalteca', published in *El Imparcial* (4–6 May 1925), attempts to analyse Guatemalan society in terms of the rift between 'la masa negra' (Indians and illiterate *ladinos*) and 'los semicivilizados' (the governing classes) (*París 1924–1933*, 26–30). The second label underlines Asturias's loss of confidence in the leadership potential of the Guatemalan bourgeoisie. 'La ignorancia de las clases que se llaman preparadas en Guatemala es algo que desconcierta', he writes (*París 1924–1933*, 28). Deeply disturbed by Guatemala's woeful lack of national will, he bemoans 'la no existencia de una realidad social guatemalteca, sino de dos realidades distintas' (*París 1924–1933*, 28).

One of the most salient traits of Asturias's early Parisian journalism is a propensity to attack his own class. This may be in part a projection of his personal insecurities—no doubt aggravated by his arrival in Paris—onto the milieu which had formed him; but the shift also has important consequences for his larger conception of Guatemalan national identity. If the bourgeoisie, the traditional agent of the nation-state, proves incapable of assuming its historical role, other groups may be obliged to shoulder the burden of national definition. Asturias's loss of faith in the bourgeoisie opens the way for his characterization of Guatemala as the land of the Maya.

While obviously daunted by certain aspects of French life, Asturias soon revised his misty-eyed images of Paris. Less than a year after his arrival, he had replaced his equation of the city with a fickle woman with the more measured (if still somewhat romanticized) vision of Paris as a combined university, library and museum: 'Para el que aspira subir, para el que viene a valer, soñador, poeta o estudiante, sabio o sacerdote, París es una universidad, una biblioteca, un museo, una historia viva de páginas imborrables, un laboratorio, un templo' (*París 1924–1933*, 32). Only the last of these images yields to romantic excess, implying a worshipful attitude towards the city and its culture; the other images all suggest a place of research and learning—endeavours which require an active, rather than a passive, relationship to French culture. This, at a superficial level, appears to be the key to Asturias's early vision of the role of the young Spanish American intellectual in Paris. At the end of his interview with Gómez Carrillo's protegé León Pacheco, Asturias breaks into an enthusiastic and covertly prescriptive account of Pacheco's place in the Parisian artistic firmament.

León Pacheco trabaja en París, se mueve en París, es una de las figuras de París, en los círculos latinos e intelectuales. Su juicio y su preparación nos hacen volver la esperanza que en presencia de las juventudes desorientadas de América habíamos perdido […]. Admira y habla siempre de hombres centroamericanos […]. Y entre una y otra idea, nos cuenta de la última humorada de Jean Cocteau, el hombre más inteligente de París, de las paradojas y de los entusiasmos de Alfonso Reyes y de la manera cómo hace don Miguel de Unamuno el pato, en papel. (*París 1924–1933*, 61)

Asturias might be writing an idealized account of his own activities. Pacheco is depicted as having achieved success and recognition ('es una de las figuras de París') through an unswerving allegiance to his native Central American culture. Asturias's list of Pacheco's subjects of conversation expresses his own order of cultural priorities. Central America comes first; but to supplement and enlarge his perspective, he maintains an acquaintance with the intellectual representatives of (*a*) Paris (Jean Cocteau); (*b*) other parts of Spanish America (Alfonso Reyes); and (*c*) Spain (Unamuno). Pacheco, in this account, incarnates the aware, emancipated Central American intellectual.

But Pacheco's literary career fizzled out; Asturias became highly successful. The apportioning of literary talent may not have been the only factor generating this disparity. The most revealing aspect of Asturias's ordering of priorities—and the one that best helps to explain why his career flourished—lies in his unexpected ranking of Paris above Spanish America. While other Spanish American writers

were wrestling with the substance of their national and continental
identities, Asturias—equipped with his Parisian-bred self-definition as
a Maya—could participate in these debates without acute personal
investment. His confrontation with France was more important. He
already knew how to define himself as a Spanish American: he was a
Maya. The question weighing upon him was how Mayan-ness (which
he construed, in emblematic form, as representing Guatemalan
national aspirations) interacted with the rest of the world. He did not,
at least during his first four years in Paris, become deeply immersed
in contemporary French literature; but the example of Parisian
prosperity and French social cohesion remained a touchstone of his
articles, a constant reproof to Guatemalan backwardness. This
dynamic tension meant that his 'liberated' focus on Guatemalan issues
was undermined by frequent references to French superiority. His
articles invoke France as a pretext for discussing Guatemala; at the
same time, France becomes a source of norms and standards to which
Asturias exhorts Guatemala to aspire. The tactic cuts both ways, on
the one hand asserting Asturias's insistence on repudiating the heritage
of Gómez Carrillo by writing about his own country, while at the
same time assessing that country in light of hegemonic European
assumptions.

The pattern repeats in article after article. A conversational ramble
through some corner of French society veers into a pointed critique
of Guatemala's prevailing social order. At times the linkage is clumsy
to the point of disingenuousness: 'Hojeando el Libro del Estudiante
de la Universidad de París (1925–26) he recordado—por contraste se
asocian las ideas—la situación precaria en que se encuentran nuestros
estudios superiores' (*París 1924–1933*, 72). In another article, Asturias
writes: 'Visitando las casas para obreros de la institución Rothschild,
he pensado en la facilidad con que entre nosotros, sobre un pie de
justicia social, podría resolverse el problema de la carestía de la
vivienda' (*París 1924–1933*, 83). The motivation behind his choice of
method is clear. As Amos Segala writes:

se advierte de inmediato cuál es el juego al que se entrega Asturias,
preocupado por deslizar mensajes que podrían resultar demasiado
desagradables o por recordar verdades bastante duras de admitir, a través del
sesgo de una experiencia directa y 'de prestigio'. Así pues, París no interviene
sólo al nivel de la información, sino de la formación. (*París 1924–1933*, p. xlvi)

This is a crucial point. When Asturias, in a dispatch from Auxerre, lauds French political pluralism, his progressive's yearning for a more liberal political culture gives way little by little to admiration of more frivolous aspects of European life. The article begins with an appreciation of the quality of regional newspapers in the French provinces and the variety of intellectual perspectives available even to French citizens residing in comparative backwaters. The variety of outlooks is interpreted as constructive rather than divisive:

En este pequeño poblado de Francia hemos encontrado varias publicaciones de importancia, algunas de extrema izquierda. Todas se ocupan vivamente de la cuestión política del momento: el arreglo financiero del país. No es la imposición de la voluntad gubernativa [...] a todos se les permite opinar y pensar en voz alta. (*París 1924–1933*, 98)

   The barely coded message for Asturias's Guatemalan readership, oppressed by the authoritarian rule of General Orellana, is clear. But what price has Asturias paid for appealing to European 'superiority' in order to make his point? As the article continues, the tone becomes prescriptive; in the prescriptions, a concern for equalling European fashion begins to compete with the expressed desire to enjoy European-style freedoms. Asturias envisages an improved Guatemala in which the city of Antigua has been converted into a university town as prestigious as any in Europe. Yet it is the students' dress, as much as their intellectual liberty, which catches Asturias's imagination. 'Por las calles memorables de la vieja ciudad vemos a los estudiantes envueltos en sus capas, con sombreros aludos, como los usan aún en París, en Salamanca, en Oxford, Bolonia y en algunas otras ciudades universitarias de Alemania' (*París 1924–1933*, 99). Having reconstructed his own identity, Asturias is beginning to make corresponding 'adjustments' in his vision of Guatemala. He yearns for the country to conform to his new, European-oriented perspective and, succumbing to a form of wish-fulfilment, allows himself to forget Guatemalan realities long enough to believe that it might actually be made to conform. The lapse is indicative of a struggle in his psyche rooted in his residual resistance to identifying himself as a Maya. If Antigua can be transformed into the equal of the Sorbonne or Salamanca, then Guatemala as a whole is capable of being elevated to European stature. If Guatemala attains a European level of progressive (implicitly bourgeois-led) development, Asturias, in order to act as the representative of Guatemalan nationalism, will not need to identify himself with the Indians whom he was brought up to disdain. The fantasy of capped students striding along beneath the volcanoes of Antigua originates in Asturias's inchoate (and deeply uneasy) sense of his role as a Maya. He can pull off the deception in Paris, but when he turns to write of Guatemala, his *ladino* training continues to recoil at the prospect of proposing any but 'modernizing', European-oriented solutions to his country's social ills.

Asturias's journalism exposes a sense of national pride badly bruised by the towering example of French integration and self-confidence. The urgency of his quest for a means of rehabilitating Guatemalan national identity often becomes painfully evident. In January 1927, nearly three years after his arrival in Europe and only a year prior to his pivotal visit to Cuba and Guatemala, Asturias published an article entitled 'Hacia una patria mejor', in which he wrote:

Los guatemaltecos que llegan a Europa con la cabeza llena de Guatemala, sentimentalismo puro, se convencen en menos tiempo del que creían que nuestro país está por hacer. Lo que primero choca y deprime al guatemalteco es su falta de nacionalidad, la impostura que a sus ojos, vista de lejos, representa la nación a la cual pertenece. En presencia de naciones donde tierras, ferrocarriles, industrias, comercio, concesiones y productos exportables corresponden a los nacionales, a los nativos del país, el guatemalteco se da cuenta, inmediatamente, de su nacionalidad de orden secundario, postizo, político, sin fundamento en las cosas, y por sus ojos abiertos, como los del que se sueña rodando en el vacío, pasan los campos de su tierra lejana, robados a los indios y vendidos por nada a los extranjeros de *capital sin corazón*. (*París 1924–1933*, 156)

In addition to expressing Asturias's wounded sense of national pride, this passage reveals a fresh source of identification with the Maya. As a member of a national bourgeoisie which has proved unable to install and codify its 'alma nacional', Asturias feels both envy of countries such as France, and frustration and outrage at the way in which greater powers—notably the United States—have bent Guatemala to their will. (He writes of his country's railways, built by US fruit companies to transport bananas to market, as 'la vergüenza del país y de sus hijos esclavos' (*París 1924–1933*, 156).) His consciousness of this situation leads to his adoption of an anti-imperialist political position. But how can such a position be symbolized? The economically privileged and culturally alienated *ladino* does not serve this purpose nearly as well as the Indian, whose dispossession of his ancestral lands is emblematic of the dilemma of the nation as a whole. When Asturias conjures up the image of the Parisian-based *ladino*, remembering 'los campos de su tierra lejana, robados a los indios y vendidos por nada a los extranjeros', he is making explicit for the first time in his writing the symbolic expression of bourgeois national aspirations through the evocation of Indian suffering which will generate much of his later fiction. The Maya becomes a versatile, conspicuous and effective icon with which to assert Guatemalan nationalism.

But Asturias had seized upon Mayan imagery because Paris, in the form of the Sorbonne and the French cultural élite, valued the 'primitive' aspect of Guatemala above all others. Asturias's awareness of this is discernible not only in his cultivation of a 'Mayan' persona but also in his account of the Parisian reception accorded 'primitivist' Latin American art. When the Guatemalan painter Humberto Garavito staged a successful exhibition in Paris in late 1925, Asturias wrote a breathless account of his triumph in *El Imparcial*. The article begins:

Garavito ha triunfado en París!, esta noticia debe propalarse por toda Guatemala con la premura del fuego en las pajas secas, entrando a las casas, a los templos, a las plazas, a los teatros; alegrándonos a todos como si se tratase de...uno de los nuestros. (*París 1924–1933*, 76)

More than a third of the article is devoted to quoting, in the original French and in its entirety, the review of the exhibition written for an unidentified Paris publication by the art critic René-Jean. The review praises Garavito's work for rendering the exoticism of the Guatemalan landscape:

Il évoque ses aspects typiques. Il évoque le pittoresque de ses habitants, ces Indiens vêtus de couleurs harmonieuses, qui juxtaposent avec audace l'éclat du rouge à la matité des noirs profonds [...]. C'est toute une vie lointaine qui surgit et s'offre à nos regards. (*París 1924–1933*, 77)

The review commends Garavito for his representational painting of 'typical' aspects of Guatemalan life. In a Paris bristling with avant-garde, often non-representational art, the Central American outsider is praised for *not innovating*: for delivering the primitive, unblemished essence of his culture to the metropolis for the metropolis's edification. The peripheral artist's finished product, charmingly naïve in its lines, becomes the cosmopolitan artist's raw material. If the Central American painter were to adopt an avant-garde approach, obfuscating the social context from which his art sprang, the metropolitan audience would be forced to grapple with the work's *artistic* content rather than with its picturesque place of origin. The peripheral artist's work would become more elaborate but less useful as an instrument with which to open the European mind to primitive artistic currents and the charms of a 'vie lointaine'. Parisian criticism, by valuing local art when it is avant-garde and foreign art when it delivers the 'truth' of distant places to a Parisian audience, strives to ensure that this does not happen. Edward Said, referring to Asturias's supporter Paul Valéry's praise of 'primitive' art from other continents in his responses to a 1925 questionnaire, argues: 'Europe's effort was to maintain itself as what Valéry called "une machine puissante", absorbing what it could from outside Europe, converting it to its use, intellectually and materially, keeping the Orient selectively organized (or disorganized)'.[4] Asturias's decision to quote a long extract in French in a newspaper many of whose readers possessed little or no knowledge of this language, underscores the extent to which he and most of his generation accepted and allowed themselves and their careers to be shaped by this hegemonic imperative. His own praise of Garavito's paintings, following his quote of René-Jean's review, reveals the prerogatives of a Europeanized eye:

Fiesta de color y de vida la de esta exposición que a jirones va mostrando a los ojos de los que, acostumbrados a los climas de Europa, se asombran al saber que entre nosotros la primavera no concluye todavía. Alegría primaveral en el cielo, en la tierra y en todo lugar [...]. Las indias envueltas en cortes rojos, con camisas blancas y en la cabeza envueltas las trenzas, se agrupan alrededor de la pila, inmóviles, con ese hierático cansancio que ennoblece a la raza de los dioses de piedra [...]. Extasis de una raza que agoniza lentamente. (*París 1924–1933*, 77)

Like the Parisian critic, Asturias lauds the bright colours in which the Maya are painted and the 'typical' aspects of Garavito's art. Where René-Jean speaks of viewing a life geographically and culturally remote from his own, Asturias depicts the Mayans as people belonging to a past era: 'la raza de los dioses de piedra'. His vision of Native culture has become far more positive than it was previously; he concedes the Mayans (whom he had earlier decried as 'anti-higiénico') the gifts of charm and spectacle. But ultimately the reference to stone gods and the romantic fuzziness of the 'éxtasis de una raza que agoniza lentamente' obscure and objectify Mayan reality.

Asturias demonstrates an awareness, not so much of Mayan culture but of Paris's willingness to embrace this culture, provided it is presented efficaciously. Near the end of the article, in a canny and prophetic insight, he writes: 'En estas ciudades cosmopolitas hay público para todo' (*París 1924–1933*, 78).

The watershed in Asturias's constitution of his creative identity was undoubtedly his Prensa Latina trip to Havana, and his subsequent return visit to Guatemala, in 1928. Coming near the midpoint of his decade in Paris, the journey enabled Asturias to test his emerging conception of Spanish American identity against a concrete social reality. Where earlier Prensa Latina jaunts to cities such as Florence, Liège and Bucharest had refined Asturias's understanding of the Latin cultures of Europe, the Havana conference gave him the opportunity to consolidate his self-image as a 'Maya' vis-à-vis Spanish America, and to elaborate his theory of 'Indo-American' identity. One detrimental result was to confirm his essential alienation from Guatemalan 'backwardness', heightening his belief in European superiority and his affinity with Europeanized interpretations of Spanish American reality. Simultaneously, the experience strength-ened the counterforce of Asturias's nationalist and anti-imperialist impulses. The trip also marked the beginning of Asturias's friendship with Robert Desnos, his personal link to the Surrealist movement, who would deepen Asturias's knowledge of contemporary French literary and artistic currents.[5]

Segala and Martin both argue that the trip to Cuba signalled the unequivocal end of any form of inferiority complex in Asturias's makeup. From this point on, they claim, Asturias wrote as a man culturally liberated. Segala argues:

Este viaje implica el final de todo complejo ante las suficiencias europeas, y francesas en particular. Por último, el descubrimiento de la realidad multirracial de La Habana habrá de constituir el *introitus* providencial para explicitar y aplicar este nuevo concepto a la realidad de su país. El *crescendo* ideológico de sus viajes corre parejas con el *crescendo* de sus desplazamientos, el viaje interior coincide con el de su cuerpo.[6]

Martin, commenting on Asturias's second dispatch from Cuba, adds: 'Asturias sigue deshaciéndose progresivamente de todo complejo de inferioridad neocolonial' (Asturias, *París 1924–1933*, 581). But the paragraph to which Martin appends the footnote containing this optimistic assertion is largely devoted to Asturias's anxious self-assurances that Havana traffic jams are just as frenetic as those in Europe. Asturias writes: 'La Habana es una ciudad viva, vivísima. Nada en cuanto actividad tiene que envidiar a las grandes capitales de Europa. El tráfico desespera al que va en lujoso coche y al que va pagando por centavos los minutos, como en París y en Londres' (*París 1924–1933*, 242). The familiar cultural reference points remain in place. Asturias's trip to Cuba undoubtedly altered his perspective, playing a crucial role in forming his identity as a writer; but the change is not as simple as Martin and Segala contend. Asturias's evolution did not consist of an untroubled 'liberation' from a series of complexes, but rather of a development built onto the framework of previous developments in his intellectual and creative formation. Asturias's experiences in Havana (and, later, Guatemala) wrought modifications in the vision of himself and his imaginative world that he had generated as a law student in Guatemala and as a writer and a postgraduate student of Mayan anthropology in Paris. The Prensa Latina trip did not, as Segala's and Martin's arguments imply, obliterate the residue of these experiences. When Asturias approached Cuba, he did so as a writer whose creative identity had been to a significant extent constituted in a European context. It is telling that in order to describe his first glimpse of Havana, he adopts a European narrative persona.

Entre los congresistas que hicieron el viaje a Europa a lo largo del Atlántico, había uno, cuya nacionalidad callo, que creía que en La Habana había que desembarcar con revólver en mano, sombrero colonial y mosquitero. Su sorpresa al llegar fue grande. La negrería que él pensaba, resultó una ciudad europea, con el trajín de los puertos franceses, con el cielo de los puertos españoles, el cielo y la simpatía, y con el sello indoamericano que da a los grupos humanos un aspecto de cosmopolitismo imponderable. (*París 1924–1933*, 243)

This narrator whose nationality has been suppressed personifies both Asturias's apprehensions with regard to his own Europeanization and his fear of how backward a Spanish American city will appear to the European colleagues in whose company he has attended previous Prensa Latina conferences. The narrator's enlightenment represents the alleviation of Asturias's insecurities. Havana's soothingly European lines ('resultó una ciudad europea') enable Asturias, paradoxically, to relax into an acceptance of his Spanish American identity. The city satisfies his need to have it both ways: Havana proves capable of matching the bustle of a French port and the limpid light of a port in Spain; at the same time, it is a locus of the 'indoamericanismo' which Asturias has assumed as his Parisian identity. He no longer conceives of Indianness as shameful or backward. On the contrary, a racially non-European identity is now portrayed as conferring upon a people 'un aspecto de cosmopolitismo imponderable'. Asturias's claim of cosmopolitanism—previously identified with Paris and Europeanization—on the part of the mixed-race populations of Latin America is of vital, revelatory importance. Asturias is able to laud his Indo-American identity precisely *because* it fosters, rather than opposes, cosmopolitanism (here understood as acceptance within the European cultural sphere). The sentence delineates the shift that has occurred in his mentality: 'indoamericanismo' has been rendered desirable by virtue of having been embraced by Europe; it thus supplies Asturias with a route in from the edge, a mode of gaining metropolitan acceptance. It is in this sense that 'indoamericanismo' can be equated with 'un aspecto de cosmopolitismo imponderable'. The Parisian origins of the insight do not, of course, entirely negate its force; Asturias's conversion into a champion of mixed-race culture is authentic and liberating. But the change is also inspired and conditioned by European expectations.

The European gaze with which Asturias first scans the Havana shoreline is evident in his effusive, estranging glorification of the city's tropical charms:

se abre a los ojos de Europa la visión, para ellos increíble a primera vista, de países en plena florescencia, de países donde se mezclan todas las razas y donde los hombres olvidan la preocupación de las fronteras, de las banderas y de los nacionalismos. ¡América para la humanidad! (*París 1924–1933*, 243)

The idealization of Spanish American experience contained in this passage occludes an important contradiction. Although Asturias will go on to praise a culture he describes as 'indoamericano', his vision promotes a *mestizo*, not an Indian, identity. It is not the survival of Mayan or Arawak cultural categories which he is celebrating, but a joyous, exotic fusion 'donde se mezclan todas las razas'. The bearer of 'indoamericanismo', in other words, is a *mestizo*. This incongruity reiterates the strategy noted above, in which the Indian becomes the emblem of the crushed aspirations of (mixed-race) *ladino* nationalism—a central motif in Asturias's later fiction.

Asturias's preoccupations in this article, identified by Segala as the central liberating moment of the Cuban trip (*París 1924–1933*, p. lix), flow from European priorities. His characterization of Spanish America focuses on attributes, such as the (debatable) absence of a concern with borders, flags and nationalism, which are accorded importance by recent European historical experience—in this case, the desire to flee the perceived causes of the First World War. Asturias closes his article with an issue which, though it may be a source of some concern to his readers, is a far more pressing consideration for Asturias himself: the question of European perceptions (especially the perceptions of his European colleagues in Prensa Latina) of Latin America.

Los salvajes mexicanos, los salvajes nicaragüenses y los bárbaros de Cuba, ya no serán desde que los periodistas de 60 grandes cotidianos europeos de París, Lisboa, Bruselas, Roma, Madrid, Bucarest, se han convencido por ojos propios que en América hay grupos humanos perfectamente organizados, con tradiciones culturales muy antiguas y glorioso pasado. (*París 1924–1933*, 243)

The reference to 'ojos propios' reiterates Asturias's abiding concern with Latin America's construction by the European gaze. While presenting himself as possessing a privileged link to the grandeur of the American past, Asturias cannot stifle his persistent *ladino* insecurities regarding the order, coherence and 'civilization' of his social milieu. His return to Spanish America throws into relief his bifurcated view of his own identity. What he wishes Europe to recognize in Spanish America is the existence of 'grupos humanos perfectamente organizados, con tradiciones culturales muy antiguas y glorioso pasado'. The phrase summarizes the contradictions inherent in Asturias's attempt to employ the pre-Columbian past as the symbolic agent of *ladino* nationalism. On the one hand his identity within the Parisian context depends upon European acknowledgement and approval of the accomplishments of the traditional cultures of the Americas; on the other hand, once reinserted into a Spanish American culture in the company of European journalists, he longs for European praise of the 'perfect organization' of societies governed by modernizing *ladino* élites such as the one to which he belongs (yet of which, during most of his time in Paris, he has been harshly critical). These disparate yearnings can be reconciled in Europe, where his 'Mayan' persona disguises his *ladino* anxieties; but exposure to Spanish America unmasks the qualified nature of his emancipation.

Asturias's outlook riddles with contradictions his commentary on racial issues. His portrayal of Afro-Cuban culture projects European needs onto the musicians whose performances he attends:

Las noches cálidas. Las noches sexuales. Las con música de negros que con sus instrumentos autóctonos modelan en carne de armonías negras, a las soñadas negras de sus amores. ¡Qué pena secreta, como cabra atrevida, salta de escalón en escalón en esta música de los sones! ¡Cómo parece llegar a las estrellas la pena de las notas de los tambores que el negro al tocar castiga con la palma de la mano cuerada o el codo o el carrillo! (*París 1924–1933*, 242)

The musicians, noble savages of the Havana night, are depicted as existing in a sphere whose emotional range and sexual spontaneity has escaped the ossifying influence of civilization. European imperatives dovetail with the priorities of the liberating ideology of 'indoamericanismo' in Asturias's re-evaluation of the cultural worth of non-white races. The Afro-Cuban musicians are simultaneously claimed and objectified, elevated and romanticized. They are characterized as 'natural' beings associated with natural images ('cabra atrevida'), yet valued for their artistic prowess, which in turn acquires worth by virtue of its contribution to the elaboration of a national culture and national autonomy. Asturias's attempts to make relevant to Guatemala the acceptance of non-white cultures that he perceives in Cuba are couched in the language of *ladino* nationalism.

Quiero sí interesar al público guatemalteco por la enorme inquietud espiritual que en La Habana y en toda Cuba se advierte, orientada a hacer valer sus propios recursos, sus haberes raciales y las manifestaciones autóctonas de las clases que antes pasaran por simiescas y detestables. El arte cubano gira actualmente alrededor del negro [...]. El literato, el pintor, el escultor y el músico forjan con esta unidad propia, un arte propio, una expresión de la vida cubana que responde en sus emociones al sentir popular [...] se orientan hacia la liberación espiritual de la isla, económica y políticamente, como el resto de la América meridional, bajo el control del imperialismo yanqui. (*París 1924–1933*, 249)

Redeemed from its 'detestable', 'simian' state by its cultural strength, the Afro-Cuban population serves the nationalistic *mestizo* artist as raw material, as a bridge to an art which will be accessible to (and thus exercise a unifying influence upon) the population at large. The Afro-Cuban is rehabilitated from the pit of racist disdain in order to be enlisted into the struggle against Yankee imperialism. The implications for Asturias's creative treatment of Guatemala's Indian population are obvious.

Yet once Asturias moves on from Cuba to Guatemala, he falls curiously silent on the question of race. The talks he delivered to students and workers during his nearly two-month return visit throb with reforming zeal. His social prescriptions focus on questions of education, social class, land reform, health, hygiene and sexual morality; these, rather than any modification in the means of conceiving racial identity, are presented as the solutions to the nation's backwardness. Lauding the achievements of the Maya no longer appears to be an option once Asturias has returned to the *ladino* milieu of Guatemala City. His sole affirmative reference to the Maya in his Guatemalan articles (nearly all of which originated as talks) is rapidly qualified, curtailed and mediated by the less threatening impulse of bourgeois nationalism.

Lo que más llama la atención al entrar a Guatemala por Puerto Barrios [...] es el tipo de mujer criolla, porque recuerda perfectamente el de las esculturas mayas: ojo rasgado hacia atrás, párpados abultados, nariz poco pronunciada y boca en medialuna. Acaso no habíamos nunca reflexionado que el tipo de belleza que define nuestro concepto de lo bello, es el tipo maya, o bien, por razones étnicas de origen más próximo, el tipo español. Un amigo me decía: Los únicos museos que visité complacido fueron los de España. Y es natural. El tipo de belleza de mi amigo se sintió estimulado, pagado, reconfortado, en los cuadros de los célebres pintores españoles. Otra amiga me decía con mucha gracia: Los únicos santos lindos son los de Guatemala. Y está claro. El tipo de santo francés, verbigracia, no nos satisface porque está lejos de nuestro ser. (*París 1924–1933*, 260)

The Mayan woman provides the *ladino* man with his ideal of beauty not because he knows and values Indian culture or because he is intimate with, and has learned to love, women of Mayan descent. The Indian woman serves as an ideal 'porque recuerda perfectamente [...] las esculturas mayas': she resembles an anthropological artifact whose worth and antiquity he has been taught to respect. The assertion, deriving from Asturias's studies at the Sorbonne rather than from his life experience in Guatemala, would have represented an exceptionally positive view of the Indian in the Guatemala of 1928; yet coming from the 'Mayan prince' of Paris, it sounds tepid. As soon as Asturias tries to elaborate upon this statement, additional ideological slippage occurs. He claims that 'nuestro concepto' of beauty is 'el tipo maya, o bien, por razones étnicas de origen más próxima, el tipo español'. Guatemalan culture may regard the Maya as a remote ideal, but the Guatemalan's blood links, Asturias insists, are with Spain. The adoption of Spain as a shield to ward off French cultural hegemony ('el tipo de santo francés [...] no nos satisface') entails a rejection of the Mayan types whom Asturias praised at the beginning of the passage. His inability to sustain his tribute to the Indian woman indicates how differently Asturias constructs his identity in the Guatemalan context. While continuing to promote *ladino* nationalism, he opts for the non-inflammatory Spanish model rather than an iconoclastic endorsement of Mayan-ness as the vehicle of this ideology. Despite his harsh criticism of Guatemala's ruling classes in the articles written from Paris, Asturias cannot bring himself to defy his own milieu to the point of publicly discarding the *ladino* as his symbol of Guatemalan nationhood. The pattern was to repeat throughout Asturias's career. Each time he returned to Guatemala he became ideologically timid and creatively sterile. Only when he was outside the country could he equate Guatemala with the Indian. At home, his immersion in the conservative, Catholic ambience of his upbringing thwarted any such identification.

The talks Asturias gave during his 1928 visit display a more restrained, pious approach than many of his polemical fusillades from Paris. Having removed himself from the cafés of Montparnasse, he also begins to place his French experience in intellectual perspective. In his preface to *La arquitectura de la vida nueva* (1928), the book that grew out of his Guatemalan speaking tour, Asturias writes eloquently of his delicate, contradictory position as a young Spanish American author trying to learn from European models without succumbing to the charms of their surface mannerisms. This preface, written after Asturias's return to Paris, demonstrates a heightened expatriate consciousness whose emerging scepticism enlarges his ability to turn his Parisian experience to his own ends. Anticipating that he will be criticized as an alienated *afrancesado*, Asturias makes clear that his goal in immersing himself in Europe is to learn to express and represent Guatemalan realities more effectively.

El que se apropia de lo ajeno para satisfacer a los suyos nunca me convenceréis que comete delito. Y eso hice: robar para los míos: hice mías las ideas ajenas para los míos. ¿Tenían hambre? No lo sé. Lo cierto es que [robé] como si hubieran tenido. Robé pan duro y no adornos. Pan duro de ideas y no adornos literarios inútiles.[7]

Four years in Paris, Asturias claims, have taught him to distinguish between the 'pan duro' of European thought and the transient superficialities of Parisian artistic fashion. The statement may reflect the tensions raised by his initial encounter with Surrealism, which probably coincided with his return to Paris and the renewal of his acquaintance with Robert Desnos, whom he had met on the journey to Cuba. While Asturias's cultural position was clearly more problematic than this staunchly independent-minded declaration would indicate, Asturias himself did evince an awareness of his growing estrangement from Guatemalan norms. His preface discloses a sensitivity to the fact that his residence in Paris has converted him into something of an outsider at home. He describes *La arquitectura de la vida nueva* as

lo que puede hacer un hombre que después de varios años de ausencia vuelve a su país por corto tiempo, cuando luchan en su alma sentimientos, se rompen doradas esperanzas y por su imperativo juvenil siente todavía la necesidad de gritar. (*La arquitectura*, 7–8)

Throughout *La arquitectura de la vida nueva*, Asturias searches for an ethical base for Guatemalan society capable of delivering reform without disdaining Catholic morality. His aspirations incarnate a personal quest writ large: Asturias wishes to give Guatemala the best of Europe—a modern, progressive society—without surrendering its Guatemalan essence, often represented in these essays by devout *ladino* Catholicism. In the two talks which the book combines as 'La arquitectura de la vida nueva', Asturias urges his secondary-school audience at the Instituto Nacional Central de Varones (his *alma mater*) to be thrifty, efficient, sober, sexually continent, fastidious in their appearance and responsible in their family lives (*La arquitectura*, 19–57). Yet this litany of traditional virtues is lacquered with a progressive veneer, in which the suppression of 'vices' such as sloth and sensuality is equated with enhanced personal freedom and a modernizing social revolution. By the end of the talk, Christianity occupies an uneasy all-purpose role as teacher of probity, catalyst of Romantic social revolution and old-fashioned dogma. It has, in other words, dropped into the slot occupied by Mayan exoticism when Asturias is in Paris. Accompanied by his European colleagues, Asturias the Maya revelled in the sensuality of the Afro-Cuban musicians of Havana; but in Guatemala, he adopts a sternly censorious attitude towards any action that hints of uninhibited sexuality, telling one youthful audience that 'debemos moralizar nuestras relaciones familiares' (*París 1924–1933*, 263). The link reconciling these contradictory positions is that each, in its particular context, works to further the goal of reinforcing the position of bourgeois Guatemalan nationalism. The Afro-Cuban musicians represent cultural autonomy, strengthening the hand of the national bourgeoisie against foreign capitalism; an efficient, disciplined working class, its sexual energy safely contained within the family structure, will have a similar effect. Asturias's recommendations may appear capricious, but his vision and goals are consistent.

Asturias draws on French authorities to buttress his analysis of Guatemala's social ills. At the beginning of 'El amor, la mujer y el niño', the long, idiosyncratic closing essay in *La arquitectura de la vida nueva*, he tells his audience at the Sociedad de Auxilios Mutuos that:

Sin ninguna modestia os confieso que mi papel se reduce a aplicar a nuestro medio la lectura de autores clásicos como Stendhal y otros, aplicación que hago con lealtad y valor, sin disimular ninguno de nuestros defectos, muchos de los cuales por no declararse en público, se agravan de día en día. (*La arquitectura*, 71)

Asturias's assumption that French intellectual constructs may be 'applied' wholesale to Guatemalan reality exposes the fragility of his vision of Guatemalan cultural distinctness. As in his article proposing the transformation of the city of Antigua into a replica of Salamanca or the Sorbonne, this preamble lays bare his bedrock belief in the guiding role of the Europeanizing bourgeoisie. Asturias's aim is to make Guatemala equal (and implicitly identical) to France or Spain; only when this proves to be an impossibility (for example, when he is personally confronted with the social integration and cultural self-confidence of Paris) does he resort to other strategies, such as the promotion of his 'Mayan-ness'.

The closing essay (*La arquitectura*, 71–124), unabashedly super-imposing European categories onto Guatemalan experience, begins by breaking down love into four types defined by Stendhal. Later pages quote Saint-Just and Marcel Prévost and one section draws heavily on the work of the Swedish feminist writer Ellen Key. The essay makes clear that even during his relatively inward-looking first four years in Paris, Asturias has come into contact with notions such as female emancipation, bourgeois hypocrisy and 'free love'. Yet the foundations of his Catholic faith remain intact (though his religious beliefs retreat into the background once he returns to Paris).[8]

Despite the relapse into *ladino* ideology evident in sections of the Guatemalan talks, Asturias's trip, particularly the visit to Cuba in the company of his European colleagues, played a crucial role in consolidating his vision of Spanish American reality. But he later acknowledged that the man he was becoming was someone whose identity he had been obliged to suppress during his stay in his homeland. Describing his departure from Guatemala, Asturias writes: 'De nuevo nacía en mí el hombre que había enterrado durante mi permanencia en [Guatemala], pero nacía más triste, más sentimentalmente estrecho para mi corazón romántico, y poco dispuesto a mis risas y bromas de estudiante' (*París 1924–1933*, 288). His experiences have enabled him to define the gap separating Europe and the Americas. In his post-1928 journalism the technique of using France as a pretext to discuss Guatemala virtually disappears. His knowledge of contemporary French society and its artistic currents improves dramatically, and portions of his journalism, such as a stultifying six-part series outlining the programmes of the main French political parties (*París 1924–1933*, 420–8), consist of little more than the imparting of the information he has gleaned. As Segala notes (Asturias, *París 1924–1933*, pp. lxv-lxxi), 1929 was Asturias's most productive year as a journalist. He published 103 articles in that year, a large number of them devoted to Guatemalan political and social problems. The issues he deals with are nearly always approached directly rather than through the mediating prism of France. (After that year, both his rate of journalistic production and his focus on Guatemala dwindled; creative work and European artistic questions, respectively, became the objects of his energies.) Asturias's themes when dealing with local issues alter little. His anti-imperialist rhetoric grows stronger (although in one instance he also warns that rhetorical excess 'nos pone en ridículo' (*París 1924–1933*, 316)), his concerns with education, national prestige and the European activities and reception of Guatemalan artists remain constant.

The emerging division in Asturias's work between what belongs to Europe and what belongs to Guatemala conceals internalized pressures. Martin writes:

Después del retorno a Guatemala en 1928, Asturias dejó de ser un escritor modernista y se hizo un escritor moderno […]. Ahora comprende mejor el mundo y su parte en él, sabe distinguir entre lo que le viene de Guatemala y lo que viene de Europa […] sabe leer la realidad y ahora podrá escribir *El señor presidente.* (Asturias, *París 1924–1933*, 593)

Martin's assessment implies that Asturias has acceded to a clearly defined emancipated outlook: that he has ascended from confusion to clarity. Yet each writer creates an individual clarity, deriving private, personal meanings from the position in which he has become inscribed within the structures governing the surrounding world; this complex of meanings is fluid and dynamic, forever evolving and shifting in response to circumstances. It is true that Asturias's assimilation of the key elements of his identity was nearly complete by the time of his return from Guatemala. Among the constituent parts of the creative persona of his novels, only the 'political exile' component of his later years was lacking. But the fact of his distinguishing more keenly between 'lo que le viene de Guatemala y lo que viene de Europa' did not in itself signal the end of his inferiority complexes. In fact, to a large extent, the journey ingrained certain neo-colonial patterns of seeing—of what Martin, while analysing them differently, terms 'leer la realidad'. When Asturias read Guatemalan reality, he did so with a gaze conditioned in large part by Europe's traditional interpretation of the 'peripheral' nations of Asia, the Middle East and Latin America in an 'Orientalist' framework which emphasized their exoticism. Edward Said writes:

'Oriental' identifies an amateur or professional enthusiasm for everything Asiatic, which was wonderfully synonymous with the exotic, the mysterious, the profound, the seminal [...] for something more than the first half of the nineteenth century Paris was the capital of the Orientalist world. (*Orientalism*, 51)

In mutated form, this Orientalist culture persisted into the early twentieth century, enjoying a wave of zealous revival in the work of the Surrealists and in novels such as André Malraux's *La Voie royale* (1930). The Surrealists' outlook expressed in extreme form the contemporary Parisian view of the 'Orient':

Mais l'Orient n'est pas seulement la patrie des Sages, c'est aussi le réservoir des forces sauvages, la patrie éternelle des 'barbares', des grands destructeurs, ennemis de la culture, de l'art, des petites manifestations ridicules des Occidentaux, des révolutionnaires perpétuels armés de la torche flamboyante et incendiaire semant sous le pas de leurs chevaux la ruine et la mort, en vue d'une renaissance. Et la révolution russe elle-même, mystérieuse parce qu'asiatique [...] ils y fondront finalement tous leurs désirs ardents, mais vagues, de révolution universelle portée par un Orient négateur et régénérateur.[9]

Asturias's response to his homeland, after a four-year absence, was to represent it in terms of the Orient: this was the vocabulary Paris had conferred upon him for describing the run-down, disorganized fringes of the Western world. One critic writes: 'The Peruvian critic Luis Alberto Sánchez reports that during the 1920s, in Paris, Asturias was an assiduous student of Orientalism'.[10] Part of the price Asturias paid for undergoing his literary apprenticeship in the Parisian milieu becomes visible in his internalization of the categories intrinsic to this discourse. Non-Western cultures, to a greater or lesser extent, all come to be included under the Oriental rubric.

Por sus mendigos parece Guatemala un villorio del lejano Oriente, de los que el Danubio ensucia con su resplandor de agua muerta cuando se va acercando al Mar Negro. El sábado es el día por excelencia. De no sabemos dónde sale un ejercito de desharrapados, costrosos y gimientes […]. Asaltan todos los lugares públicos […] sortean el paso de los vehículos con dificultad […]. Esto a la vista de las autoridades, que no se han preocupado de poner una barrera al mal que con el tiempo va en aumento. (*París 1924–1933*, 270)

Asturias's description of his re-encounter with his homeland is written from the outside looking in; the account might be the work of an imperial traveller witnessing the confusion and disorder of a marginalized, 'Oriental' society whose internal dynamics remain veiled in mystery. Having grown up in Guatemala, Asturias is presumably accustomed to (and comprehending of) the authorities' tolerance of ragged hordes. By imputing to him an ignorance of such matters, his narrative arrogates for him a position within the metropolitan sphere. In its apparent catering to a non-Guatemalan readership (though written for a Guatemalan newspaper), the article could almost belong to the literature of colonialist encounters with 'primitive' cultures.

Asturias's appalled reaction to Guatemalan 'backwardness' emerges even more strongly in a lurid, flagrantly unsuccessful short story he wrote during his stay. 'El guardián del puente de Las Vacas' (*París 1924–1933*, 276–81), a tale of blood-spattered death on a railway line, displays revulsion towards the country and its inhabitants; the characters are both crude and cruelly caricatured. The journalism Asturias wrote after his return to Paris, while less hysterical in its rejection of Guatemala, betrays the same loss of confidence in Spanish American worthiness. Where he had earlier depicted Paris as a university from which the active, questing Spanish American intellectual could extract the learning that he required for his private purposes, in the post-1928 articles the role of the Spanish American visitor is depicted as being more passive. European learning, though acquired for the purpose of furthering the goal of Guatemalan (or Mexican or Argentine) national autonomy, becomes a superior, transforming entity bestowed upon the grateful visitor rather than a storehouse which the Spanish American ransacks in order to select the elements likely to be of use to him. In a 1929 article on one of the student leaders instrumental in the overthrow of the Estrada Cabrera dictatorship, Asturias writes: 'Después de una docena de meses en Europa, regresa Jorge Alvarado a Guatemala con un importante bagaje intelectual' (*París 1924–1933*, 384). (Alvarado had completed an advanced medical diploma.) Europe is seen as the privileged site of the knowledge which Guatemala must acquire in order to progress. In a near-reversion to the ideology of *El problema social del indio*, the Europeanization of Guatemala's youth is presented as the country's best hope for the future. Asturias's article on Alvarado concludes: 'La vuelta de la juventud ya preparada llena de regocijo los corazones de quienes todo lo esperamos de ella. Un optimismo vuelve con cada joven que regresa' (*París 1924–1933*, 384).

Yet this influx of Europeanized young people is expected to create a Spanish America that is not only more modern, but also more politically independent. In another 1929 article, Asturias praises a group of Uruguayan students: 'Valiosos elementos de la juventud uruguaya que habían estudiado en Europa, intentaron al volver a su país la organización de un partido socialista viable' (*París 1924–1933*, 377). At the end of the article, revealing the roots of his socialist sympathies, he calls for 'una conducta nacional, nacional y sólo nacional' (*París 1924–1933*, 378). His vision of the Spanish American intellectual's Parisian residence has become laden with feelings of responsibility towards the homeland. Living in Paris has taken on the aura of a high moral duty, a deadly serious preparation: the crucial act is that of returning and contributing with European-gained expertise to the homeland's improvement.

During 1928 Asturias refreshed his memories of Spanish American reality and deepened his knowledge of contemporary France. Possessing a more informed, up-to-date grasp of both societies than he had a few months earlier, he underwent a shift in his perceptions, widening the gap between Europe and the Americas in his imaginative vision. This rift brought with it a more acute sense of inferiority; he came to portray the relationship between Europe and Spanish America more as one of tutelage than he had done immediately prior to his trip. In lamenting, for example, that in Guatemala, 'la ideología de sus dirigentes más avanzados es ideología de 1789' (*París 1924–1933*, 379), he accepted the primacy of European history and patterns of development. At the same time, in his work, what Europe was teaching Spanish America was often how to remain independent of the United States. In one article this implicit connection becomes explicit as Asturias, equating the French and Guatemalan struggles for cultural autonomy, offers his readership the model of the Parisian theatre's 'batalla decisiva contra la producción extranjera, y sobre todo norteamericana, que asalta París' (*París 1924–1933*, 390).

The conflicting forces of cultural subservience and national self-assertion, mingling constantly in Asturias's make-up, applied an unremitting tension to his conception of the role of the Guatemalan artist in Paris. If the duty of the 'prepared' young intellectual was to carry his learning back to Guatemala, how could Asturias, having turned 30 a few months after his return to Paris, justify remaining in Europe? His journalism of this period reflects his preoccupation with this inconsistency in its accounts of two other Guatemalan artists resident in Paris, the composer Alfredo Wyld and the painter Carlos Mérida. The looping, incessantly qualified structure of Asturias's defence of Wyld's decision to remain in Europe betrays his own contradictory emotions:

Wyld es un bellísimo ejemplo de lo que puede un apasionado por el arte, cuando sin elementos en el suelo que le vio nacer, árido para la florescencia artística, se ve obligado a buscar en otros techos el pan y el abrigo del alma que en sustentándole le hacen partícipe en el banquete cultural del mundo, aunque sea de una miga muy pequeña, muy pequeña. (*París 1924–1933*, 403)

The sentence's contorted length betrays Asturias's own confusions. Apparently still reeling from the conditions he witnessed during his visit to his homeland, Asturias blames Wyld's presence in Paris (and by implication his own) on Guatemala's being 'árido para la florescencia artística'. Ultimately, though, egotistical motives such as access to the 'banquete cultural del mundo' do not suffice: Asturias requires a more developed rationale for remaining in Paris. He finds it, as his article on Mérida shows, in the notion of nationalist self-assertion; of the Guatemalan artist not merely enjoying Europe's cultural wealth, but contributing to swaying the global balance of cultural power by subverting the European dominance which in other ways Asturias appears to subscribe to and uphold.

En Mérida lo fundamental es su temperamento americano y americanizante de todo lo europeo. Su originalidad es racial, si se puede hablar así, es decir, es la originalidad del artista maya que sintió en sus venas la sangre de muchas razas viejas, permitiéndole el lujo de captar en el universo estético lo que iba con su simpatía y transformarlo en personalísima expresión de sus monumentos, de sus vasijas, de sus obras de arte. (*París 1924–1933*, 430)

Asturias's assertion of cultural autonomy—of 'Americanizing' Europe's cultural riches—immediately transforms itself into a hymn of praise to the ancient Mayan artist. (The shift in verb tense, from 'es' to 'sintió', makes this clear.) Within the Parisian context, the creative Guatemalan becomes *de facto* a Maya. Artistic creation and the adoption of a Mayan persona, in Asturias's imaginative framework, have become inseparable: both are outgrowths of the artist's presence in Paris.

Yet in becoming a Maya, Asturias was not merely acting out a role determined by European requirements (although this was often the form his self-image, and even his early fiction, assumed). Responding to European demands in the way he presented himself, and even in the material about which he chose to write, Asturias none the less pursued a trajectory which sought to describe a narrative space within which the Spanish American writer could become universal without sacrificing his distinctively Spanish American concerns. In a 1931 article praising Arturo Uslar Pietri's novel *Las lanzas coloradas* (1931), he writes:

El escritor americano había sido hasta ahora local o europeo. Se quedaba en el pueblo y escribía como en el pueblo, aprovechando el lenguaje pintoresco del paisaje, lo anecdótico, lo fácil, lo familiar, todo esto sin profundidad por falta de convencimiento, con los ojos puestos en las revistas extranjeras, ventanas sobre lo universal, a lo que secretamente aspiraba; o salía a Europa y en el ambiente del viejo mundo se lavaba el sudor sudamericano y corría al cultivo de formas literarias en boga, cerrando los ojos propios voluntariamente, para ver con los ajenos […]. Hay en toda nuestra literatura un olvido de lo propio que desconcierta y puede afirmarse que hasta la fecha se está haciendo la literatura americana, en el preciso sentido de la palabra americano, no americano local puramente pintoresco, o americano europeo, sino americano universal. (*París 1924–1933*, 452–3)

This creative fusion of local and European elements, of autochthonous cultural concerns and universalizing structures, overflowed
from Asturias's journalism to become the central goal of his own early
fiction.

Notes to Chapter 3

1. Darío, cited by Gerald Martin, 'Asturias y *El Imparcial:*', in Asturias, *París
    1924–1933*, 799.
2. Aníbal González, *Journalism and the Development of Spanish American Narrative*
    (Cambridge: Cambridge University Press, 1993), 85.
3. Asturias, *París 1924–1933*, 23.
4. Edward W. Said, *Orientalism* (London: Routledge & Kegan Paul, 1978), 251.
5. The journey was also significant in another way: in Havana Asturias and Desnos
    encountered the 23-year-old Cuban writer Alejo Carpentier, recently released
    from prison and facing possible imminent rearrest. Carpentier escaped to France
    on the return voyage, borrowing Desnos's passport. Asturias's arrival in Cuba
    thus became the starting point of Carpentier's own eleven-year Parisian
    apprenticeship. See Carpentier, *La novela latinoamericana en vísperas de un nuevo
    siglo* (Mexico, D.F.: Siglo Veintiuno, 1981), 97.
6. Segala, 'Introducción del Coordinador', in Asturias, *París 1924–1933*, p. lix.
7. Asturias, *La arquitectura de la vida nueva* (Guatemala: Editores Goubaud y Cia.,
    1928), 7.
8. For a more complete discussion of *La arquitectura de la vida nueva*, see Stephen
    Henighan, 'Asturias's *Arquitectura*: A Novelist's First Construction', *Journal of
    Hispanic Research* 2/3 (Summer 1994), 385–92.
9. Nadeau, *Histoire du Surréalisme*, 109–10.
10. Richard Callan, *Miguel Angel Asturias* (New York: Twayne Publishers, Inc.,
    1970), 53.

CHAPTER 4

Approaches to a Self:
Asturias's Parisian Fiction
to 'La Barba Provisional'

Asturias's early short stories, with the exception of a few minor sketches and the melodramatic 'El guardián del puente de Las Vacas', written during the 1928 visit to Guatemala, chart a rising curve in his interest in literary technique and, more problematically, in his ability to convey a detailed rendering of Guatemalan society. Neither *Un par de invierno* nor either of Asturias's first two short stories was explicitly set in Guatemala. After his arrival in Paris, locale, whether Guatemalan or European, became an increasingly important element in Asturias's short fiction.

The first story Asturias wrote in Europe may have been 'Las Señoritas de la Vecindad', published in the November 1924 issue of the Guatemalan student magazine *Studium*. Asturias's *ladino* Catholic approach to his material remains firmly fixed; the first-person narrator issues unironic judgements such as: 'Mi amigo es casado y católico, suficientes cualidades para juzgar a un hombre'.[1] The narrator's friend tells him the story of the peasant Jacinto. Though manifestly of Mayan origin, Jacinto is identified simply as a man who 'había venido de Oriente, de uno de esos pueblecitos silenciosos de Oriente' (*NC*, 136). 'Las Señoritas de la Vecindad' predates Asturias's enrolment in Georges Raynaud's seminar at the Sorbonne and his adoption of a 'Mayan' persona. Given its publication date, the story may even have been written prior to Asturias's arrival in Europe.

As in *Un par de invierno*, Asturias's critique of social injustice is blunted by his *ladino* blindness to racial inequality as one of the sources of this injustice. Yet for the first time in his fiction, the story takes place in Guatemala (although the setting remains unstated). Jacinto is presented as the inheritor of the modernizing Liberal tradition of late nineteenth-century Central America which, impregnated with positivist assumptions, had shaped Asturias's own ideology.

Al hablar de la guerra, cruzaron los corredores de la imaginación: el tatarabuelo que murió para las guerras de independencia, en unión de dos hijos; el bisabuelo que murió en la Arada; el abuelo que salió mal herido el ochenta y cinco, un hermano que avanzaron [*sic*] el noventa y tres y su padre que murió cuando fueron a poner a Zaldívar en El Salvador. (*NC*, 139)

The peasant Jacinto becomes the protagonist of the bourgeois Liberal epic. The opening reference to the Wars of Independence is succeeded by approving allusions to the leaders of late nineteenth-century Central American Liberal positivism. 'El ochenta y cinco' was the name commonly given to the suicidal invasion of El Salvador launched by the Liberal Guatemalan president Justo Rufino Barrios (1873–85) in a futile attempt to subject all of Central America to Liberal ideas.[2] 'El noventa y tres' appears to refer to the power-struggle which resulted in the emergence of Barrios's Nicaraguan counterpart, the Liberal strongman José Santos Zelaya (1893–1912). Asturias's unusually affirmative mention of the leader of a neighbouring country, the Liberal reformer Zaldívar, who ruled El Salvador from 1876 to 1885, before being overthrown by a general of similar tendencies, completes the trinity of Central American Liberal demigods.[3]

While 'Las Señoritas de la Vecindad' imagined a Guatemala in which the aspirations of *El problema social del indio* had been realized, wishfully presenting the peasantry as racially neutral and imbued with the progressive positivism supported by the bourgeoisie, the story marked a significant development in Asturias's literary language. The tale incorporates Guatemalan expressions such as *guates*, *caites* and *milpa* both into its dialogue and into its narrative passages. Oddly, considering that the story was published in a Guatemalan magazine, ten of these terms are defined in a 'Tabla de los Modismos Usados'. The words are italicized in the text. Like the inclusion of the glossary, the italicization signals Asturias's self-consciousness in using terms from outside the realm of literary Spanish. The generally standardized language of the dialogue, however, avoids tortured *costumbrista* transcription of regional accents. This may be due to Asturias's lack of familiarity with these accents. While the slang expressions Asturias includes in the text often derive from Native words, the story contains no phrases in major Mayan languages such as Quiché, Cakchiquel or Mam. As with Asturias's racially blank portrait of Jacinto, his language imposes a *ladino* linguistic norm on the entire cast of characters, asserting a Guatemalan cultural unity—and implicitly an 'alma nacional'—which does not in fact exist. The story's 'frame' structure serves simultaneously to arouse sympathy for the poor and hold them at a safe distance. The narrator's friend is inspired to recount the tale of Jacinto when a group of countrywomen ('las Señoritas de la vecindad') meander past his house 'como náufragos que el mar arrojó a costas lejanas' (*NC*, 133). Before he can sympathize with the peasants, though, the narrator must first establish the distance separating his life from theirs. His friend, who is to tell Jacinto's story, echoes Asturias's thesis when he says: 'toda esta gente es de piedra. Se calientan al sol y se hielan en invierno, sin importarles frío ni calor. No tienen voluntad: nacen sordos, se reproducen ciegos y mueren insensibles' (*NC*, 134). Jacinto overcomes these limitations through the breadth of his experience. Having left his native patch of earth to fight in 'la guerra'—possibly the Mexican Revolution—he passes through 'la Ciudad' on his way home and is seduced by its cosmopolitan charms. The imagery associated with the city is insistently technological, decadent and copulatory. Jacinto's clash with the intoxicating speed of urban life renders him dissatisfied with peasant existence.

Quería volver a la Ciudad eléctrica; la Ciudad inteligente, esplendorosa frontera de histerismo, con los cabellos enredados en los peines de los postes y su carne de mujer besada continuamente por los astros. La Ciudad de los ovarios eléctricos. Quería volver al amor sin fin de aquella hembra barata que se dejaba besar, como una cosa inútil. (*NC*, 145–6)

The extravagance of Asturias's descriptions, calling up an atmosphere far more frenetic than that of the sleepy milieu of 1920s Guatemala City, suggests that these passages may be a transcription of Asturias's own seduction by the verve and energy of London or Paris. Elsewhere, evoking the cultural price exacted by the city of its inhabitants, he writes: 'La Ciudad abusiva que obliga a los hombres a dislocamientos absolutos, compleja como una alcoba femenina, sorda a los llamados virtuosos' (*NC*, 141). The crisis of adaptation to the city gradually takes over the story, shouldering aside the theme of social injustice. Jacinto is stripped of his importance as an individual or even as a member of Guatemala's deprived classes. The problem confronted by the story mutates from that of impoverished peasants roaming the street of the city to the less socially charged theme of dislocation, waywardness, the ineffable distance separating individuals in the urban environment. The image of the countrywomen passing down the street becomes recast as a symbol of alienation, absolving the *ladino* bourgeoisie of responsibility for the poverty of the lower classes. The narrator's friend says: 'Estamos condenados a ver pasar […]. Nuestro ver pasar no conoce la tristeza de los finales, la noche sin camino de los "nunca más", el ahogo de los imposibles, las columnas de Hércules' (*NC*, 148–9). When the narrator enquires about Jacinto's fate in the city, his friend replies: 'Nada, amigo mío, esa historia como todas las de todos los días, no tiene final […]. ¡Qué importa al mundo un tío que hice vivir y traje a la Ciudad para que muriera de hambre y dos Señoritas condenadas a la desgracia!' (*NC*, 149). Metaphysical speculation displaces social criticism. While it is possible that the narrator does not concur with his friend's scornful attitude, he neither voices his objections nor includes details which undermine his friend's observations. He appears, in fact, to be learning a lesson; the story gives the friend, rather than the narrator, the last word.

'Las Señoritas de la Vecindad' represents a more subtle, literary elaboration of the yearnings evident in Asturias's thesis. Removed from his homeland and grappling with the divided identity of the expatriate, Asturias effaces the Mayan reality whose assimilation he recommended as a student. The quest for the 'alma nacional' flattens the craggy disjunctures of Guatemalan society. Asturias's imaginative universe is idealized in the sense that it depicts a Guatemala where his proposals have already been put into effect. Having dispensed with the Mayan world through his acultural depiction of Jacinto, Asturias proceeds to write off *ladino* responsibility for the poor by way of a Romantic doctrine of unbridgeable distance between people. The one authentic preoccupation left unresolved at the story's end lies in the disorientating effects of the individual's adaptation to 'la Ciudad'. This tension becomes more clearly focused in the first pieces of fiction Asturias attempted subsequent to his arrival in Paris; abstract dislocation yields to explicit, if unsatisfactory, efforts to dramatize the rifts between European and American experience. Asturias did not possess a strong talent for this sort of writing—arguably he did not command a sufficiently broad experience of either Guatemalan or European society to pit their cultural idiosyncrasies against each other—and most of his stories dealing with this material are unpublished and/or unfinished. The final lines of an unfinished, untitled story written in one of Asturias's Paris notebooks highlight the problem. A tale of a trans-Atlantic voyage, it ends with an encounter between French and Spanish American passengers. One of the Spanish Americans says:

> —El francés es un tipo que no nos cae bien nunca porque no es como nosotros; y para mejor que así sea porque tiene por cada virtud unos defectos muy graves.
> Un grupo de franceses en el [illegible] a veinte pasos:
> —Francia y después nada. ¡Qué atraso el de España! ¿Inglaterra? Bueno, pero sobre todo Francia.[4]

At this point the story ends. Having made his observation about French arrogance, Asturias has nothing more to say. 'Sacrilegio del miércoles santo', a semi-religious allegorical dialogue between three men who meet in the Place de la Sorbonne in an imprecise era mingling the seventeenth and twentieth centuries, relies on a similar reduction of its characters to national types. Written in 1925 but left unpublished until 1971, the story reflects the contradictions of Asturias's first months in Paris. The narrator's wry description of the statue of Auguste Comte 'que busca en la materia la explicación del Universo' (NC, 153–4), hints at a newly ironic approach to French intellectual deities; at the same time, though, the character of the Latin American la Sota conforms to the European imagination's projection of its own repressed sexuality onto the exotic Americas. The Knave is both devoutly religious and sexually insatiable:

> La Sota se puso de pie, arrebozóse en la capa y, persignándose dijo salir en busca de una mujer.
> —Jamás he dormido solo—adujo—, pues, cuando era niño dormía con mi madre que de Dios haya. He dormido con más de veinte mil mujeres negras, sin exageración, callándome las rubias, las mulatas, las amarillas. (NC, 156–7)[5]

Attempting to satisfy his lust, la Sota rapes a woman who turns out to be Joan of Arc. The exotic foreigner has violated European sanctity. In the story's final sentence, he cries out for absolution. More an exposition of inchoate anxieties and half-articulated obsessions than a honed work of art, 'Sacrilegio' suggests the existence of powerful tensions in Asturias's (by this stage ongoing) conversion of his identity to that of a Parisian Maya. The devout Guatemala City *ladino* fears the outrageous persona likely to be attributed to him in his new guise as an embodiment of the primitive. Like la Sota, Asturias's exotic Parisian incarnation is destined to scandalize his traditional religious and social values.

'Florentina', the most successful of Asturias's European short stories, explores the alternative path that lay open to him: immersion in European culture, the elaboration of a neo-*modernista* creative identity. Published in September 1925 in the Guatemalan newspaper *América Central*, 'Florentina' echoes the work of Gómez Carrillo more powerfully than any of Asturias's other stories or sketches. Inoculated against replicating Gómez Carrillo's infatuation with the 'myth of Paris', Asturias none the less superimposes many of Gómez's trademark excesses on Florence. Europe is presented as the scene of grand romantic gestures, ancient civilizations and multiple literary allusions. In a story barely ten pages in length, Asturias alludes to Dante, Tolstoy, Maeterlinck, Velázquez, Heinrich Heine, Ernest Renan and various episodes and figures from the Bible. Repetitions of heavy-handedly significant phrases such as 'El Arno pasaba con lentitud de entierro' (*NC*, 165, 166) heighten the atmosphere of artificiality and contrivance. The Spanish American narrator, having arrived in Florence on the rebound from an unspecified romantic disappointment, takes advantage of his encounter with a compatriot, an expatriate sculptor, to commiserate over their respective deceptions. Asturias's Florence, like Gómez Carrillo's Paris, saps his protagonists of vigour, reducing them to a worshipful enervation before the ancient civilization enveloping them: 'Más tarde, en algún rincón (venerables rincones de Florencia) [...] le hablé de los amores civilizados, de las pálidas carnes de Ninón, de las explicaciones psicológicas' (*NC*, 164). The narrator's compatriot falls in love with a miserably poor Florentine girl who comes to model for him. The narrator, meanwhile, seeks 'mi cura en las catedrales y las bibliotecas, reanudando mis charlas con sacristanes y bibliotecarios, leyendo y rezando en la creencia de que las heridas de amor se curaban con telarañas e ideas filosóficas' (*NC*, 171).

The sculptor's lover throws herself in the Arno, conforming to Gómez Carrillo's contention that such cities abound in 'mujeres que se suicidan por amor'. The sculptor destroys the statue he has made of her without vanquishing his grief—a truth the narrator expresses by way of imagery drawn from the myth of the Garden of Eden (*NC*, 174). The story offers a taste of the variety of writer into whom

Asturias might have evolved had he not reconstituted himself as a 'Maya': a kind of latter-day Gómez Carrillo whose scatterings of European cultural references were interspersed with Christian religious imagery; a more moralizing, Catholic boulevardier. Lacking Gómez Carrillo's panache and lumbered with a rigid allegiance to Christian dogma, Asturias probably would have remained a very minor writer of fiction. His rediscovery of Guatemala through the angle of the Maya afforded him access to a vast social and mythological panorama. No matter how problematic his 'Mayan' identity may at times have become, it is vital to bear in mind that it was the adoption of this focus which enabled him to develop into a significant creative intelligence.

Among Asturias's remaining early short stories, three stand out from the ruck of vague religious parables and minor sketches. Two of these stories were written shortly after his enrolment in Georges Raynaud's seminars; the third, which follows his early novel *El Alhajadito*, was written in response to his meeting with the Surrealist Robert Desnos during his journey to Cuba.

'El Lucas', subtitled 'cuento de Guatemala,' marks a radical departure from the languid tone and ethereal ambiance of 'Florentina'. Written in Paris in 1926, it opens with a sequence whose brisk self-assurance bespeaks a writer confidently in control of his material.

> El Médico oyó a la mujer y quedóse callado: actitud extraña en un médico de pueblo. Nada podía la ciencia y el Lucas—indio de oro le llamaban los indios—, dentro de unos momentos dejaría de existir. La mujer por su parte guardó silencio: al fin y al cabo aquél no hacía sino confirmar el dicho del curandero, llamado con anterioridad y con más fe por la familia del herido.
>
> En el rancho, a medio tapesco (tapesco, cama de cañas colgada del techo) estaba el Lucas con el cráneo roto. La cobija negra le cubría hasta la nuca. Su cara recordaba los ídolos mayas que se encuentran removiendo la tierra donde hubo ciudades.
>
> La mujer dijo a su marido lo que afirmaba el Médico de su próximo fin:
> —*Chapa-jut-zimcacamik.* (NC, 185)

For the first time in Asturias's work, the reader is undeniably in Guatemala; the setting, which remained unstated in the generic Central American blur of 'Las Señoritas de la Vecindad', is made explicit in the subtitle. The story plunges into the tension at the heart of Asturias's own identity: the conflicting roles of Maya and *ladino* in Guatemalan society. Asturias's depictions of this struggle generate an authentic emotional force by comparison with which the puffed-up sensitivities of the expatriates in 'Florentina' feel bogus. Asturias's growing confidence in the validity of Guatemalan experience and language are signalled by his decision not to italicize Indian-derived expressions such as '*tapesco*'. While this term is explained, others such as '*nahual*'—the creature with whom an Indian is identified and whose spirit protects him—are not. The lone snatch of Quiché dialogue, though its meaning is spelled out beforehand, remains untranslated. Asturias enjoys mixed success in integrating his exposition of local customs into the forward flow of the narrative. The primacy of the traditional, spirit-dominated world in the Indian mind appears relatively unobtrusively, in the narrator's observation that the doctor 'no hacía sino confirmar el dicho del curandero, llamado con anterioridad y con más fe por la familia del herido'. On the other hand, the doctor's reactions become the subject of a clumsy narrative intervention in the story's opening sentence: 'actitud extraña en un médico del pueblo'.

The story portrays the Maya as losing his battle for survival against the *ladino*. The opening scene, describing Lucas on his deathbed, conjures up the familiar Asturian image of the Maya's face as resembling 'los ídolos mayas que se encuentran removiendo la tierra donde hubo ciudades'; once again, the Maya is linked to the past. He survives in the modern era as a picturesque freak, a curiosity that cannot endure. The doctor 'experimentaba por el indio una profunda simpatía hecha de lástima y respeto. La simpatía que se experimentaba por el árbol que corta en pedazos el hacha del leñador' (*NC*, 186). The image of the Maya as a tree chopped up by the woodcutter's axe underlines his status as an anachronism whose disappearance, though regrettable, constitutes an inevitable result of human advancement (though Asturias's phrasing also allows for the possibility of irony, critical of the doctor's stance). As the doctor arrives at Asturias's grandparents' country house to tell the story of how Lucas received his wounds, the story shifts from a non-dramatized third-person narration to the voice of personal reminiscence: 'aunque en ese tiempo yo era muy niño, recuerdo bien que el médico dijo así' (*NC*, 186). No longer privy to the thoughts of either the Maya or the doctor, the reader shares the infant Asturias's passive position as the tragedy unfolds. The structure serves to emphasize the inevitability of events; no intervention is possible since the modification of the narrative voice has eliminated the omniscient perspective that would have permitted the rendering of moral judgements. The Maya has betrothed his daughter Agustina to the son of another Maya; the customary exchange of gifts has taken place: 'El trato, pues, estaba hecho' (*NC*, 186). When Agustina takes the son of a wealthy *ladino* family as her lover, Lucas tries to prevent their union. He surprises Agustina and the *ladino* making love on a river bank. Assisted by his *nahual*, the rattlesnake, he drags the *ladino* away from his daughter, provoking a struggle on a precipice.

Agarrados cuerpo a cuerpo trataban de quebrarse uno a otro, de quebrarse por la cintura, por la nuca, por las rodillas [...] el indio y el ladino parecerían, agarrados como estaban, un animal de dos cabezas o las tenazas formidables de un alacrán junto al abismo. (*NC*, 188)

In this description, Guatemala becomes a two-headed beast rearing towards an abyss. The country's lack of integration, its unresolved dual identity, threatens both of its main component elements with destruction. The Maya wins the physical struggle, but when his daughter threatens suicide if he kills her lover, Lucas lets him go and, in despair, hurls himself over the cliff. The miscegenation promised by the liaison of the Maya woman and the *ladino* man can only mean death for the full-blooded Maya. The story marks an evolution beyond the prescriptions of *El problema social del indio*. The appreciation of Mayan culture instilled in Asturias by the influence of Raynaud's seminars (evident, also, in his use of Quiché) has reformed Asturias's outlook to the point where he acknowledges that the integration required by the 'alma nacional' will entail the annihilation of vibrant, valuable cultures. The insights make Asturias's creative vision more tragic and complex; his fiction gains correspondingly in authenticity and feeling.

'La venganza del indio', apparently written either shortly after or shortly before 'El Lucas' (it was published in *El Imparcial* in May 1926), moves beyond this insight to provide a more subjective evocation of rural Guatemalan reality. The anthropological assertions of narrative authority, such as the use of Quiché, the explanation of Mayan customs and the observations on the attitudes of country doctors, yield in this story's opening pages to the intuitive knowledge of a narrative voice firmly rooted in the reality it is describing. The barrier which in the earlier story divided the language of the narrator from that of the characters dissolves in the opening sentence of 'La venganza del indio'.

Luis Ramos había dicho en la chichería que su querida era, aunque ladina, la más gente del pueblo, para que lo oyeran todos, y la más fiel, para que lo oyera su rival, un ladino que la esperaba en el río y según decían se iba a bañar con ella el rato menos pensado. (NC, 193)

Ramos's lover la Chila is an outsider in the village, a *ladina* who has moved there and settled down with Ramos to the general surprise of the community. Their liaison shocks local society, not because she is beautiful and he ugly, 'sino porque era indio' (NC, 194). The arrival in the district of the municipal secretary Don Jerónimo, another *ladino* outsider, heightens the tension inherent in la Chila's relationship with Ramos. Drawn together by their common language, la Chila and Don Jerónimo become the subject of prurient gossip.

A su llegada hizo amistad con la Chila, no sólo porque era la más gente del pueblo, como decía Ramos, sino porque hablaba español. Y la Chila fue y la Chila vino en las conversaciones de don Jerónimo, dando lugar a que entre los indios se decían cosas muy feas de decir. (NC, 194)

Throughout these passages, Asturias's language remains mimetic of the rural social milieu. The rhythms of the final sentence cited above reflect the singsong exchange of gossip; the previous citation employs the term *chichería* (a rural bar in which corn beer is served) unexplained and unitalicized. Ramos's father is introduced into the narrative as 'El tata de Ramos'; the substitution of the Quiché word for the Spanish *padre* helps to immerse the reader in the ambience of rural Guatemala. Yet Asturias's rendering of this locale through a mixture of colloquial Guatemalan Spanish, rural speech rhythms and occasional Mayan words, remains problematic. The narrative voice is an artificial construct. As the story makes clear, the language of the village is Quiché; but the story is written in Spanish. The speech rhythms Asturias imitates are those of Spanish-speaking Guatemalans, albeit peasants whose conversations are spiked with Mayan words. As the story drifts deeper into Native mythology, Asturias is obliged to relinquish the spicy pungency of his colloquial mimicry for a mystical, incantatory tone. Where the rendering of Mayan village gossip in the first part of the story could rely on the existing and (to Asturias through his childhood recollections) accessible tradition of Spanish-language rural speech, the summoning of the spirits to avenge the cuckolded Ramos's honour in the latter half of the tale must create a language of its own. This enterprise is more perilous, inevitably less authentic but richer in possibilities of generating a sense of veri-similitude than the writing of the opening pages. The first half of the story perpetuates Asturias's submerged project of assimilating the Maya into *ladino* reality by presenting *ladino* speech as though it were the Maya's natural utterance. The story's concluding pages represent Asturias's inaugural venture into new territory: the reconstruction in Spanish of Native cosmology and Mayan perceptions of reality (though the assumptions behind even this enterprise would remain fraught with contradictions). As the three participants in the lovers' triangle sit drinking aguardiente, 'Don Jerónimo y la Chila hablaban en español' (*NC*, 197). Ramos, meanwhile, plays the marimba, calling up the spirits placed at his disposal by his father's visit to the wisest witch in the district. Through the incorporation in parentheses of the refrain 'Nana, nanita de mi alma, te voy a dar cacao' (*NC*, 195, 197, et seq.) in support of an explosion of supernatural events and extravagant imagery, Asturias gives the Maya his revenge.

se oía reptar por los zacates una culebra cascabel, con la mano firme acercó a las pajas del rancho la brasa de su puquiete. Una nube en forma de alacrán vino a quitar la luna. Mil látigos de fuego azotaron el bosque. No se escuchó lamento humano, apenas si el río iluminado a trechos de oro y sangre parecía repetir la voz del indio viejo: Nana, nanita de mi alma, te voy a dar cacao.
(*NC*, 198)

As in 'El Lucas', the Maya's guardian spirits are the rattlesnake and the scorpion. Here, though, the Maya, by calling upon magical forces, obtains his rough justice: la Chila and Don Jerónimo are burned to death by 'un corazón de fuego' (*NC*, 198). Asturias's evocation of Native magic remains somewhat externalized, as is made clear by his resorting to a phrase such as 'bajo la acción de un poder extraño'. But for the first time in his work Guatemala's conflicting racial groups are dramatized as the bearers of radically different yet equally authentic conceptions of reality—*ladino* materialism and Mayan animism respectively. 'La venganza del indio' holds the two forces in a tensed balance, its language favouring first the *ladino* then the Maya. If, in a reversal of the fatalism and covert assimilationism of 'El Lucas', this story permits the Maya to win a round by depicting the *ladino* couple as being literally consumed by ancestral magic, Asturias's presentation of Native imaginative concepts remains stagey and tentative. In its cascade of thunderbolts from heaven, the Maya's revenge differs little in mythological form from the wrath of the Christian god. Yet the story's striving for a more natural, colloquial and autochthonous literary language, combined with its (in Asturias's writing) unprecedented validation of Mayan realities, surpasses the mere realization that the destruction of Mayan culture represents a tragedy. For the first time, Asturias moves beyond sympathy to devote his creative energy to an imaginative revival (albeit in exoticized and clichéd terms) of the cultures he had until recently disdained.

Having dredged up and expressed this central tension in his imaginative personality, Asturias quickly set it aside. A year after writing 'El Lucas' and 'La venganza del indio', he made his first sustained attempt at a novel. The result, El Alhajadito (1961), has the most muddled publication history of any of his works other than El señor presidente. A note in the back of the first edition states: 'Este libro, escrito en París en 1927, fue sacado del manuscrito en Buenos Aires en 1960, y acabóse de imprimir el 14 de julio de 1961'.[6] The confusion as to what was written when is compounded by the novel's disjointed structure and radically varying tones. The long opening section, written in relatively rich language and narrated in the third person, offers a continuous narration of the fantastic events engulfing the heir to a family dynasty inhabiting a never-never land on the edge of a lake. The short middle section, narrated in the first person in simpler but more poetic and controlled language, describes a journey at sea. The third section consists of a fragmented narrative interspersed with brief children's fables. The three sections read as if written by different writers, or by the same writer at disparate stages of his career. Couffon notes that the novel 'apparaît comme cassé par le milieu [...]. La première partie [...] constitue un tout et pourrait fort bien être détachée'.[7] The stylistic rupture dividing the first part of the novel from the second and third sections (with which it shares only the most tenuous links of character, plot or image) suggests that this is probably the narrative Asturias wrote in Paris in 1927. The two subsequent sections, in their more accomplished prose style and far more deft deployment of the techniques of fantastic writing, appear to have been added later—perhaps several decades later. The critic Bellini, a close friend of Asturias, claims that the author rewrote the entire manuscript prior to publication: 'rielabora sostanzialmente il libro in anni recenti, pubblicandolo nel 1961'.[8] This analysis will focus on the opening section, as this is the only part of the novel which was almost certainly written in Paris in 1927.

The imprecise fantasy-land in which the action of El Alhajadito unfolds appears to denote Asturias's abandonment of important themes that he had only just begun to confront. At a connotative level, however, the novel focuses on the issue which lay at the heart of Asturias's life during the 1920s: the question of how the individual constitutes his identity. The boy protagonist's passage from an almost total absence of self-awareness to a clearly differentiated sense of his place within a sprawling social network is emblematic of Asturias's own delineation of the contours of his identity during his Paris years. Jacques Lacan, for example, has argued that the infant's process of self-definition serves as a paradigm recapitulated by all subsequent acts of identification. Malcolm Bowie, in his discussion of Lacan's theory of the mirror-phase, explains:

> Identification in all its forms is the repetition of an infantile narcissistic rite. But where the infant has at least the virtue, as Lacan sees it, of provoking a schism that he cannot control, adult knowledge-seekers—psychologists, say—mechanically reapply identificatory procedures that seek to disguise their delusional origins [...]. Early identifications are a destiny in embryo, a blueprint for the future.[9]

Substituting 'novelists' for Bowie's 'psychologists', *El Alhajadito* appears not only as an allegory of Asturias's rebirth as a 'Maya', but also as a source of clues to his underlying identificatory 'blueprint'. The boy's lack of identity at the beginning of the novel is matched by his lack of a mother. While the appearance of a grandfather figure early in the book suggests that the male pole remains recoverable, the female principle continues to be irredeemably absent. This sense of absence, most clearly dramatized in the figures of María Tecún and the other vanished, unreachable women in *Hombres de maíz*, supports the contentions of critics who have argued that Asturias's identification with Mayan realities stemmed in part from his worshipful, dependent, unresolved relationship with his comparatively dark-skinned mother.[10] A Lacanian reading of *El Alhajadito*, interpreting the allegorical construction of the boy's identity as revealing both current cultural tensions and childhood patterns of identification, corroborates the connection between Asturias's relationship with his mother and his equation of Guatemalan identity with Mayan-ness.

The action of *El Alhajadito* takes place not in the recognizably Guatemalan social environment of 'El Lucas' and 'La venganza del indio', but in a landscape whose defining characteristic is 'el monte. El monte verde. Toda clase de monte. Más allá, el mismo monte. Y más allá, el mismo monte' (*EA*, 10). One of the rare details which hints that the boy protagonist's world may in fact be situated in

Guatemala is the fact that the members of his army of braided servants are at one point identified as Indians: 'la servidumbre fantasmal de indios trenzudos' (EA, 26). (Other details, such as the presence of aguacate fruit and the use of the word zopilotes to refer to buzzards, indicate a Caribbean Basin, though not necessarily a specifically Guatemalan, setting.) Cheymol has parlayed the Indian reference into a critique of the blend of expatriate nostalgia and colonized mentality which he sees as inspiring El Alhajadito.

Tel est ce Guatemala primitif, colonial, qu'Asturias se plaisait à évoquer: un grand domaine en ruines, appartenant à de riches seigneurs d'origine espagnole (les Alhajados), peuplée d'une armée de domestiques indiens avec leurs cheveux noirs peignés en tresses, et de pêcheurs, de bohémiens, de nomades organisés en un cirque minable. Tout ce décor, évoqué par des images somptueuses, sert une évidente nostalgie.[11]

There is no doubt that the setting of El Alhajadito consists of a fantasy-land of the sort which epitomizes European visions of exotic far-away places. In this sense, Asturias is supplying his implied European reader with confirmation of predigested illusions, acquiescing to another culture's romanticized conception of his identity. Yet the setting of El Alhajadito is so misty and phantasmagoric that it is difficult to criticize the novel as a portrait of Guatemala. The setting, even though it presents a distorted and subservient picture of 'far-away places', is of secondary importance to Asturias's meticulous investigation, through the novel's opening chapters, of how the individual undertakes the process of assembling his identity. In this sense, El Alhajadito may have represented a necessary pause for reflection in Asturias's creative trajectory. Immersed in an intense questioning and reconstitution of his own identity (1927 appears to have been the year of his most committed participation in Georges Raynaud's seminars on Mayan culture)[12] Asturias not surprisingly began to develop an interest in the process by which identities were formed.

The protagonist of El Alhajadito begins the novel as a tabula rasa in absolute stasis. Sensations and observations impact upon him, shaping his personality and consciousness. 'Bigotes de miel de caña de azúcar' (EA, 9), the novel begins. Through his perception of the taste and appearance of the syrupy sweetness on his face, the boy is awakened to the salient traits of his environment. The first page and a half of the opening chapter consist of a catalogue of impressions narrated in impersonal fashion by a disembodied consciousness: 'El zumbido

ligero del insecto al ataque y el ronco zumbido del insecto golpeado'
(*EA*, 9). Not until the second page of the novel does a verb appear
that takes the third person singular pronoun as its subject.

> Los gallineros quedaban del otro lado de la casa. Sólo que volaran. Pero él
> las habría sentido pasar sobre los patios, mitad volando, mitad arrastrándose.
>   El corredor aquél. Aquel *su* corredorcito. Una mañana descubrió una
> cáscara de aguacate. Un guacalito. No le dio importancia. (*EA*, 10)

The accumulation of impressions and observations forges the boy's
identity as a subject. He becomes capable of conceiving of himself as
an agent ('él las habría sentido pasar') who shapes his vision of the
world through his perceptions. This awareness of self enables the boy
to lay claim to his place of origin. Like Asturias himself, recasting his
identity in Paris, the boy develops a sense of belonging to a particular
locale ('*su* corredorcito'; original emphasis); his identification with
that place establishes his approach to his environment, setting his angle
of vision. The novel dramatizes the boy's dawning recognition of the
fact that the adoption of a given identity implies a choice of actions
and perceptions: 'Para estar presente en su corredorcito tenía que estar
ausente de otros muchos lugares' (*EA*, 17). At the same time, the boy
learns that affiliation with a specific place does not confer imaginative
suzerainty over that spot. Like Asturias coming to grips with the
contradictions of Guatemalan society, the boy learns that he is neither
the only inhabitant of his place of origin nor the sole arbiter of its
nature. The *corredorcito* presents a reality which he must uncover rather
than merely decreeing its essence.

> ¡Cuántos ojos, no sólo sus ojos [...] gotitas de agua viva, luminosas gotitas
> de agua inteligente! ¡Cuántos movimientos en la oscuridad! No sólo él se
> movía en el corredorcito. Las arañas se disparaban en largas puntadas de
> hilván apresurado, las cucarachas indecisas, tontas, los ratones sin más ruido
> que el escabullimiento. ¡Y él que creía estar solo y ser el único dueño del
> corredorcito! (*EA*, 13)

The boy's initiation into the limitations of his own perception and
his discovery of the multiplicity of intelligent eyes which are also
imposing their respective visions on his *corredorcito* leads to his
discovery of time and the imagination. The arrival in the *corredorcito* of
an enfeebled old man—later revealed to be his grandfather—prompts
the boy to observe: 'Hay un momento en la vida en que se empieza
a decir *fui*' (*EA*, 17). As the old man falls asleep, the boy yields to a

child's fantasy of an attack by bandits. Asturias depicts the mysteries to which the psyche provides imaginative access as the persistence of vestiges of the past:

Las realidades misteriosas, el pasado palpable en lo impalpable, presente en lo que no se tocaba, en el aire que respiraban, en el agua que bebían, en las raíces de los árboles gigantes, en los esqueletos del cementerio sumergido, en los ojos del viejo que cabeceaba de muerte en un sueño dulce. (*EA*, 19)

Imagination, then, grows out of the decay of past realities. Asturias conceives his creative impulses as springing from the residue of the Mayas' ancient grandeur. In similar fashion, the boy's vision is engendered by his perceptual inventory of the *corredorcito*, itself a remnant of the mansions constructed by the illustrious dynasty of which he is the last wayward descendant. This sprouting of his imagination sharpens the boy's awareness of the limitations of his own static vantage point within the *corredorcito*. The fourth chapter ends: 'Estaba como siempre inmóvil en el corredorcito, de pie o sentado, la espalda apoyada en la pared o en un pilar' (*EA*, 19). The boy begins to chafe against his restricted vision, seeking a crack ('rendija') which will enable him to scrutinize the outside world: 'Si encontrara en el corredor, en *su* corredorcito, la más mínima abertura para espiar tanto misterio' (*EA*, 22). His initiation into the larger world occurs once the boy, liberated by the disappearance of the older generation, assumes his 'autonomous' identity.

When his sickly grandfather vanishes in a rainstorm—members of this family disappear rather than dying; their return never ceases to be a possibility—the boy finds the mantle of family responsibility thrust upon him. For the first time in the novel, the protagonist is named. His father having been the Alhajado, he is called the Alhajadito. The revelation comes as a surprise and brings immediate responsibility. A stranger tells him: 'Desde anoche es Su Merced el dueño de todo esto, por haberse ausentado el abuelo, y como a dueño y Alhajadito, le pido permiso para instalar un circo' (*EA*, 30). Naming, Asturias contends, is not an act of volition or choice, but an imposition from without. Others name us as a function of where we are situated; we may choose our *corredorcito*, but we cannot control others' characterizations of the significance of our selection of a particular stance or allegiance. Furthermore, the names we take up are freighted with traditions and expectations with which we are unfamiliar. The diminutive in the boy's new title exhorts him to act like a replica of someone else. This is both a constraint and the beginning of the possibility of growth. Bowie, explicating Lacan, writes:

> The identification of oneself with another being is the very process by which a continuing sense of selfhood becomes possible, and it is from successive assimilations of other people's attributes that what is familiarly called the ego or the personality is constructed. (*Lacan*, 30–1)

Yet the boy does not remember his father, El Alhajado, with whom he is identified; nor does the reader see him pass through a succession of such identifications. Rather, emphasizing the political and cultural implications which Asturias is giving the experience of identity-building, the boy must contend with the burden of a name whose significance he cannot fathom, a tradition that he has been told is his yet which remains largely inaccessible to him. The parallels with Asturias's (externally imposed) discovery in Paris that he was a 'Maya' are obvious. El Alhajadito can scarcely credit the manner in which he is being addressed. The opening sentence of the next chapter underlines his new identity's external provenance: 'El Alhajadito se oyó nombrar por primera vez *Alhajadito*' (*EA*, 30). The boy's doubts concerning the authenticity of this identity provide a suggestive echo of the crisis provoked in Asturias by Georges Raynaud's assertion: 'Vous êtes maya'. Asturias portrays personal identity as the interaction between the observations gleaned by an active human consciousness defined by its location and perspective, and the labels attached to the individual by others. Identity is constituted through a dynamic process in which free will and innate qualities play minor roles. Asturias's account of El Alhajadito's self-realization reflects his own acquiescence in the 'primitive' role Parisian literary and artistic circles demanded of him—or at least implies that not much resistance can be offered to a powerful Other's depictions of one's nature. This Other is portrayed as unitary, the encounter with the Other as a single cataclysmic shock rather than the more subtle layering of 'successive' identifications described by Lacan. Identity as El Alhajadito comes to experience it consists of a struggle to attain a sense of authenticity within the boundaries of a culture imputed to be the subject's own, but with which the subject himself has been allowed only a glancing, unsatisfactory acquaintance: it is alienated, neo-colonial identity.

The arrival of the circus, midway through the opening section of the novel, explores the implications of this discovery. The deliberate, almost claustrophobic account of El Alhajadito's piecing-together of his identity in the confines of the *corredorcito* yields to the fast-paced, often slapstick description of the struggle for control of the circus after the death of its *jefe*, Don Antelmo Tabarini. Though El Alhajadito's presence fades during these sections, his status as narrative consciousness occasionally yielding to those of members of the circus, the theme of the integration of the psyche remains at the forefront of Asturias's work. The Rabelaisian antics of the circus performers and their battles with the local fishermen provide Asturias with an external reality upon which to test the relationship between the individual's construction of his own identity and his perception of his society. El Alhajadito's installation as the heir of an august lineage about which a paucity of hard facts are available obliges him, like Asturias, to imagine the past he does not know: 'imaginaba lo que creía que las criadas le callaban de sus antepasados' (*EA*, 37). This reliance on his imagination challenges the boy's faith in an objectively verifiable material reality, inducing him to accept the value of beliefs, legends and images which may not be objectively 'true'. The construction of such myths constitutes his sole defence against being passively labelled by the gaze of a more powerful Other (in this case, the world of adults). El Alhajadito discovers that he can accept the label yet alter its meaning, undermining the Other's controlling definition of his identity. But this stance entails the adoption of certain philosophical principles. In order to hew out an autonomous space, an identity over whose contours he will be able to exercise a degree of control, El Alhajadito must renounce any belief in positivist reasoning: the free play of the imagination necessary to the construction of enduring personal myths requires a disregard for empirical proofs and positivist categories. El Alhajadito initially experiences difficulty in accepting this reality. He cries out to the Mal Ladrón, the deity whom he worships: '—¡No permitas que me pierda como imagen en el mundo de la fantasía! ¡Enduréceme para que no salga de la realidad, de lo positivo, de lo material! ¿Por qué dejas que me aparte de tu ejemplo en lo ficticio?' (*EA*, 38).

The turmoil of the mortal struggle between the circus performers and the hunchbacked fisherman Surilo forces El Alhajadito to reassess the value of the imagination. After Surilo is wounded (he takes refuge, significantly, in the *corredorcito*), fishermen and circus performers offer competing explanations of the events leading to his injury. El

Alhajadito realizes that 'Cada quien en este mundo fabrica su verdad' (*EA*, 44). This insight represents a movement beyond the realization that individual perceptions spring from a given angle of vision, in the individual's allegiance to his *corredorcito*, or that a *corredorcito* may be the shared property of many eyes. El Alhajadito is progressing towards a view of the world in which an implicit relativism frees the individual to propagate nearly any myth that suits his purposes. It is a universe which justifies the strategies of a writer of fiction. As Surilo confronts a painful death, El Alhajadito comforts him with words he knows to be a myth:

> Tirado largo a largo en el corredorcito, las moscas comiéndole la sangre de las heridas, como si fuera miel colorada, Surilo se quejó con la cara pegada a la pared.
> El Alhajadito, olvidado de sus antepasados prácticos y positivistas, para quienes sólo existía la materia, se acercó a decirle:
> —¡Surilo, mañana estarás en el paraíso [...]! (*EA*, 47)

The image of honey with which the novel opened, provoking the boy's first trickle of self-awareness, here signals El Alhajadito's passage to a level of consciousness in which he accepts the need to give myth priority over reality. As Asturias, the former positivist sociologist, must learn to submit to the superior 'reality' of myth in order to develop into an accomplished writer of fiction, so El Alhajadito must undergo a similar transition in order to come to terms with and take command of his new realm. Even after he is initiated into the mysteries of his heritage by the wise fisherman Mendiverzúa, who enables him to disentangle legend from reality in his family history, El Alhajadito continues to place a high value on his imaginative faculties. His consolidation of his control over his realm after the departure of the circus and his discovery of the 'true' stories of his ancestors seem only to strengthen his belief in the value of myth-making and the imagination.

> Atado al corredorcito por una cadena de pasos infantiles....el Alhajadito se relame el gusto a miel de caña que tenía en los labios cuando lo descrubrió, aquella mañana, como el único sitio en la casa que por estar abandonado y no tener dueño, podía ser suyo. Fue suyo. En su imaginación, pero fue suyo. ¿Qué otra cosa es la propiedad sino imaginación? Imaginativamente se adueñó del corredorcito. Nadie le disputó el derecho adquirido por su sola fantasía. ¿Qué otra base tiene la propiedad, sino la ficción? (*EA*, 74)

This doctrine of ownership by fiction holds important implications for Asturias's own career. Though not a Maya, he may take possession of the Mayan past through his creative immersion in its mythology. He will make his version the authentic one by allowing the Mayan universe to inhabit his imagination. El Alhajadito demonstrates an analogous approach to external realities when he abandons his search for an angle of vision capable of providing him with direct access to the mysteries of the larger world. Understanding that persuasive accounts of historical experience are summoned up from within, 'ya no corría en busca de la rendija que daba al misterio' (*EA*, 74). His experience of the outside world (represented by the circus) has taught him the primacy of the world within. El Alhajadito learns to superimpose the inner world on the outer, the private fiction on the historical 'fact'. By playing the role of a reincarnation of his ancestors, El Alhajadito successfully propagates the illusion that his dynasty has fulfilled its mythological destiny and returned to its traditional domain.

Volvían los Alhajados. Los señores de la casa regresaban. Así lo decían a todos, los trenzudos barbilampiños al ver pasar al Alhajadito, jinete en un caballo negro, ir de cacería con su escopeta al hombro […] vivir en una palabra como vivieron sus antepasados […] los Alhajados volvían en la manera de ser del Alhajadito, en sus gustos, en sus modales, en sus preferencias (*EA*, 82)

The power of the charade, the capacity of the imagination to mould popular perceptions, constitutes Asturias's response to the problem of having one's identity defined by the gaze of a more powerful Other. The generation of myths is portrayed not merely as a private obsession but as a means of projecting one's vision into the public sphere. By acting out his fantasy of overlordship, dressing in black and riding a black horse, El Alhajadito convinces his servants and neighbours that the dynasty of his ancestors has returned. In a similar vein, by playing the role of the Mayan prince of Paris, Asturias remade himself through force of will into the inheritor and reincarnation of a vanquished empire. Asturias portrays individual identity as the dynamic product of the interaction between a consciousness engendered by meticulous stock-taking of its environment and labelling on the part of the eyes and voices of more powerful external figures; the individual enhances his margin of manoeuvre and succeeds in stamping a distinctively personal interpretation onto the label which has been projected onto him, by taking imaginative possession of his role and acting it out according to his peculiar interpretation of its meaning. The world becomes a battle of competing fantasies; the individual who possesses his imaginative universe most thoroughly will invest particular, personal myths with the credibility necessary to enforce their acceptance as 'truth'. The constitution of individual identity is inseparable from the struggle for the way in which the world is to be interpreted and the relative significance assigned to each of its component parts.

El Alhajadito hears himself being defined, by adult voices, through his connection with a dynastic tradition (that of the Alhajados) and a place (the *corredorcito*) which defines and delimits his angle of vision. This externalization of the self causes the rupture which triggers self-definition. Jacques Lacan, using the paradigm of the 'petit homme', writes of this process:

L'assomption jubilatoire de son image spéculaire par l'être encore plongé dans l'impuissance motrice et la dépendance de nourrissage qu'est le petit homme à ce stade *infans*, nous paraîtra dès lors manifester en une situation exemplaire la matrice symbolique où le *je* se précipite en une forme primordiale, avant qu'il ne s'objective dans la dialectique de l'identification à l'autre et que le langage ne lui restitue dans l'universel sa fonction de sujet.[13]

Lacan situates his model in a bourgeois, patriarchal European society; Asturias sets his young protagonist in a semi-feudal position in an imaginative universe that is non-European and whose laws appear closer to those of fantasy than of reality. El Alhajadito and the 'petit homme' share Lacan's pre-linguistic, 'primordial' stage of identification. They differ in age: Asturias, who construes identification more directly in terms of the individual's role in society, makes his protagonist old enough to dress in black and ride a horse. By contrast, Lacan's 'petit homme' is an infant. The construction of El Alhajadito's identity in terms of his role in society—that of a feudal lord rather than a problematic bourgeois subject—simplifies his trajectory by comparison with that of his European counterpart. A single identificatory act establishes El Alhajadito's role; unlike Lacan's young subject, he does not pass through a 'dialectical' progression of identities. He grasps his role, or theme, then worries at it and refines it. This pattern, more easily applicable to the development of the embryonic artist than to that of the human infant, pinpoints the preoccupations guiding Asturias's narration of the development of El Alhajadito's identity. Like Lacan's 'petit homme', Asturias's little boy remains acutely conscious of the alienating falsehood underlying his newly integrated identity. Taking over the family dynasty intensifies, rather than subdues, his alienation. His new identity is incessantly threatened with dissolution by his participation in rituals preparing for the moment when his authority will be superseded by that of his revenant ancestors.

Pero este decir y redecir que el Alhajadito era el retrato de sus padres y abuelos, tíos y abuelos-tíos, no quitaba que la casa grande se moviera siempre en espera del regreso de los desaparecidos. Salones, comedores y alcobas los esperaban. La servidumbre procedía como si ya tuviera noticia de la vuelta de los enlutados personajes. Noche tras noche mullían las camas profundas [...]. Noche a noche se encendían candelabros y lámparas. (*EA*, 82–3)

A similar contradiction plagues Asturias. The quest for the integrated Guatemalan 'alma nacional' which prompts his adoption of a Mayan persona, is at odds with the interests and goals of the Mayan peoples with whom he has identified himself. Any substantial growth in the power of Guatemala's Indians would make more explicit the opposition between Maya and *ladino*, rendering even less likely the realization of the stable, integrated (implicitly Europeanized) Guatemala for which Asturias yearns. The alternative solution—the integration of the country around an Indian 'alma nacional'—which Asturias's Mayan posture would seem at times to support, enlists Asturias, like El Alhajadito on the final page of the opening section of the novel, as an accomplice in the obliteration of his own essence. In the miraculous case of a resurgent Mayan empire attaining dominance in Guatemala, Asturias would be in the same position in which El Alhajadito would find himself were his ancestors to return: his identity would lose all coherence. Only the tension of advocating the per-petuation of a fragile, defeated world whose strength can never be restored confers a measure of integration upon these identities; at the same time, this contradiction burdens both El Alhajadito and Asturias with identities wracked by alienation. (In Asturias's case, this alienation is compounded by his problematic relationship with French literary culture.) In Lacanian terms, the temporal dialectic which hurls the formation of Asturias's identity, like that of El Alhajadito, into the turbulent waters of history, taxes the subject with a fragmentation and alienation which will persist throughout his development. In this sense *El Alhajadito* serves as a metatext for Asturias's entire *obra*: it is the novel which lays bare the procedures of identification underlying the creation of Asturias's subsequent works of fiction.

Most critical commentary on *El Alhajadito* has emphasized its fairy-tale setting. Uslar Pietri is virtually alone in interpreting the novel in a naturalistic vein. The boy's world, he maintains, 'no era nada extraordinario sino el mundo normal en que podía crecer un niño en Guatemala'.[14] (Cheymol, as noted earlier, views the novel as the work of a consciousness afflicted by nostalgia and prone to consider the homeland as 'primitive'.) Most other critics have depicted *El Alhajadito* as evidence of the growing impact of Surrealism on Asturias during the late 1920s. Couffon writes of passages 'où réalisme et surréalisme se mêlent pour créer un climat d'enchantement et de drôlerie' (*Asturias*, 74). Bellini, while emphasizing the novel's theme of 'il richiamo della fantasia e in essa la necessità di un'evasione spirituale', also points out what he considers to be 'tinte accesamente surrealiste' (*La narrativa*, 200–1, 198). Sáenz weaves her sole mention of the novel into a discussion of Surrealist theories of art:

Conciliar lo real con lo soñado en una superrealidad para lograr que el inconsciente se expresara con mayor libertad, era uno de los própositos de la escuela [...]. Algunas de estas expresiones oníricas quedan reflejadas en *El Alhajadito* como preocupaciones estéticas. (*Genio y figura*, 44)

However, she does not pursue the implications of her insight concerning the liberation of Asturias's unconscious in this novel. The Guatemalan poet and critic Alaide Foppa pushes the Surrealist connection even further than does Sáenz, writing:

El Alhajadito está situado en un Guatemala intemporal, donde los elementos reales aparecen en situaciones irreales. Si de surrealismo debe hablarse a propósito de Miguel Angel Asturias, este libro y *Mulata de tal* son los que mayormente lo manifiestan.[15]

If Uslar Pietri's contention that El Alhajadito grows up in what many Guatemalan children would regard as 'el mundo normal' seems far-fetched, the argument that the novel arose out of Asturias's engagement with Surrealism is equally difficult to sustain. No agreement exists as to when Asturias became aware of the Surrealist movement and began to adopt certain of its aesthetic values and procedures, such as automatic writing. Carmen Vásquez suggests that Asturias had already taken up the Surrealist banner well before his encounter with Robert Desnos on the voyage to Cuba in 1928. She credits Asturias's subsequent sidetrip to Guatemala with liberating him from Surrealist influence: 'Ce retour a provoqué l'abandon du courant surréaliste suivi à l'époque par quelques-uns de ses amis dont Desnos. Il annonçait sa propre vision du monde, celle qu'il aimait appeler "réalisme magique".[16] In fact, Asturias did not apply the designation 'magical realism' to his work until 1948;[17] contrary to what Vásquez implies, he never claimed to have coined the term. Amos Segala adopts a position diametrically opposed to that of Vásquez, maintaining that Asturias knew little of Surrealism and did not (consciously, at least) experiment with its artistic tenets until after his meeting with Desnos: 'Hasta este mismo año [1928], Asturias sólo conocía de oídas las discusiones de Montparnasse, pero Desnos—a quien encontró en el barco que lo conducía a La Habana—se los [sic] relataría de primera mano.'[18] Most of the available evidence supports Segala's claim that Asturias possessed only a vague inkling of Surrealist credos prior to 1928.

The only conscious exercise in Surrealism among Asturias's uncollected early short stories, 'La barba provisional', was published in March 1929. In reference to this story, Asturias recalled: 'Escribí el cuento a mi regreso de un viaje a Cuba [...]. Los otros invitados eran escritores franceses como Robert Desnos' (NC, 22). Asturias and his critics have often described the exercises in automatic writing in which the young Guatemalan and his Spanish American colleagues engaged during their Parisian apprenticeships. In his later years Asturias was fond of portraying these exercises, like his own connection with Surrealism, as dating from the movement's earliest days. In 1966, on his final visit to Guatemala, he gave a student audience this description of the Paris he discovered upon his arrival:

Había llegado Tristán Tzara, había terminado un poco el dadaísmo, y comenzaba Breton y comenzaban los surrealistas a lanzar sus manifiestos y a impulsar la creación puramente mecánica. Nos entusiasmó a nosotros esta idea de podernos sentar a la máquina de escribir o frente a una cuartilla y empezar a escribir mecánicamente, procurando la no intervención de la inteligencia [...]. Con Arturo Uslar Pietri [...] hacíamos ejercicios de esta clase [...]. Poníamos el papel y empezábamos a escribir en esta forma casi mecánica, de donde salieron muchos textos que también publicaron en esta revista que se llamó Imán.[19]

Yet Imán, a one-issue magazine including texts by Asturias and Alejo Carpentier, was published in April 1931.[20] And according to Uslar Pietri, Carpentier—who escaped to Paris from Cuba on the return voyage of the ship which had taken the Prensa Latina journalists to their conference—was a regular attendant at the café gatherings where Asturias practised automatic writing.

> Según los años y las estaciones cambiaban los contertulios de la mesa. Casi nunca faltábamos Asturias, Alejo Carpentier y yo [...]. Pasábamos de la conversación al poema. En un papel del café escribíamos, renglón a renglón, sin concierto, a paso de manos y de mentes, largos poemas delirantes que eran como un semillero de motivaciones o caóticos extractos, llenos de palabras inventadas. Las que pasaron a la literatura y las que se quedaron en aquellos papeles debajo de la mesa. (*Fantasmas*, 15–17)

The translator Jean Cassou corroborates Uslar Pietri's account, recalling:

> En la época en que traducía yo *La vorágine*, de José Eustasio Rivera, nos reuníamos para almorzar todos los miércoles en un pequeño café de la calle Montparnasse Asturias, Uslar Pietri, Alejo Carpentier, Guillermo Valencia, Eduardo Avilés Ramírez, Lara Pardo y yo. (Asturias, *París 1924–1933*, 744)

The presence of Carpentier dates Asturias's ventures into automatic writing as belonging to the years after 1928. But perhaps the strongest evidence of Asturias's lack of awareness, prior to his meeting with Desnos, of the Surrealist ferment on his doorstep comes from his journalism. The year of Asturias's arrival in Paris, 1924, has been described by one critic as 'la grande année du surréalisme'.[21] It was the year of the publication of André Breton's *Manifeste du surréalisme* and *Poisson soluble*, Louis Aragon's *Une vague de rêves* and Robert Desnos's Surrealist fiction *Deuil pour Deuil*. Over the next year, the Surrealists became embroiled in a succession of scandals: they published their pamphlet *Un cadavre*, violently attacking Anatole France just as a national funeral was being prepared for him; they provoked a much-reported brawl at a banquet to voice their opposition to the Rif War and French colonial policy; in a hostile open letter to Paul Claudel they denounced France as a 'nation de porcs et de chiens'.[22] Asturias gives no evidence of having been aware of any of these highly public events. The Surrealists continued to agitate and experiment—often on themes of direct relevance to Asturias—throughout his first four years in Paris. Jacqueline Chénieux-Gendron notes that 'La seconde exposition de la Galerie surréaliste, en mai 1927, présente des toiles d'Yves Tanguy avec des "objets d'Amérique": de [la] Colombie britannique, du Nouveau-Mexique, du Mexique, de la Colombie et du Pérou' (*Le Surréalisme*, 32). It is almost impossible to imagine Asturias not attending such an exhibition had he been aware of its existence. Since his journalism served as a virtual diary of his cultural preoccupations, and often drew upon his encounters with French society in order to launch critiques of Guatemalan reality, it is difficult to conceive of him attending such an exhibition without writing about it.

The most plausible explanation of Asturias's silence is that, in 1927, he possessed at best a glancing acquaintance with Surrealist activities and philosophy. Both his journalism and his notebooks corroborate this hypothesis. The 440 articles Asturias filed for *El Imparcial* between 1924 and 1933 do not contain a single mention of André Breton, Paul Eluard, Louis Aragon, Philippe Soupault, Benjamin Péret, Jacques Vaché, René Crevel, Yves Tanguy, Max Ernst or Antonin Artaud. Robert Desnos and Man Ray are mentioned once each, the former in 1931, the latter in 1929. By contrast, Jean Cocteau, the Surrealists' arch-foe, receives five mentions; one of the few traces left by the growing Surrealist 'influence' on Asturias is that his characterizations of Cocteau grow less complimentary. In November 1925 Asturias describes Cocteau as 'el hombre más inteligente de París'; by November 1931 he is writing that 'Cocteau […] ha sido siempre un valor liquidado entre los hombres de su tiempo' (*París 1924–1933*, 60, 464). Aside from his adoption of the Surrealists' disparaging view of Cocteau, it is nearly impossible to isolate evidence of the impact of Surrealist theories in Asturias's journalism. He never explicates or grapples with Surrealist concepts, and no Surrealist figure's name appears prior to 1929. Asturias's notebooks from the 1920s and 1930s contain reading notes on Guatemalan history and drafts of short stories. His sole attempt to define his relationship with Surrealism occurs in a random jotting in a notebook apparently dating from the late 1950s or early 1960s: 'El surrealismo me ayuda a encontrar en mí, si se fuese, las excentricidades'.[23]

The fantasy of *El Alhajadito*, then, belongs to a mode predating Asturias's familiarity with Surrealist conjurings of a dense, sensually surprising 'superreality'. The novel is essentially an allegory of identification. While Asturias did not know Lacan (at this point publishing his first papers), his composition of *El Alhajadito* appears to have nearly coincided with his discovery of Freud, whom he quoted with apparent familiarity during his 1928 speaking tour of Guatemala. Asturias's emphasis, in his talk 'La arquitectura de la vida nueva', on Freud's study of dreams as manifestations of suppressed desire and a necessary escape from reality parallels his praise of dreams in *El*

Alhajadito. '¡Cómo podía ser que tanta realidad desembocara en tanto sueño!', El Alhajadito marvels towards the end of the opening section (*EA*, 75). Asturias's reading of Freud led naturally to his study of a young boy's definition of his identity. As Bowie writes: 'For Freud, identification is the mainspring of the psychical apparatus' (*Lacan*, 32). Asturias chose to dramatize this process through the allegory, a form already familiar to him from his youthful attempts at Christian allegories such as 'El toque de ánimas' and 'La línea de una nube blanca (Judea)'. The richness of Asturias's language in many of the descriptive passages seems to stem from a residual tendency towards *modernista* elegance supplemented by a passion for the writers of French decadence, such as Lautréamont and Remy de Gourmont. The setting, while differing significantly from 'el mundo normal' of a Guatemalan boy, derives from a systematic exaggeration of such traits of bourgeois *ladino* life as the centrality of the big house, the presence of teams of servants, the ranking of individuals within society on the basis of their *apellidos*. This depiction is enhanced, as Cheymol has argued, by the need to present Guatemala as 'primitif, colonial', in order to conform to French expectations of Guatemalan reality. The result is certainly not realism, but—despite having been rewritten prior to publication by an older Asturias who was anxious to establish his Surrealist lineage[24]—*El Alhajadito* scarcely draws upon Surrealism for its fantastic elements.

By the time he wrote 'La barba provisional', Asturias had become familiar with the Surrealist vision of life as an integrated act of rebellion whose manifestations included the creation of spontaneous, idiosyncratic works of art. Yet despite exhibiting various Surrealist traits, 'La barba provisional' invokes the anxiety of the exile rather than the revolt of the revolutionary artist.

In so far as the story serves as a homage, the object of Asturias's esteem is not Surrealism as a movement but Robert Desnos, both as an individual and as author of *La liberté ou l'amour!* (1927). Asturias's encounter with Surrealism is inseparable from his friendship with Desnos. His failure to become more deeply immersed in Surrealist debates or to read more widely in Surrealist writings may be largely due to André Breton's expulsion of Desnos from the movement in March 1929, only two weeks after Asturias completed 'La barba provisional'.[25]

Facing the choice between preserving his friendship with Desnos and frequenting mainstream Surrealist circles (the bitterness of the split did not permit hangers-on to maintain ties with both Breton and the dissidents)[26] Asturias clearly opted for Desnos.[27] At the time, Surrealism appears to have represented for Asturias an incidental component of his literary friendship with Desnos. The creed did not exert a strong claim on his allegiance, and it was only thirty years later that he began, retrospectively, to enlist himself in its ranks. The passionate, fractious Desnos's continued advocacy of Asturias's writing—in 1931 he sent the manuscript of *Leyendas de Guatemala* to Gallimard, recommending that they publish it[28]—provides virtually irrefutable evidence that Asturias did not patronize Breton after the March 1929 schism.[29] Asturias's potential access to the movement, therefore, was confined to the period between May 1928, when he returned from Guatemala, and Desnos's expulsion in March 1929. Despite his later assertions of having been intimately acquainted with the movement's central figures, it is unclear which of the Surrealists Asturias actually met or whether he read their works during his years in Paris. On the evidence of his journalism and his often imprecise summations of Surrealist aesthetics, Desnos's short novel *La liberté ou l'amour!* is the only Surrealist volume that one may be almost certain Asturias had read. He mentioned the novel—though mangling and altering the meaning of its title—in an article published in the Havana newspaper *Diario de la Marina* (Asturias, *París 1924–1933*, 925); 'La barba provisional' is inextricably entwined with Desnos's text.

Asturias's allusions to Desnos in 'La barba provisional' constitute a troubled, much-qualified declaration of allegiance to the Surrealist project as Desnos had presented it to him. Prior to the 1929 purge, the Surrealists were fond of praising one another in their books. In *Le Paysan de Paris* (1926), for example, Louis Aragon refers to 'Robert Desnos, ce singulier sage moderne'.[30] The mannerism served to reinforce the Surrealists' solidarity in their efforts to bring to fruition a collective endeavour; by referring to each other, they underlined the primacy of their tightly bound—and ultimately destructively enforced—group identity over their individual creative egos. In 'La barba provisional', Asturias introduces as a character 'Robert Desnos, poeta y escritor surrealista que […] dice en su último libro: ¡Yo nunca tuve amigos, mis amigos, todos fueron mis amantes!'.[31] In making this distinctively Surrealist gesture of solidarity, Asturias goes beyond the mere acknowledgement of the impact of French literary culture on his prose: he inscribes himself in the Surrealist brotherhood, knitting his text into the web of Desnos's writings through a recognized method

of professing loyalty.[32] In fact, Asturias pushes this melding of creative
identities farther than did the Surrealists themselves. He not only
refers to his creative colleague, but cites from his work. (Asturias
balances his homage to Desnos with references to, though no quotes
from, the Guatemalan poet Carlos Samayoa Aguilar.) Linking himself
to a foreign tradition, across a language barrier, Asturias misquotes—
or rewrites—Desnos. He also attributes the cited line to Desnos
himself. In fact, the sentence appears in a section of *La liberté ou
l'amour!* entitled 'Monologue du Corsaire Sanglot devant une
boutique de coiffeur rue du Faubourg-Saint-Honoré'. Sanglot—
arguably a sort of *alter ego* for Desnos—begins his monologue: 'Je n'ai
jamais eu d'amis, je n'ai eu que des amants'.[33] Asturias's rendering
of the sentence is more emphatic than the original; he adds an
exclamation mark and translates the indirect 'je n'ai eu que'
construction with the more forceful and assertive '¡todos fueron mis
amantes!'. The effect is to transform the opening sentence of a
reflective soliloquy into a bold provocation. Playing up the
outrageousness of Desnos's words, Asturias presents Surrealism—and
by implication French literature and European culture—as a source of
rebellion. The self-justification he musters for his overt identification
with a European literary school is to depict that school as revolutionary. Asturias's insertion of the additional clause 'mis amigos' into
his translation both heightens the scandalousness of the declaration
(the speaker is, in effect, claiming his readers as lovers) and reinforces
the theme of connection: the added bond between Desnos (in
Asturias's translation; Corsaire Sanglot in the original) and his readers
(of whom Asturias is obviously one) provides an additional textual
thread uniting Asturias and Desnos. 'La barba provisional', then, is not
a story written under Surrealist 'influence', but a work produced by
Asturias's engagement with, and transmutation of, the specific textual
tones and features of *La liberté ou l'amour!*.

   Julia Kristeva has written: 'Tout texte est absorption et transformation d'un autre texte. A la place de la notion d'intersubjectivité
s'installe celle d'*intertextualité*, et le langage poétique se lit, au moins,
comme *double*'.[34] This doubling permeates 'La barba provisional'.
Kristeva, writing on Lautréamont, argues that 'ce procédé de dialogue
entre les discours s'intègre à tel point au texte poétique qu'il devient
le lieu indispensable de la naissance du sens de ce texte' (*Sémeiotiké*,
196). 'La barba provisional' generates meaning through its sparring
with the differing discursive tradition of *La liberté ou l'amour!*.

Asturias's rewriting of that tradition's modes, mannerisms, linguistic tics and image-clusters invests his text with a duality in which the reader observes a fledgling Spanish American modernity both parodying and paying obeisance to the weight of European tradition disguised in the brash, avant-garde garb of Surrealism. This interplay between two semiological systems serves to amplify the story's basic theme of the exile's anguished search for his identity. The narrator, ill at ease with both his European and American identifications, is trapped in a linguistic field whose tensions and contradictions mirror those of his own confused sense of self.

Asturias's invocation of Surrealist motifs alters the rhythms of his prose, bringing the eloquence of long, clever sentences, extended by multiple subordinate clauses, into a style which, on the evidence of *Leyendas de Guatemala* (completed at roughly the same time), normally alternated between florid linguistic profusion marked by stylized repetition, and pseudo-Biblical diction intended to recall the sacred texts of the Mayas. The language of 'La barba provisional' is unrelentingly literary, delighting in its own manicured sophistication. Asturias's delving after images worthy of the Surrealist stamp generates an elaborate, self-conscious prose style. In the opening scene the narrator enters a Parisian bar frequented by prostitutes and orders a cup of milk.

Reconfortado en mi físico con aquella blanca diezmillonésima parte de una vaca, tomando contacto con los seres y las cosas que me rodeaban, vine a darme cuenta de que cerca de mí había una... ¡dos!, porque en ese momento entró otra, y otra, tres... cuatro... cinco... seis... siete. El café se llamaba 'Las once mil vírgenes,' aunque de todo tenían, menos de vírgenes. (*BP*, 223)

Asturias's Surrealist-influenced attempt to conjure reality in surprising ways produces the somewhat strained image of the glass of milk as the ten-millionth part of a cow. His inverted introduction of the prostitutes as virgins borrows from Guillaume Apollinaire's pornographic novella, *Les onze mille verges* (1907), which was re-habilitated by Surrealism. Like Asturias's story, *Les onze mille verges* describes a protagonist from the fringes of the Latin world (in this case, Bucharest) who has realized his dream of living in Paris.[35]

Asturias's invocation of virginity also stems indirectly from Desnos's Freudian depiction of Corsaire Sanglot's quest for knowledge: 'Et la pensée de Corsaire Sanglot suivait une piste au cœur d'une forêt vierge' (*LA*, 28). Asturias appropriates this image in the final paragraphs of 'La barba provisional' as a way of symbolizing his divided narrator's quest for knowledge: 'Mi última noche de América la pasé corriendo por una selva oscura [...]. Iba detrás de un mono blanco como una estrella, como un serafín de la selva virgen, y no le pude alcanzar' (*BP*, 241). Having ushered into his text this image of virginity, through his echo of Desnos's portrayal of the quest for knowledge as a race through a virgin forest, Asturias proceeds to systematize it, welding it (shorn of its Desnosian sexual resonances) into the structure of his short story. In order to prepare for the image's appearance at the end of the story, he introduces it, through his ironic reference to the prostitutes, in the initial scene. In this way, the tone and meaning of the story's opening and one aspect of its symbolic unity are spawned by Asturias's loan of an image from Desnos's novel.

Asturias borrows other images from *La liberté ou l'amour!*. Vásquez suggests that the character of Sisil is 'une évocation possible' ('Une amitié méconnue', 200) of Desnos's female protagonist Louise Lame. Yet, perhaps owing to the differences between their respective discursive traditions, Asturias's Sisil soon recedes from view, while Louise Lame remains important throughout *La liberté ou l'amour!*. Lame's presence is crucial to Desnos's portrayal of Corsaire Sanglot's pursuit of liberty through the uninhibited expression of his sexuality. The development of Lame's character is subordinated to Sanglot's quest, which nevertheless cannot be dramatized without her compliance. Writing out of the more constrained Hispanic prose tradition, Asturias cannot share Desnos's penchant for glorying in explicit sexual description. The scene in which the narrator and Sisil, finding themselves without the money to pay for a hotel room, cavort and caress one another in a swimming pool, is discreet to the point of ambiguity. Where Desnos's narrator applauds his characters' enjoyment of oral sex ('Je vous salue bien bas baisers de la chair. Moi aussi j'ai plongé ma tête dans les ténèbres des cuisses' (*LA*, 27–8)), Sisil continues to wear her 'traje de baño' (*BP*, 227) during even her most prolonged moment of physical contact with Asturias's narrator. Asturias has appropriated Desnos's tactic of beginning his narrative with a sexual encounter. But the device does not permit him to express adequately his central preoccupations, which concern the exile's confusions of identity rather than the projection of an ethos of revolt through sexual energy; Sisil disappears from the text within a paragraph of emerging from the swimming pool. Asturias's means of subordinating his female protagonist to his particular themes is to use the narrator's lingering memories of his encounter with her to set up the crucial opposition between his Spanish American and French identities, represented by his respective emotional bonds with Carlos Samayoa Aguilar and Robert Desnos.

Carlos Samayoa Aguilar se le parece a Sisil de una manera desconcertante, apasionadora, triste. Con temor estrechaba la mano del poeta ahora que volví a mi país. Sus ojos, infusiones de agua de mar, me devolvieron al recuerdo de Sisil, que estoy tentado de llamar Carlota, agregándole los apellidos de mi amigo.
Robert Desnos […] también se parece a Sisil...
La hermandad de ojos entre Sisil, Samayoa Aguilar y Desnos me sigue turbando el corazón. A ella la trataba a veces como a un hombre, sin saber el motivo, sin presentirlo siquiera, y a Samayoa Aguilar, le vi a veces los ojos turbados como a una mujer. ¡Ay, aquel amor tan natatorio y tan sutil, enterrado en París y resucitado en los ojos de un amigo! (*BP*, 229–30)

The confusions of sexual identity expressed in this passage are an outgrowth of Asturias's intertextual absorption of the governing motifs of Desnos's novel. On a strictly symbolic plane, the narrator's apparently unstable sexual identity ('a ella la trataba a veces como a un hombre') and imaginary androgynization of his compatriot Samayoa Aguilar offer an initial paradigm of the divided self whose dilemmas will be dramatized more fully in the story's later pages. At a practical level, the passage serves as an intertextual bridge linking the gambit of sexual-encounter-as-opening, which Asturias has pilfered from Desnos's differently directed text, to the motifs of duality, division and confused identity which occupy the thematic centre of his own work. This transitional passage exemplifies the 'dialogue entre les discours' which Kristeva posits as the source of meaning in literary texts; it displays in undigested form the doubling which elsewhere is more subtly integrated into the surface of Asturias's prose.

Viewed from this perspective, the narrator's swim with Sisil makes possible, or gives birth to, the more highly articulated depiction of his doubleness during the remainder of the story. Asturias captures this fact through his punning employment of 'natatorio' to evoke both swimming and birth. Asturias introduces the concept of punning early in 'La barba provisional', when the narrator prevaricates at Sisil's initial invitation to accompany her to the swimming pool: '—[…] cómo podría dárseme la idea desagradable de un baño a estas horas sin hacérseme dudar entre un calambur o la verdad sin medias tintas, es decir con las piernas desnudas' (*BP*, 225). The choice between a 'calambur' (a borrowing from the French *calembour*) or the truth 'sin medias tintas', itself a *double-entendre*, boils down to no choice at all. Both terms illustrate the instability of meaning and essential doubleness lurking behind the story's language. Asturias's treatment of basic phrases and key motifs is fraught with the tension instilled by his awareness of the pressure being exerted by European tradition on his constitution of his 'independent' Spanish American creative identity. This pressure is evident in his characterization of the image of the voyage to America and his problematic use of the expression 'hero'.

Desnos, articulating his disgusted rejection of European civilization, draws on Latin American imagery in his quest for freshness, spontaneity and exoticism. His vision of Latin America is unrelentingly romantic. He evokes 'aventuriers en pantalon blanc hantés par l'idée du prochain paquebot qui les emportera vers les casinos d'Amérique du Sud et les amours plus fatales' (*LA*, 37). A long poem (a homage to, and parody of, Arthur Rimbaud's 'Le bateau ivre') introduces the prose text of *La liberté ou l'amour!* and provides an explicit rendering of this outlook.

> Ils enverront longtemps à l'horizon fragile
> L'appel désespéré des Christophe Colomb
> Avant que, répondant à leur prière agile,
> Quelque sauvagerie y marque son talon.
>
> Et que, pilote épris de navigation
> Dont le sillage efface aux feux d'un soleil jaune
> Ton sillage infamant, civilisation!
> Un roi nègre, un beau jour, nous renvoie à la faune (*LA*, 11)

European civilization, like any Christopher Columbus, is gliding towards the hostile coast of a primitive, 'savage' world. Desnos's rehabilitation of the 'roi nègre' (an image whose customary connotations are of servility perpetuating European dominance) exemplifies the Surrealists' enraged enlistment of the downtrodden world beyond Europe's borders into their campaign against their own cultural traditions.

Asturias absorbs these Surrealist themes. In a story dramatizing his efforts to recuperate the outlines of his American identity, he nevertheless offers a clichéd, Europeanized vision of American realities. America, he states, is a continent whose passions remain free of the deadening effects of European civilization. He initially presents this outlook in a tongue-in-cheek manner that seems intended to ridicule European stereotypes while ostensibly acquiescing to them.

En América donde sobre los Andes van los hombres con los pies desnudos, me daba la barba una gran expresión de bandolero que había dejado el caballo atado en la esquina y andaba en busca de una mujer a quien besar o de un hombre a quien matar. Amor u odio... (*BP*, 240)

Yet the narrator's tone soon modulates into a language less resistant to the romanticizations which Europe wishes to impose upon America. The 'amor u odio' pairing leads Asturias into a digression which, while still playful and eloquent, betrays a documentary earnestness absent from the paragraph's opening sentence. The passage continues:

Eso tiene de peculiar América, y los que hemos vivido dos o tres años lejos ya no nos acostumbramos a vivir desnudos, es decir a vivir amando u odiando, prefiriendo términos menos expuestos a la intemperie y tal vez muy cerca de la indiferencia. Poblaciones, gentes, universos enteros se aman y se odian en aquel Continente divino, y no se concibe la indiferencia hacia nada que existe. Amor u odio, conservar o destruir... (*BP*, 240)

America becomes a continent of irreducible oppositions and undiluted passions, conforming to the Surrealists' need to banish the indifference endemic to modern life—an indifference which expatriate Spanish Americans such as the narrator find themselves absorbing in Europe. In his descriptions of America, Asturias projects the image of untamed savagery demanded by the assumptions generating such texts as *La liberté ou l'amour!*. The ironic phrasing of 'aquel Continente divino' hints at an effort to mock these clichés while continuing to recite them. Ultimately, though, the narrative does comply with Desnos's categorization. Asturias absorbs the ideology of Desnos's text, stages an initial insurrection against its vision of American identity, but eventually succumbs to its tenets— while providing some evidence of residual misgivings. The ironic tone expressing the narrator's sense of cultural duality springs from the intertextual tensions binding together, while failing to reconcile completely, Desnos's and Asturias's respective characterizations of America.

Asturias's grappling with the notion of heroism reveals a similar internalization of European preoccupations. The search for gestures capable of assuming heroic resonance is one of the sublimated forces motivating Corsaire Sanglot and Louise Lame's anarchic actions in *La liberté ou l'amour!*. The novel's insistent images of death and cemeteries, most notably in chapter VI, 'Pamphlet contre la mort', dwell upon the shadow of the First World War without ever naming the event. When Louise Lame 'dies' (she returns to life in later chapters), her funeral procession is described in enigmatic, vaguely military terms: 'Le convoi suivait une avenue' (*LA*, 61). The narrator mourns Louise with the words: 'Mon esprit lui est soumis comme au fusil la balle' (*LA*, 64). The chapter ends with an embittered exchange of dialogue harshly critical of the ethos of a society willing to sacrifice its youth on the battlefield: '—Mais la mort?/—C'est bon pour vous' (*LA*, 65). In opposition to the conception of heroism as the willingness to submit to a premature, patriotic death, Desnos promotes the pursuit of love as an activity entailing truly heroic risks. At the same time, by implanting the mythological figure of a siren in a modern house, he acknowledges the inherent incompatibility of this vision with the streamlined context of the post-war world.

Le paysage où se meuvent nos héros [Corsaire et Louise] est composé, ne l'oublions pas, d'une maison moderne au rez-de-chaussée de laquelle une sirène blanche se prépare à de sanglantes aventures, au troisième étage de laquelle des hommes aventureux sont prêts à risquer pour l'amour des dangers sensationnels. (*LA*, 79–80)

Given the discrepancy between routinized societal romanticizations of love and the searing honesty of feeling sought by his protagonists, Desnos admits only the most visceral, even perverse, expressions of love into his refined conception of heroism. In the novel's final pages, Corsaire 'liberates' thirty-two schoolgirls from the clutches of their tyrannical headmistress. 'Et que fit le héros d'une si troublante aventure?' the narrator asks (*LA*, 107). Having curtailed the headmistress's nightly ritual of beating two girls selected at random, Corsaire elects to beat the entire class. He is assisted in his night-long brutalization of the girls by the headmistress, who turns out to be Louise Lame.

Il y eut une étreinte entre lui [le Corsaire] et la terrible maîtresse qui avait assisté, sans mot dire, aux actions de son amant.
  Encore une fois, Louise Lame et le Corsaire Sanglot se sont rencontrés.
(*LA*, 108)

In the framework of a corrupt society, Desnos contends, the savage authenticity of feeling expressed in sadism offers access to emotions habitually smothered by the hypocrisy of convention. Not only do Louise and Corsaire rediscover each other, but by torturing the girls they introduce them to love. 'Elles se souviendront des événements de la nuit. L'amour et la jalousie ensemble tortureront leurs âmes [...].

Bientôt même et pour mieux évoquer ce matin tendre où elles rencontrèrent l'amour, elles entreprennent de se meurtrir elles-mêmes' (*LA*, 108). In deliberately outrageous, *épater-le-bourgeois* fashion, Desnos portrays Corsaire's role in proliferating the honesty of feeling characteristic of beatings and flagellations (as opposed to hypocritical bourgeois dissimulations of one's true emotions) as establishing Corsaire's heroism. Debased by its propagandistic wartime usage, the notion of heroism, in Desnos's optic, may still be re-habilitated through acts of revolt.

Asturias's first allusion to heroism demonstrates his awareness of the particular resonances evoked by the idea in the climate of post-First World War Europe. Sisil, indicating a deep line in the palm of her hand, tells the narrator: 'Este fue mi primer amor... y quién sabe si el último. Murió en la guerra [...]. Un héroe' (*BP*, 224). Sisil's declaration that her pre-war first love may prove to be her last introduces the prevailing European mood of disillusionment. The narrator shows that he has absorbed this European distrust of 'heroic' acts when he reflects: 'No sé por qué dan miedo los héroes' (*BP*, 224). The narrator's outlook, although not based on personal experience of the war, reflects European apprehensions. The First World War and the homogenized banality of post-war capitalism have deprived Europeans of the latitude to make genuinely heroic gestures, but heroism remains possible in less world-weary societies. When the narrator goes to the cinema, he attends 'una película de guerra, titulada *Verdun*' (*BP*, 234). His body divides in two, his clean-shaven Parisian incarnation remaining in the audience while his bearded Spanish American self (albeit with his beard trimmed in French style) ascends to the screen. 'Y esa noche fui héroe, de barba negra subí a la gloria, desde donde en vano trato de pescar un aplauso para utilizarlo como gillette y rasurarme. Con aplausos se rasuran los héroes' (*BP*, 235). If social approval tames heroes by 'shaving' them, the hero himself, in this case, is complicit in his own shaving. Asturias's narrator is applauded in his bearded, 'savage' Spanish American incarnation, but he longs to parlay the applause into a means of integrating himself into the clean-shaven, 'civilized' domain of the Parisian audience: 'trato de pescar un aplauso para utilizarlo como gillette y rasurarme'. Asturias's choice of the verb 'pescar', reiterating the story's recurrent fish imagery, identifies Surrealism (whose flagship symbol is Breton's *poisson soluble*) as the potential agent of his integration into the Parisian milieu. But Asturias's narrator yearns for both Parisian acceptance *and* a more self-confident and satisfying accommodation with his Spanish American roots. Asturias's situating of heroism in otherness—the self projected on a cinema screen—arises from his intertextual transmutation of Desnos's conception of heroism as a rebellion in search of emotional authenticity. Like Desnos, Asturias seeks truth of feeling; unlike Desnos, he believes that the heroic achievement of this truth will be found in the constitution of a coherent (in this case, Spanish American) identity. Given his European vantage point, this desired Spanish American identity remains a foreign entity, an object outside his present being. For Desnos, a stable conception of the self, such as that sought by Asturias's narrator, would belong to the realm of bourgeois illusion. Surrealism, then, may offer Asturias part of the solution to his dilemma, but by virtue both of its European origins and of its relentlessly anarchic tendencies the internalization of Surrealist tenets also forms part of his problem. The primary tension animating 'La barba provisional' springs from the ways in which the narrator's residence in France, and his growing ties with French writers and French literary culture, leaves him feeling torn, divided and increasingly alienated from his Spanish American 'essence'. Asturias's discussion of heroism reworks Desnos's presentation of the concept in such a way as to make it express this sense of division.

In an echo of Lacan's metaphor of the mirror-phase, the narrator's personality ruptures during the moment prior to his plunge into the swimming pool with Sisil. Observing the pool, he feels incited to 'romper aquel clarísimo espejo, no con mi imagen, con mi persona, como en un sueño' (BP, 226). The statement establishes the rift between the narrator's 'imagen' and his 'persona', confirming the bifurcation of his self into two halves which refuse to cohere. Where the Lacanian subject assumes the armour of an alienating identity, constituting himself in history through an imperfect synthesis of his conflicting self-images, the narrator of 'La barba provisional', unlike the protagonist of El Alhajadito, appears unable to initiate the dialectical integration central to Lacan's 'image morcelée du corps' (Lacan, Ecrits I, 93–4) (or, in this case, the 'morcellement' dividing 'imagen' and 'persona') revealed by the surface of the swimming pool. The evocation of the 'persona' as engaged by dreams, and the narrator's subsequent description of his frolicking in the pool with Sisil as 'aquel extraño amor de peces' (BP, 226), associate his mental fragmentation with, respectively, the activity most vaunted by Surrealists (dreaming) and the most salient Surrealist symbol (the fish).

The narrator's split identity is inextricably linked to his interaction with Desnos's literary aesthetic.[36]

Craving wholeness, the narrator visits his consulate. He describes himself 'dirigiéndome […] al consulado de mi país en busca, nada menos, que de repatriación' (*BP*, 230). The final word demands to be read literally: disoriented by his union with Sisil, bearer of Surrealist Parisian culture, the narrator seeks the consolation of union with his *patria*. His confusions of identity increase upon being told that the consulate has closed for a 'semana inglesa', leading him to think that the porter has mistaken his query for a request to visit 'el consulado del Soberano de la Gran Bretaña y todas las Indias' (*BP*, 231). This fantasy of British domination over the entire Caribbean both heightens the narrator's confusions and underlines his basic insecurity regarding the solidity and integrity of his *patria*. He cannot be certain that the bases of the autonomous Spanish American identity that he wishes to consolidate do, in fact, exist. The scene exposes the political weakness of the narrator's homeland as an important factor in rendering him vulnerable to French cultural domination.

The narrator's insecurity with regard to the contours of his identity is underlined by his encounter with the 'zurcidoras de medias' who declare: 'Este señor, antes tenía barba' (*BP*, 231). The prophets' employment as darners of socks recalls the image of the narrator's entering the swimming pool with Sisil 'sin medias tintas'; they are stitching together Parisian garments to cover the narrator's cultural nakedness. The narrator himself reiterates the point through his repetition of the phrase: '¡Me zurcían la vida!' (*BP*, 232, 239). His receptiveness to the sock darners' designation of him as Marcel Orfie, a bearded English nobleman who lost his memory after an injury suffered in the First World War, demonstrates the narrator's essential malleability: 'De veras tal vez era inglés' (*BP*, 232). Like El Alhajadito, and to some extent like Asturias himself, the narrator bows to the definition of an alien gaze.

> ¿Qué sabía yo si a pesar de rasurarme todos los días, esta buena mujer habíame visto alguna vez con barba o que de un otro que pareciéndoseme mucho llevara pelos en la cara […]?
>
> […] No es cierto, tuve deseos de gritarle, pero luego me convencí de si no era yo el que habiendo perdido la memoria, había olvidado mi vida anterior, lo que era antes.
>
> […] Un noble inglés que perdió la memoria en la guerra, estuve a punto de creerme después de oír a las zurcidoras. (*BP*, 231–2)

The narrator's encounter with the sock darners confirms the existence of his two irreconcilable selves, the bearded and the clean-shaven. But it leaves unclear the respective significances of the two identities. The next scene attaches specific meanings to these two images. 'Obligado a no rasurarme por la falta de dinero' (*BP*, 233), the narrator recounts, he begins to sprout a beard symbolic of his resurgent Spanish American identity. 'La cara se me fue poblando de una selva rala, de pelos en los que reinaba la más absoluta anarquía [...] espejo de esa parte de mi vida que había olvidado en no sé donde' (*BP*, 233).

Foreshadowing the 'selva virgen' through which he will run in his futile search for knowledge in the story's final paragraphs, the narrator associates his beard with the primitive anarchy Surrealism has assigned Spanish America as its role in the liberation of the European psyche. The savage 'selva' of his beard, even while sprouting sparsely on his expatriate's face, mirrors the Spanish American life and history which the narrator has forgotten as a result of his prolonged stay in Europe. The beard features a moustache which he describes as 'Mi bigote oriental, de Confucio, de Buda y de Cristo' (*BP*, 233), underlining the way in which, under the Parisian Orientalist rubric, Spanish American 'savagery' is conflated with other exotic modes of life. Scraping together enough money to go to the barber, the narrator has his beard 'tallada a la francesa' (*BP*, 233–4). It is this beard, cut to suit French norms, which earns him the applause of the cinema crowd. Mistaking him for Marcel Orfie, the spectators acclaim him as a war hero, when 'se dividió y subdividió mi cuerpo' (*BP*, 234). The self who ascends to the cinema screen sports a Spanish American beard tailored in such a way as to enable him to pass for a European. The obdurate separateness of his two selves prevents the narrator's seated half from assuming the image on the mirror of the screen as part of his irredeemably fissured identity. He appears unable to achieve what Lacan would view as the essential if terminally flawed process of bringing the alien self into the psyche. The film of a life which both is and is not his own provides the narrator with a source of happiness: 'Antes soñábamos para ser felices, ahora vamos al cinematógrafo' (*BP*, 237).[37] At the same time, the film reinforces the story's emphasis on the fact that the narrator's lack of a coherent identity leaves him alienated from a significant portion of his own experience: 'El personaje de este asunto, que en el fondo soy yo, viéndose con barba recordó' (*BP*, 237). By maintaining the third-person narration in this sentence, the text holds the narrator's two incarnations apart. At the same time, Asturias emphasizes the sovereign role of the imagination in shaping the individual's world. During the dream-sequence in which the narrator envisages himself assuming the guise of the deceased Marcel Orfie in order to 'return' to his Other's widow, he says: 'La esposa del marido en el fondo es él, su pensamiento de ella' (*BP*, 238). Later, recalling his trans-Atlantic crossing, he writes: 'En el mar, en la muerte, en la vida, siempre estamos solos, todo lo demás son ficciones' (*BP*, 239).

As in *El Alhajadito*, the world is revealed as infinitely pliable, subservient to the creative individual's overmastering imagination. The insight takes on an added piquancy in 'La barba provisional' through its connection with the plight of the exile. No longer belonging fully to either Europe or America, the narrator possesses his imaginative universe so thoroughly *because* little else in his life offers him certainty or stability. The exile's imagination constitutes his one ever-present piece of baggage; but even this most intimate possession is irredeemably fissured. As the story progresses, the narrator views his own essence as increasingly savage, foreign and forgotten; he shrinks to a mere shadow of his *alter ego*, the European war hero Marcel Orfie.

Marcel Orfie tomaba a las mujeres y me las pasaba ya seducidas—conseguía mujeres, oficio propio de héroes—y yo, por mi parte, las pasaba al que en mí era el yo que sabía olvidar, al de la barba, cruel como un domador de circo, moroso como un estudiante rico, desatento como un santo de palo, molesto para dirigirle la palabra como una tortuga que nunca sabemos de primera intención si está muerta.

Marcel Orfie, el desmemoriado inglés con que me confundieron las zurcidoras, tanto se me parecía, que he llegado a creer que era yo. (*BP*, 241)

The apparent fusion of the narrator's two formerly irreconcilable selves is realized not by a movement towards synthesis, however fraught, but by a process of absorption—the transition from expatriate to immigrant—which elides the narrator's Spanish American identity. His rush through the 'selva virgen' of America in pursuit of 'un mono blanco, blanco como una estrella'—a source of light which he may pursue but never catch—leads him to the ship which will transport him back to Paris. Boarding, he confuses the surface of the ocean with 'la piscina' (*BP*, 242) and searches the ship in vain for Marcel Orfie, in whom he has invested his identity. In Orfie's absence, the narrator's defined, if subordinated, sense of self vanishes; he relapses into a primitive, anonymous savagery.

En el fondo negro, caverna del troglodita, loco, erizados los cabellos, anestesiado por el miedo, estaba un hombre—yo—con la cabeza vuelta y las manos en actitud defensiva. Todo mi ser temblaba, sudando [...]. Por mi cara pasó una ola de acero afiladísimo, una navaja de barba para rasurar tritones y viejas desilusionadas de la eficacia de los depilatorios. (*BP*, 243)

Still trapped outside himself, the narrator at last experiences the shaving which he had hoped would integrate him into the Parisian cinema crowd. Yet the imagery the text offers to describe this event both deflates him and reinforces his ambiguous position. The powerfully anti-romantic association of 'viejas desilusionadas de la eficacia de los depilatorios' is accompanied by an allusion to Triton, a minor Greek sea god traditionally depicted as a man with a fish's tail. Recalling the Parisian swimming pool in which the narrator immersed himself in the water of Surrealist assumptions and 'aquel extraño amor de peces', the Triton image underlines the narrator's status as a hybrid creature—neither fish nor man—completely at home neither in the Parisian world nor outside it. The Surrealist fish returns in the story's penultimate paragraph to demolish the narrator's status as a hero and decree his subordination to Parisian artistic requirements. '—Tu barba, tú no eres Marcel Orfie—me dijo un pez—nos pertenece, exigua parte del mar de los sargazos que no tienes porque llevar en la cara' (*BP*, 244).

For Paris, the narrator is not a hero; his 'savage' beard serves as a component of the natural and the primitive (in this case driftweed from the Sargasso Sea) which enables Parisian writers to generate texts such as *La liberté ou l'amour!*, in which the Americas become symbolic fodder with which to beat down bourgeois assumptions. Shorn of his beard, the narrator no longer passes for Europe's image of a hero; but in being deprived of the 'selva' on his face, he has lost his American identity. He is left, in the story's final sentence, desperately trying to recuperate his savage essence—'en el piso me quedé buscando la barba' (*BP*, 244)—as the ship leaves harbour, bearing him back to Europe. His inexorable restoration to the European milieu, this time as a cultural cipher, dramatizes the narrator's sense of being depleted by Europe's exploitation of his 'native' artistic material. 'La barba provisional' represents not only Asturias's imaginative absorption and transformation (to use Kristeva's terms) of a specific Surrealist text; it also provides an allegory of the cultural anxieties instilled in him by his long residence in Paris and his increased integration—as witnessed by his greater familiarity with French politics, literature and public issues in his post-1928 journalism—into French life. Extending beyond a mere homage to Desnos, the story provides an account of Asturias's subconscious worries that alliances with French writers such as Desnos might adversely affect his relationship with his Spanish American creative material. His intertextual reworkings of key motifs in Desnos's novel act as a counterweight to French appropriations of Spanish American imagery. If *El Alhajadito* demonstrates a certain pandering to the implied European reader's romanticized vision of Guatemalan reality, 'La barba provisional', written by an Asturias more fully engaged with his Parisian surroundings, dramatizes the cost of such distortions. *El Alhajadito* describes the constitution of individual identity; 'La barba provisional' delineates the threat, for the expatriate artist, of that identity's potential disintegration.

Notes to Chapter 4

1. Asturias, *Novelas y cuentos de juventud*, ed. Claude Couffon (Paris: Centre de Recherches de l'Institut d'Etudes Hispaniques, 1971), 133. Henceforth *NC*.
2. 'To consolidate Liberal power in Guatemala required friendly rulers in Honduras and El Salvador.' Hector Pérez-Brignoli, *A Brief History of Central America* (Berkeley: University of California Press, 1989), 87. Barrios himself was killed in one of the opening battles of the campaign.
3. Leslie Bethell (ed.), *The Cambridge History of Latin America: Volume V c.1870 to 1930* (Cambridge: Cambridge University Press, 1986), describes the disastrous consequences of Zaldívar's reforms for the rural population (pp. 202–4).
4. Le Fonds Asturias, Bibliothèque nationale, Paris. Carnet de travail numéro 3, 16.
5. La Sota's vices anticipate Cardoza y Aragón's extraordinary summation of Asturias's own character: 'Fue sibarita, glotón, bebedor y de muchacho o de adulto nunca durmió solo'. Cardoza y Aragón, *Miguel Angel Asturias*, 27.
6. Asturias, *El Alhajadito* (Buenos Aires: Goyanarte, 1961), 143. Henceforth *EA*.
7. Claude Couffon, *Miguel Angel Asturias* (Paris: Editions Seghers, 1970), 74.
8. Giuseppe Bellini, *La narrativa di Miguel Angel Asturias* (Milano: Istituto Editoriale Cisalpino, 1966), 189.
9. Malcolm Bowie, *Lacan* (Cambridge, Mass.: Harvard University Press, 1991), 37.
10. This position is taken most unequivocally by Prieto, *Archeology of Return*, 115–18.
11. Cheymol, *Miguel Angel Asturias dans le Paris des années folles*, 160.
12. Cheymol writes: 'En la reseña de los seminarios del año 1926–27, se puede comprobar que "MM. Asturias et de Mendoza ont pris une part active à la discussion."' ('Miguel Angel Asturias entre latinidad e indigenismo: los viajes de Prensa Latina y los seminarios de cultura maya en la Sorbona', in Asturias, *París 1924–1933*, 877).
13. Jacques Lacan, *Ecrits I* (Paris: Editions du Seuil, 1966), 90.
14. Arturo Uslar Pietri, *Fantasmas de dos mundos* (Barcelona: Seix Barral, 1979), 25.

15. Alaide Foppa, 'Realidad e irrealidad en la obra de Miguel Angel Asturias', in *Homenaje a Miguel Angel Asturias*, ed. Helmy F. Giacoman (New York: Las Américas Publishing Company, 1972), 147.

16. Carmen Vásquez, 'Miguel Angel Asturias et Robert Desnos: Une amitié méconnue', *Revue de Littérature Comparée* 222 (Apr.-June 1982), 203.

17. See Martin, *Journeys through the Labyrinth*, 145.

18. Segala, 'Introducción del Coordinador', in Asturias, *París 1924–1933*, p. lxv.

19. See Hugo Cerezo Dardón *et al.* (eds.), *Coloquio con Miguel Angel Asturias* (Guatemala: Editorial Universitaria Guatemala, 1968), 7.

20. Cheymol, *Années folles*, 41–2, describes the creation and contents of *Imán*.

21. Marie-Claire Dumas, *Robert Desnos, ou l'exploration des limites* (Paris: Klincksieck, 1980), 364.

22. Jacqueline Chénieux-Gendron, *Le Surréalisme* (Paris: Presses Universitaires de France, 1984), 60. See Elyette Guiol-Benessaya, *La Presse face au surréalisme de 1925 à 1938* (Paris: Editions du Centre National de la Recherche Scientifique, 1982), 11 (for reactions to the 'sauvage bataille' at the banquet) and 215–58 (for important articles from newspapers on both sides of the debate over the Surrealists' impact on French society).

23. Le Fonds Asturias, Bibliothèque nationale, Paris. Carnet de travail numéro 26, 32.

24. Carlos Rincón, in 'Nociones surrealistas, concepción del lenguaje y función ideológico-literaria del *realismo mágico* en Miguel Angel Asturias', in *Escritura: Teoría y Crítica Literarias*, iii. 5–6 (Jan.–Dec. 1978), 25–62, argues persuasively that Asturias's identification with Surrealism was largely retrospective and that, for political reasons, Asturias showed the greatest desire to portray his writing as an outgrowth of the Surrealist movement during the years 1959–64. See especially pp. 37–8. The single striking lapse in Asturias's project of furnishing himself with a Surrealist lineage dating from the movement's earliest days comes in his *Life* interview with Rita Guibert, where Asturias states with disarming candour: 'I was a student when [S]urrealism first appeared but my earliest contact with it was in 1929 or 1930 when I had already left the Sorbonne'. Guibert, *Seven Latin American Writers Talk* (New York: Alfred A. Knopf, 1972), 135.

25. For a description of the 1929 rupture in the Surrealist movement see Nadeau, *Histoire du Surréalisme*, 170–95.

26. After his expulsion, Desnos wrote of his former mentor: 'Breton est méprisable parce que sa vie et ses actions ne sont pas en rapport avec les idées qu'il prétend défendre; parce qu'il est hypocrite, lâche, affairiste [...] et que son activité s'est toujours développée dans un sens contraire à la vie, à l'homme et à la vérité.' Desnos, *Nouvelles Hébrides et autres textes, 1922–1930* (Paris: Gallimard, 1978), 474.

27. Alejo Carpentier, who signed *Un cadavre*, the dissidents' polemic against Breton, emphasized in a 1977 radio interview that the rift between the Breton faction and the dissidents was irreparable: 'Fue la escisión y seguí con ese grupo'. Virgilio López Lemus (ed.), *Entrevistas Alejo Carpentier* (La Habana: Editorial Letras Cubanas, 1985), 355. In a 1975 interview, Carpentier identified the 'Deux Magots' group with which he became associated as consisting of Desnos, Artaud, Leiris, Vitrac, Prévert, Bataille, Queneau, Masson, Miró and Buñuel (p. 282). Carpentier does not mention Asturias in this context, and no evidence exists to

suggest that Asturias, despite his friendships with both Carpentier and Desnos, frequented 'Les Deux Magots'.

28. Vásquez, 'Une amitié méconnue', 199. Gallimard rejected the manuscript in May 1931.

29. Philippe Soupault writes of Desnos's legendary reversals of allegiance: 'L'homme le plus passionné que j'aie jamais connu. C'était [...] un vrai "copain". Mais par contre le plus violent de mes ennemis. Capable des colères les plus noires et des éloges les plus dithyrambiques. La mesure n'était pas son fort.' *Mémoires de l'oubli, 1923–1926* (Paris: Lachenal & Ritter, 1986), 31.

30. Louis Aragon, *Le Paysan de Paris* (Paris: Gallimard, 1926), 110.

31. Asturias, *NC*, 230. Henceforth, quotes from 'La barba provisional' will be identified by *BP*.

32. Desnos returned the favour many years later by referring to Asturias in 'Feu', his poem about international solidarity with Spain during the Civil War. Invoking 'la libre jeunesse du monde', Desnos mentions, among others, 'ami du Guatemala, Asturias tout ironie et sentiment'. Desnos, *Destinée Arbitraire* (Paris: Gallimard, 1975), 155–6.

33. Desnos, *La liberté ou l'amour! suivi de Deuil pour Deuil* (Paris: Gallimard, 1962), 91. Henceforth, quotes from *La liberté ou l'amour!* will be identified by *LA*.

34. Julia Kristeva, *Séméiotiké: Recherches pour une sémanalyse* (Paris: Editions du Seuil, 1978), 85.

35. 'Le beau prince Vibescu songeait à Paris, la Ville-Lumière, où les femmes, toutes belles, ont toutes aussi la cuisse légère' (Apollinaire, *Les onze mille verges* (1907; Paris: Editions J'ai Lu, 1973), 15).

36. The 'extraño amor de peces' also invokes Lautréamont's romantic encounter with a female shark in *Les Chants de Maldoror*: 'Ils tombèrent brusquement l'un contre l'autre, comme deux aimants, et s'embrassèrent avec dignité et reconnaissance [...]. Enfin je venais de trouver quelqu'un qui me ressemblât!' (Lautréamont, *Les Chants de Maldoror* (1869; rpt. Paris: Flammarion, 1990), 180–1). The allusion to Lautréamont, who was raised in Montevideo, recapitulates the theme of the Spanish American odyssey to Europe. Asturias was a passionate reader of Lautréamont well before his own arrival in Europe or Lautréamont's resurrection at the hands of Surrealism. See Asturias, *América, fábula de fábulas*, 82–4 (Caracas: Monte Avila Editores, 1972).

37. This phrase echoes Desnos's article 'Le rêve et le cinéma' in *Cinéma* (Paris: Gallimard, 1966), 104. Desnos writes: 'A défaut de l'aventure spontanée que nos paupières laisseront échapper au réveil, nous allons dans les salles obscures chercher le rêve artificiel'. Vásquez ('Une amitié méconnue', 202) draws attention to the similarity, although it is unclear whether Asturias had read Desnos's article (published in *Paris-Journal* in Apr. 1923, roughly a year prior to Asturias's earliest possible date of arrival in Paris) or whether, as seems more likely, he absorbed the comparison from Desnos in conversation.

CHAPTER 5

Leyendas de Guatemala:
The Poetry of the Divided Self

Leyendas de Guatemala, probably begun two or three years before 'La barba provisional' and completed at approximately the same time, constructs a bulwark—yet a bulwark whose architecture is conditioned and infiltrated by the assumptions and dualities inherent in the writer's Parisian residence—against the disintegration explored in 'La barba provisional'. On the one hand *Leyendas* offers Paris a far richer lode of Guatemalan exoticism than *El Alhajadito*; on the other hand, while conforming to Parisian expectations of the marvellous, *Leyendas* deforms Orientalist assumptions by virtue of the fact that the 'explorer' who is transmitting this magical world back to his Parisian readership is not himself a Parisian, but a native Guatemalan. Asturias's acquiescence to the hegemonic culture carries within it his re-definition of that culture's categories.

Leyendas de Guatemala, perhaps more than any other work by Asturias, courted a European audience. The book was published in Madrid in 1930; it is unlikely that more than a handful of copies trickled back to Guatemala. Asturias did not owe the inauguration of his literary career to acceptance by a Spanish American readership; it was with the publication of Francis de Miomandre's French translation of the *Leyendas* in Marseille in 1932 that Asturias started to become well known as a writer. The book won the annual Prix Sylla-Monsegur for the best foreign work translated into French. Once again it was France whose taste and cultural dictates defined Asturias, confirming him in his role as a writer of fiction. Cheymol writes: 'Asturias est le premier grand écrivain contemporain de l'Amérique hispanique que l'édition française ait lancé' (*Années folles*, 177). The significance of *Leyendas de Guatemala* lay in its role in bringing to European attention an imaginative picture of Guatemalan reality.

Bellini writes: 'Le *Leyendas de Guatemala*, raggiungo un risultate immediato, per lo scrittore, quello di liberare il mondo guatemalteca dai limiti angusti di una geografia che lo condannava all'oblio, imponendolo improvvisamente all'attenzione europea, nella sua più complessa sostanza spirituale' (*La Narrativa*, 20). But Asturias's expression of Guatemala's 'sostanza spirituale', moulded to fit the cultural space French attention would allot it, entailed the adoption of certain poses. Luis de Arrigoitia's summary captures the contradictory nature of Asturias's success in *Leyendas de Guatemala*.

Miguel Angel Asturias atrapa su presa y logra exponerla por primera vez a las miradas de los cultos europeos: mitología maya, exuberancia tropical, preciosismo expresivo y suntuario del oriente americano [...]. Cuando con el surrealismo la cultura europea se abre a las expresiones primitivas por considerarlas más auténticas, entonces aflora plenamente la América indígena, la América mágica que había estado dormida durante siglos de imitación y de inhibición pueril frente a los esquemas, cánones y preceptos europeos.[1]

The resurgence of the Mayan world is both authentic *and* counterfeit. It is stimulated by the expectations of a French audience and requires the acting-out, on Asturias's part, of French Orientalist fantasies. The reliance on myth obscures certain particularities of Guatemalan history, rendering this history innocuously assimilable, despite its elements of incompatibility with the European tradition, into the worldview of a Parisian reader. But Asturias also succeeds, with no deeper background in Mayan culture than Raynaud's seminars at the Sorbonne and his memories of visits to his grandparents' country house, in creating a language capable of giving voice to the animist mentality of rural, peasant Guatemala. Asturias did not write in the 'authentic' voice of Mayan Guatemala (which would, in any event, have been illiterate and spoken in Quiché). His achievement in *Leyendas de Guatemala* was to create what Mario Vargas Llosa has called 'las mentiras verdaderas': fictions which distort reality in such a way as to capture its essence.[2]

Asturias's European readers, though, needed to be persuaded of the validity and trustworthiness of this unknown writer from a backward country. The 1930 Spanish edition of *Leyendas de Guatemala* established its authenticity through the inclusion of 'dibujos alucinados reproducidos de los códices mayas'[3] and an 'Indice alfabético de modismos y frases alegóricas'. The French translation, as was the custom with works by writers considered *indigènes*—notably with books written in French by African writers from the French West African colonies—included an 'authorizing' preface by a respected French cultural figure,[4] in this case Paul Valéry. Welcoming the *Leyendas* as a source of invigorating strangeness, Valéry wrote:

Rien ne me parut plus étrange,—je veux dire de plus étranger à mon esprit, à ma faculté d'attendre de l'inattendu—, que ces histoires-rêves-poèmes où se confondent si bizarrement les croyances, les contes et les mœurs de tous les âges d'un peuple composite, tous les produits capiteux d'une terre puissante et toujours convulsive, en qui les forces des divers ordres qui ont engendré la vie après en avoir dressé le décor de roche et d'humus, sont encore menaçantes et fécondes, comme prêtes à créer, entre deux océans, à coups de catastrophes, de nouvelles combinaisons et de nouveaux thèmes d'existence.[5]

Valéry's introduction continues in a similar vein for three more paragraphs before concluding with the recommendation that 'Une dose, de temps à autre, de cet elixir guatémaltèque est excellente *contre* bien des choses' (Couffon, *Asturias*, 32). Though the advice is meant to be droll, Valéry's underlying assumption of naïve Spanish American spontaneity reviving a jaded, world-weary Europe remains unequivocal. Valéry's commentary incorporates *Leyendas* into the process of European self-renovation: Guatemala expands the cultural menu available to a disillusioned, discredited European civilization, offering 'de nouvelles combinaisons et de nouveaux thèmes d'existence'. These fresh, hybrid forms are the product of a land where 'les forces de divers ordres [...] sont encore menaçantes et fécondes', in contrast to Europe, where technology has subdued nature. In fact, Valéry portrays nature, in the Spanish American context, as enjoying priority over humanity, shrinking human existence to a mere offshoot of 'le décor de roche et d'humus'. The Spanish American man, hence, is a natural creature, an outgrowth of the 'botanique aberrante' (Couffon, *Asturias*, 32) from which he emerges; as such, he can restore the urban European to the realm of natural forces from which Europe has become alienated. The European subordinates the Spanish American to the quest for his lost natural essence. Spanish American art which caters to this usage, such as *Leyendas de Guatemala*, collaborates in the suppression of the complexities, historical peculiarities and humanity of its own society.

But as Valéry's introduction demonstrates, the hegemonic traffic does not travel solely in one direction: Asturias has succeeded in insinuating some of the values of his nationalistic, *ladino* bourgeois ideology into the European's discourse. When Valéry writes of 'ces histoires-rêves-poèmes où se confondent si bizarrement [...] les mœurs de tous les âges d'un peuple composite', he is on the one hand annulling the distinct epochs of Guatemalan history in order to generate a single intoxicating image of a magical land—a tendency encouraged by Asturias's treatment of his nation's history in his opening sketch. But Valéry also refers to Guatemalans as a 'peuple composite', demonstrating that he has absorbed the ideology of *mestizo* primacy which Asturias had been promoting since *El problema social del indio*. (*Leyendas de Guatemala*, like *El señor presidente*, posits the *mestizo* as the Guatemalan 'norm'; it is only with the publication of *Hombres de maíz* that Asturias allows the Mayan persona cultivated in his Parisian artistic life to take over, at least at a denotative level, as the governing symbol of Guatemalan nationhood in his fiction.) Through his adoption of dominant European cultural forms—indeed, his self-appointment as the prime agent in transmitting the core of Guatemalan life to Paris—Asturias has hewn out a space allowing him to temper the Parisian vision of his country with elements of his own concerns. By assuming the gaze of the superior Other, he has occupied a territory previously barred to him. The question of Asturias's relationship with French culture is not as charged as that of a writer from a French colony. But Asturias does present a vision of Guatemala in many ways tailored to a French optic. In order to inhabit a French space, he takes up French assumptions (which in some instances coincide with his own bourgeois *ladino* preconceptions).

The structure of *Leyendas de Guatemala* makes plain the divisions rending Asturias's psyche. The book takes the form of tales told to a principal narrator by two rustics. Like many works employing this technique, *Leyendas de Guatemala* opens with an introductory sketch setting the scene and recounting the principal narrator's meeting with the two 'güegüechos de gracia', Don Chepe and Niña Tina, who recount to him the five original *leyendas* (the long final story, 'Los brujos de la tormenta primaveral', and the play 'Cuculcán', were added in the 1948 Buenos Aires edition; Martin argues, on the basis of both internal and external evidence, that these pieces were not written until the 1940s).[6] What makes *Leyendas de Guatemala* unusual is that instead of the customary introductory sketch describing the narrator's arrival in the remote district which serves as the setting for the tales that follow, Asturias presents his reader with *two* such sketches. The first, 'Guatemala', provides a distanced overview of the country; the second, 'Ahora que me acuerdo', is subjective and phantasmagoric. This dual introduction is followed by a blank page containing the title 'Leyendas'; the five tales told by the 'güegüechos' follow.

'Guatemala' offers the (implicitly foreign) reader an introduction to a country about which he or she is presumed to know little. At the same time, the sketch's presentation of the country is designed to produce a portrait which will correspond to the European reader's preconceptions and prejudices about such countries. Not only the reader, though, but also the narrator (and close behind the narrator, the implicit author) is becoming acquainted with Guatemalan reality. The narrator presents his penetration of the village as a return which is also in an important sense an arrival: a personal stock-taking spawning an artistic communion with the nation from which he has become geographically separated. The arrival motif is established in the opening sentence: 'La carreta llega al pueblo rodando un paso hoy y otra mañana'.[7] The absence of a human subject in this sentence sets the pattern for the paragraphs that follow: a roving, disembodied camera eye, its angle of vision responding in large part to European preconceptions and limitations in knowledge, performs an imaginative inventory of the village. At the same time, as this sentence indicates, the language is local and colloquial. The narrator speaks in a Guatemalan voice even as he indulges the foreign reader's imaginative demands. His omniscience enables him to provide an account not only of the village's physical appearance and social dynamics but also of its myths and fantasies. The opening paragraph, tracing a curve from the social realm to the mythological, reproduces in miniature the evolution of the introductory sketch as a whole. The paragraph concludes with a non-judgmental description of the beliefs of the two (at this point still unnamed) 'güegüechos': 'han visto espantos, cuentan milagros y cierran la puerta cuando pasan los húngaros: esos que roban niños, comen caballo, hablan con el diablo y huyen de Dios' (*LG*, 13).

The narrator records these legends without embarking upon the flood-tide of fantasy. Like the narrator of 'La barba provisional', he has become estranged from his Spanish American essence; he can

approach his own nation only through sceptical, distanced observation. The second paragraph lapses into a naturalistic description of
the village's social divisions. The narrator's overview of Guatemalan
history begins only when he abandons the naturalistic mode and
submits to flights of fantasy to which neither he nor his readers can
comfortably lend credence: 'Como se cuenta en las historias que
ahora nadie cree—ni las abuelas ni los niños—, esta ciudad fue
construida sobre ciudades enterradas en el centro de América' (*LG*,
13). The proviso that no one believes the legends of the past frees the
narrator, little by little, to immerse himself in Guatemalan mythology,
imagining into existence the country he no longer knows intimately
(and, if one carries this point over to the historical author, the country
he never knew intimately as Paris expects him to know it: as a Maya,
a representative of past ages, rather than an alienating, modernizing
ladino bourgeois).

The next paragraph continues the process of gradual modulation
into a world of fantasy: 'Existe la creencia de que...' (*LG*, 13). After
this paragraph, such qualifications disappear: the fantasy world is
presented straight, without apology; the narrator ceases to speak as
one standing outside that world. This transition is made possible by
the introduction of the narrative conceit of the 'Cuco de los Sueños',
who guides both reader and narrator through the telescoped Mayan,
colonial and mythological planes of Guatemalan history. The narrator
presents the Cuco de los Sueños as the product of an awakening
within his own consciousness: 'despierta en el alma el Cuco de los
Sueños' (*LG*, 14). (Yet once again the verb is not linked to a specific
subject; the narrator remains too alienated from his Guatemalan being
to possess an identity sufficiently defined to permit the usage of
personal pronouns.) Engendered by an amorphous, expatriate
narrator, the Cuco de los Sueños combines a clairvoyant vision of
Guatemalan existence with a tendency to present his perceptions in
ways compatible with the stance of a European or European-oriented
mind. The Cuco de los Sueños serves as the agent of the narrator's
unconscious. In conformity with Freudian (and Surrealist) doctrine,
the unconscious is portrayed as holding the keys to the individual's
masked core of identity. While providing narrator and reader with
imaginative access to Guatemalan reality, this conceit betrays its
European provenance in its tendency to universalize the motifs it
uncovers, collapsing the particularities of Guatemalan history into
shimmering, ahistorical images:

El Cuco de los Sueños hace ver una ciudad muy grande—pensamiento claro que todos llevamos dentro—, cien veces más grande que esta ciudad. Es una ciudad formada de ciudades enterradas, superpuestas, como los pisos de una casa de altos […]. ¡Libro de estampas viejas, empastado en piedra con páginas de oro de Indias, de pergaminos españoles y de papel republicano! […] Por las escaleras suben imágenes de sueño sin dejar huella […]. De puerta en puerta van cambiando los siglos. En la luz de las ventanas parpadean las sombras. Los fantasmas son las palabras de la eternidad. El Cuco de los Sueños va hilando los cuentos. (LG, 14–15)

The final sentence, acting as an incantatory invocation of Guatemalan history, is repeated throughout the story. The Cuco de los Sueños threads together tales from different eras of the Guatemalan past, linking them in a such a way as to facilitate their contemplation by outside observers. In creating this linkage, however, the Cuco effaces the particularity of specific epochs. While he recognizes the differences dividing the era of 'pergaminos españoles' from that of 'papel republicano', his present-tense narration, in which 'de puerta en puerta van cambiando los siglos', breaks down the barriers between distinct periods, blending them into a unified vision. This tendency towards simultaneity, in which cities of different times and civilizations become simply components of a larger, overarching whole—'los pisos de una casa'—advances the aims both of the European penchant for 'universalization' (which takes possession of foreign cultural products by claiming key images of other cultures as 'pensamiento[s] que todos llevamos dentro') and of the ladino bourgeois urge to depict Guatemalan history as the integrated emanation of a unified 'alma nacional'. Each paragraph in the succeeding pages sketches events in a Mayan or colonial city, collapsing all of these vignettes into what is implicitly a single time-frame.

En la ciudad de Palenque, sobre el cielo juvenil, se recortan las terrazas bañadas por el sol. […]
En la ciudad de Copán, el Rey pasea sus venados de piel de plata por los jardines de Palacio. […]
En la primera ciudad de los Conquistadores—gemela de la ciudad del Señor Santiago—, una ilustre dama se inclina ante el esposo. […]
En Antigua, la segunda ciudad de los Conquistadores, de horizonte limpio y viejo vestido colonial, el espíritu religioso entristece el paisaje. (LG, 15–18)

While conflating these varied times, places and events, the eye that perceives and communicates them betrays a clear hierarchy of cultural values. It is not merely that different stages of Mayan evolution are flattened into a single picturesque fresco, or that the story's peculiar intermingling of Mayan and colonial history breeds numerous anachronisms. The more important point is that the story's structure induces an implicit subordination of *lo guatemalteco* to *lo europeo*; within the Guatemalan context, it subjugates Mayan realities to the realization of the national unity striven for by the *ladino* governing class. The description of Quiriguá displays the narrator's alienation at work.

El Cuco de los Sueños va hilando los cuentos. La arquitectura pesada y suntuousa de Quiriguá hace pensar en las ciudades orientales. El aire tropical deshoja la felicidad indefinible de los besos de amor. Bálsamos que desmayan. Bocas húmedas, anchas y calientes. Aguas tibias donde duermen los lagartos sobre las hembras vírgenes. ¡El trópico es el sexo de la tierra! (*LG*, 15)

The passage blares an appeal to European Orientalist romanticizations of peripheral societies. The continuation of the impersonal narration enables the narrator to link Quiriguá with the cities of the Orient without attributing the observation to any particular authority or source. The city's architecture 'hace pensar' of the cities of the Orient. Whoever may be nurturing this parallel, it is certainly external to Guatemala in its origins; the connection is crafted to evoke a predigested image embedded in the European imagination. Yet the link is made to appear inevitable. The narrator reinforces Guatemala's role as a reservoir of liberating exoticism through the image of alligators dozing in warm water on virgin young women. The final sentence posits the existence of a division between cerebrally based Europe and the spontaneous, sexual tropics. A precondition for this vision of the country lies in the suppression of the various historical traditions contributing to Guatemalan reality. Asturias's blend of times and civilizations veils a scarcely disguised hierarchy of values in which the colonial city represents an implicit advance over its Mayan counterpart.

Continuing to employ the impersonal mode, the narrator introduces the transitional paragraph connecting these two phases of Guatemalan history with an image of ascent: 'La memoria gana la escalera que conduce a las ciudades españolas' (*LG*, 17). For the first time in the sketch, a first-person verb appears, albeit in the plural form: 'Vamos subiendo la escalera de una ciudad de altos: Xibalbá, Tulán, ciudades mitológicas, lejanas, arropadas en la niebla' (*LG*, 17). The Cuco de los Sueños guides the reader through these realms to the 'higher plane' of the Spanish colonial cities. The vignettes Asturias offers of these cities differ from the vignettes of the Mayan cities in that the characters are named and the scenes contain dialogue; unlike the Mayan characters, the Spaniards are permitted to speak for themselves. Despite his cultivation of the Mayan past, the narrator's consciousness grows more alert as he tours the colonial cities. His sense of personal identity becomes integrated only as the Cuco de los Sueños approaches Guatemala City. Less than a page before the end of the sketch, the narrator begins to speak in the first person.

Las primeras voces me vienen a despertar; estoy llegando.¡Guatemala de la Asunción, tercera ciudad de los Conquistadores! [...] Me llena de orgullo el gesto humano de sus muros—clérigos o soldados vestidos por el tiempo—, me entristecen los balcones cerrados y me aniñan los zaguanes abuelos. [...]
    —¡Mi pueblo! ¡Mi pueblo, repito, para creer que estoy llegando! (*LG*, 20)

The final sentence emphasizes the provisional nature of the narrator's depiction of his homeland. As he writes earlier in the sketch: 'La memoria es una ciega que en los bultos va encontrando el camino' (*LG*, 17). Like the protagonist of *El Alhajadito*, the narrator of 'Guatemala' is able to establish himself as a subject and speak in an independent voice only once he has undertaken a full accounting of his surroundings. Unlike El Alhajadito's examination of his *corredorcito*, however, the narrator's tour of Guatemalan history and mythology is haphazard and arbitrary. His need to imagine his homeland into existence overrides the claims of verisimilitude. His structure of his Guatemalan tour—rising through the Mayan cities both historical and mythological to the smaller colonial cities and finally to his home in Guatemala City—has the effect of assimilating the Mayan heritage into the identity of the *ladino* metropolis. This organizational scheme cuts both ways, subordinating the Mayan past to bourgeois imperatives while at the same time, for the benefit of the implied European audience, 'Mayanizing' Guatemala City. The story marks Asturias's assumption of a Guatemalan identity which Paris will recognize. Yet although the tale culminates in a moment of communion between the narrator and the Guatemalan people (the final words are '¡Mi pueblo! ¡Mi pueblo!' (*LG*, 21)) the remote 'aerial view' narration ensures that people—even a narrator with a recognizable personality or a name the reader knows—are notably absent from the sketch.

    The shorter second instalment in the book's double introduction,

'Ahora que me acuerdo', provides the previously alienated narrator with a myth of origins which ultimately deepens his confusion. Despite having achieved self-definition through his return to the *ladino* metropolis of Guatemala City, in the second story the narrator offers an account of his past and his estrangement from his roots that is almost entirely dependent on Mayan motifs. This paradox illustrates the confusions inherent in Asturias's cultural posture vis-à-vis Paris: though his home is Guatemala City, the legitimacy of his stance as the representative of that place and culture flows—in French eyes and, increasingly, in his own—from his identification with the Mayan past. The destruction of linear time required by this merging of past and present is established early in 'Ahora que me acuerdo', when Niña Tina states that the influence of the *chipilín* tree 'me privó de la conciencia del tiempo' (*LG*, 22). The narrator responds by offering an account of his departure from his homeland, couched in allegorical terms: '—Les dejé una mañana de abril para salir al bosque a caza de venados y palomas y, ahora que me acuerdo, estaban como están y tenían cien años. Son eternos. Son el alma sin edad de las piedras y la tierra sin vejez de los campos' (*LG*, 22). The narrator identifies himself, at this time, as having been 'primitivo, inhumano e infantil […] me llamaban Cuero de Oro' (*LG*, 22). Through his association with Don Chepe and Niña Tina, he is linked to a mystical, semi-mythological past. As he ventures into the wilderness, 'el vuelo del milano y mi paso despertaron el eco de las tribus errantes que vinieron del mar […]. Aquí fue donde comenzó su vida' (*LG*, 23). The narrator's *alter ego* witnesses the tribes' invocations of their gods, yet as night falls he becomes disoriented, losing touch with the tribes and hence with his own identity. The phrase 'noche delirante' (*LG*, 25, 27 et seq.) repeats in this story much as 'El Cuco de los Sueños va hilando los cuentos' does in the first sketch. Where 'Guatemala' describes the narrator's tenuous achievement of communion with his homeland, 'Ahora que me acuerdo' outlines a more acute, unresolved crisis of an absence of connection with that homeland's cultural sources. Despite his participation in the Mayan myth of origins, the narrator's bond with the Mayan world proves to be hopelessly frail. Lacking any other identity to fall back upon, he grows increasingly lost: '¡No existe nada! ¡No existo yo que estoy bailando en un pie!' (*LG*, 25). Approaching the four roads which cross before Xibalbá, the mythological capital of the underworld, he discovers that 'los cuatro caminos éranme vedados' (*LG*, 26). The cascade of increasingly chaotic imagery that assaults the narrator over the next page and a half underlines the fragmentation of his personality. Three jaguars with differing symbolic associations 'vinieron a disputar mi vida' (*LG*, 26). The snake, linked elsewhere in Asturias's early fiction with the protective *nahual* figure of Mayan mythology, here puts in a disconcerting appearance. Snakes of four different colours climb 'el camino de mi epidermis blando y tibio para el frío raspón de sus escamas' (*LG*, 26).

The narrator's attempts to descend to the core of the Mayan imaginative world—and thus to the heart of the identity which he has appropriated as his own—only deepen his pain and bewilderment. He starts to grow roots, but they soon become 'innumerables y sin nombres' (*LG*, 27), depriving him of the defined identity the image of roots would seem to promise. He finally concludes that: '¡A medida que taladro más hondo, más hondo me duele el corazón!' (*LG*, 27). Having interrupted Don Chepe and Niña Tina on three occasions, the narrator at last recognizes that the stories they wish to tell him are essential to the integration of his shattered psyche. 'Pero acuérdeseme ahora que he venido a oír contar leyendas de Guatemala y no me cuadra que sus mercedes callen de una pieza' (*LG*, 27). This phrase reveals the true meaning of the story's title. What the narrator has remembered is not an organically whole culture, but rather the limitations of his own knowledge of the Mayan world; by the end of the sketch he has been reduced to disorientation and, ultimately, silence. The five *leyendas* which follow, therefore, perform the function of constituting the narrator's identity by synthesizing, however imperfectly, the warring halves of his personality, attempting to realize the process which the narrator of 'La barba provisional', having been denuded of his Spanish American identity, was unable to initiate.

But *Leyendas de Guatemala* projects a different dynamic of cultural identity. In 'La barba provisional', the narrator was torn between European culture and a waning Spanish American essence with which his prolonged residence in Europe was causing him to lose touch. The dichotomy presented by the twin introductory sketches of the *Leyendas* is more subtle. Unlike the anxieties animating 'La barba provisional', the tensions expressed by *Leyendas* do not repose on an assumption of 'pure' cultural essences. 'Guatemala' focuses on expatriate alienation *as a condition*; 'Ahora que me acuerdo', which plants the narrator among the myths of an 'authentic' (i.e. Mayan) Guatemala, ends with his confession of estrangement from these myths. Rather than dramatizing the encroachment of European culture upon a fixed Spanish American identity, *Leyendas* portrays a clash between a Guatemala seen from without and the country as viewed from within—a conflict which inevitably involves the recurrent tension in Asturias's life and work between *ladino* and Mayan perceptions of Guatemalan reality. The narrator is depicted as not belonging fully to either the outside or the inside; only by synthesizing his two flawed visions may he hope to arrive at a viable identity merging cosmopolitanism and tradition. The pattern recapitulates that described by the protagonist's evolution in *El Alhajadito*: the integration of the self, echoing Lacan's account, propels the subject into history through a process of assuming an alienating identity—in this case, that of the Maya—as one's own.

The five *leyendas* attempt to reconcile the tensions embodied in the book's double introduction by subordinating traditional motifs and images to personal ends. The stories engage in a rich syncretism in which pagan and Christian religious symbols, like pre-Columbian and colonial settings, are juxtaposed for reasons that are intimate and irrational. Attempts to interpret *Leyendas de Guatemala* as an unadulterated emanation of Mayan culture—a commentary upon the *Popol-Vuh*, for example—are unlikely to produce rewarding readings. As Luis de Arrigoitia argues:

> El lector, al adentrarse en estas leyendas, siente la tentación de trazar la presencia en ellos de los textos precolombinos, de desentrañarlo todo a la luz de las referencias documentales. Pero eso es inútil [...]. Lo que en apariencias no pasa de ser un ejercicio arqueológico de especialista, es en lo más profundo una experiencia única, personal, lírica, subjetiva, irrepetible. (Giacoman, *Homenaje*, 41–2)

The critic who has made the most sustained effort to read *Leyendas* as a transcription of Mayan mythology is René Prieto. Prieto's *Miguel Angel Asturias's Archeology of Return* (1993) is remarkable for accepting at face value both Asturias's 'Mayan prince' pose and his claims in later life to have become deeply immersed in the Surrealist movement from his earliest days in Paris. Prieto contends that the key to *Leyendas de Guatemala* is that 'The author's aim is to teach the reader that his homeland is a nation of nations even if the forces that be do everything in their power to squelch the past and homogenize the culture' (*Archeology of Return*, 49). This romanticized reading takes Asturias's scrupulously cultivated public persona as a given and translates it back into the text. Prieto's analysis is sustainable only in so far as Asturias is proposing a *mestizo* national identity, with the Maya serving as emblem, rather than a Spanish one; given the evidence of Asturias's journalism in 1928–9, even this reading would be extremely generous. Charles Minguet, in his discussion of these issues, describes *Leyendas de Guatemala* as '[t]rabajo de puro ladino, efectuado con una ideación reflexiva y premeditada sobre un imaginario autóctono y con un código lingüístico no indígena'.[8] In addition, Prieto's analysis takes for granted that the author's stated ideology (as Prieto interprets it) is expressed directly by the text, without distortion or psychological mediation.

Prieto also argues: 'The most obvious structural devices underlying the *Leyendas* are conspicuous borrowings from Breton, Tzara and Eluard' (*Archeology of Return*, 249). His depiction of Asturias's imagistic techniques as transcriptions of rhetorical devices developed by the Surrealist inner circle assumes that Asturias was much more conversant with the tenets of Surrealism than the available evidence will support. As was argued in Chapter 4, Asturias probably possessed only the vaguest notion of Surrealism prior to his meeting with Robert Desnos in 1928—by which time the *Leyendas* were nearing completion. His potential exposure to the movement ended a few months later with Desnos's expulsion. No proof exists that Asturias read any major Surrealist text other than Desnos's *La liberté ou l'amour!* during this period. Carlos Rincón notes that 'Las diversas declaraciones de Asturias sobre el tema [del sueño] no muestran un conocimiento de escritos como *Poisson soluble*'. Rincón goes on to point out that: 'Al hablar de *l'écriture automatique*, puede decirse que lo que Asturias hacía era casi siempre, en realidad, aludir a su propia experiencia'.[9] He was not, in other words, an initiate of Breton's Surrealism. His technical innovations remained creatures of his perpetually evolving identity. The results, as Minguet argues, 'tienen muy lejanas relaciones con la vanguardia surrealista y rebasan ampliamente los hallazgos literarios del surrealismo' (Wentzlaff-Eggbert, *La Vanguardia*, 410).

The idea that Asturias, eminently in control of both doctrines, consciously mingled Surrealist technique and Mayan mythology to achieve his literary-ideological ends produces strained, unconvincing readings. In his treatment of 'Ahora que me acuerdo', Prieto writes:

In the case of Golden Skin's fragmentation and denial of self, Asturias turns to the notion of polarity in order to describe the process of his perpetual transformation. The importance of this process in his fiction likewise explains the leitmotif in this section of the story: 'Noise is followed by silence as the sea is by the desert'. ([*Leyendas*] 26) As Eluard was fond of saying, the expansion of the poetic consciousness depends on the always present possibility of shifting from one extreme to the next. Asturias has this notion in mind when he describes characters that pull and tug at their own limbs until they split themselves in half. [...]

Because to the surrealists creation always implies the clash of contraries, it follows that the holocaust described by Golden Skin should have rebirth as its sequel. (*Archeology of Return*, 53–4)

Prieto's approach is doubly unconvincing in its programmatic conception of literary creation and its assertion of an admiring, encyclopedic command of Surrealist doctrines on Asturias's part. Prieto provides no evidence to support his claim that Asturias possessed this sort of knowledge or that (contrary to the available evidence) he had even read Surrealists other than Desnos. Yet he goes on to imply that Asturias borrowed artistic concepts from Antonin Artaud's *Manifeste du théâtre de la cruauté* (1932),[10] builds an extended analysis of 'Guatemala' on Asturias's purported 'sustained use' of the Surrealist technique of 'l'un dans l'autre', refers to an André Breton poem as 'a source of rhetorical inspiration for Asturias', and contends that 'The truth is, if the author of the *Leyendas* latches on to the notions of physical fragmentation and schizoid personality with such vengeance, it is because he is truly smitten with the process of transformation essential to surrealist hope' (*Archeology of Return*, 48, 56, 53). This lack of sensitivity to Asturias's anguished position as an expatriate, as revealed by his journalism and 'La barba provisional,' lies at the core of Prieto's misreading of *Leyendas de Guatemala*. Asturias's acute sense of personal fragmentation (and his interest in the process of transformation) stems from his historical and social position; it is a condition which he attempts to express through literature, not an artificial pose derived from literary enthusiasms which he almost certainly did not possess.

In a similar vein, Asturias adopts Mayan images—the use of the snake as a *nahual* figure, the four roads crossing before Xibalbá, heart of the Mayan underworld—in order to twist them to his own ends, investing them with resonances that are personal rather than traditional. Prieto's pronouncement that 'It is impossible to deny that the young author who was in the process of writing down the *Leyendas* was generally considered a specialist in Mayan culture' (*Archeology of Return*, 32) is as irrelevant as it is dubious. The pattern of the Mayan images' recurrence in *Leyendas* is governed by Asturias's artistic and narrative requirements rather than by Mayan tradition. The 'culebra' appears in 'Leyenda del Volcán', deprived of its *nahual* role (*LG*, 31); the image of 'cuatro caminos,' severed from associations with Xibalbá, returns in 'Leyenda de la Tatuana' (*LG*, 41). The related phenomenon of Asturias's religious syncretism has confused critics wishing to categorize *Leyendas de Guatemala*. Bellini writes:

L'essenza e l'originalità delle *Leyendas de Guatemala* sta, infatti, parti-colarmente, nella riuscita ricreazione di un'atmosfera biblica, quella stressa che permea il libro sacro dei 'quichés,' di cui le *Leyendas* finiscono per essere la continuazione magica. (*La narrativa*, 23)

At the opposite extreme, the Spanish critic Carlos Meneses has argued that 'La actitud religiosa que tan frecuentemente se halla en estas Leyendas, es claramente española'.[11] Both critics are correct in their respective observations but mistaken in their analyses. *Leyendas de Guatemala* is neither a magical continuation of the *Popol-Vuh* nor a collection of Spanish Catholic fables. The book pilfers indis-criminately from both of these traditions, combining its gleanings according to the whims and requirements of the implicit author's personal psychology, in order to imagine into existence an identity for a remote, polarized nation lacking an integrated sense of itself. Hierarchical distinctions reflecting Asturias's bourgeois nationalist ideology emerge in the *ways* in which these elements are combined. The opening lines of 'Leyenda de la Tatuana', one of the most 'Mayan' of the pieces, offer a recreation of the epic voice of native mythology, albeit in a post-Conquest environment:

El Maestro Almendro tiene la barba rosada, fue uno de los sacerdotes que los hombres blancos tocaron creyéndoles de oro, tanta riqueza vestían, y sabe el secreto de las plantas que lo curan todo, el vocabulario de la obsidiana—piedra que habla—y leer los jeroglíficos de las constelaciones. (*LG*, 41)

Yet even this immersion in the Mayan view of reality is 'impure', containing in its interpolated explanation of the significance of obsidian within the Mayan context a nod in the direction of the European reader. While the inclusion of such an explanation effectively destroys the authenticity of the Mayan voice, the narrative attempts to rescue the illusion of verisimilitude through the use of metaphorical language intended to evoke an Indian mentality: 'la piedra que habla'. This strategy in itself betrays a reified hierarchy of cultural values, since it implies that the Maya hear one another's speech in this picturesque, metaphorical way. Paul Julian Smith, commenting on a similar tendency in the depiction of native speech in Rosario Castellanos's novel *Balún Canán* (1957), writes:

Castellanos retreats into a gnomic oracular style bristling with calques. Thus the literate Felipe refers to the law extending civil rights to Indians as 'the paper which speaks'. The problem is not whether or not such an idiom exists in the Tzeltal language. It is that by reproducing the idiom in Spanish, Castellanos returns her Indian characters to a state of picturesque naïvety.[12]

Asturias's entire enterprise is freighted with extravagant mythologizations, with tactics designed to capture the attention of the European reader seeking fresh marvels. Yet the creation of startling images is not in itself sufficient; such images must bear the stamp of cultural authenticity. Later in 'Leyenda de la Tatuana', the narrator writes: 'Después de un año de cuatrocientos días—sigue la leyenda— cruzaba los caminos de la cordillera el Mercader' (*LG*, 43). The attention-grabbing quaintness of the 400-day year (which exists in the Mayan calendrical system, but which, like 'la piedra que habla', would not be heard as quaint by a Mayan audience) is validated by the interjection of the claim that the story originates in a legend; the reader accepts the 400-day year as an element of his or her narrative immersion in the anomalies of an alien universe, rather than viewing the image as artificial or strained. Having established this background, Asturias prepares the reader for the story's fantastic conclusion, in which the female protagonist escapes from prison in a boat which has been tattooed onto her arm.

As the native voice which opens 'Leyenda de la Tatuana' proves unable to sustain its 'pure' Mayan essence, a similar erosion of cultural homogeneity occurs in 'Leyenda del Cadejo', one of the most Spanish of the tales in its diction and one of the most Catholic in its preoccupations. The story opens:

Madre Elvira de San Francisco, prelada del monasterio de Santa Catalina, sería con el tiempo la novicia que recortaba las hostias en el convento de la Concepción, doncella de loada hermosura y habla tan candorosa que la palabra parecía en sus labios flor de suavidad y de cariño. (*LG*, 36)

Enfolded in a world of piety, the novice lives 'en la dulce compañía de Dios' (*LG*, 36). The language of this story does not suffer from the inconsistencies of cultural perspective apparent in the opening paragraph of the 'Leyenda de la Tatuana'. No obvious disjuncture appears between the novice's imaginative universe and the language employed to describe it. Yet the opening sentence's inverted presentation of time suggests that the novice's certainties rest on unstable ground; the lush flora and fauna outside her window contain pagan mysteries that lie beyond the grasp of the Christian belief system and Western linear time. The entry into the novice's quarters of the 'hombre-adormidera' (*LG*, 37), whose name associates him with this natural richness, threatens her faith with the mystery of prophecy—'le cortarán la trenza', he tells her (*LG*, 38)—while forcing her to confront her own dormant sexuality. In a trait emphasized by Paul Valéry in his preface to the French edition, the narrator depicts the clash between Christian and pagan outlooks as presenting the novice with access to new forms of life: 'Un abanico de realidades posibles se abría en torno suyo' (*LG*, 38–9). Her growing awareness of the sexual dimension inherent in these hybrid lives becomes focused on her braid: 'en su trenza estaba el misterio' (*LG*, 38). As with the Mayan worldview in 'Leyenda de la Tatuana', the novice's undiluted Christian outlook proves impossible to sustain. In a universe throbbing with sensuality and populated by pre-Columbian mysteries, the shoes the novice has inherited from a paralysed nun who has died come to symbolize the death-in-life of her shackled convent existence. Dressed in the dead nun's shoes and confronting the natural force of the 'hombre-adormidera', the novice teeters on the brink of succumbing to the call of witchcraft and sensuality:

Entre un cadáver y un hombre, con su sollozo de embrujada indesatable en la lengua, que sentía ponzoñosa, como su corazón, medio loca, regando las hostias, arrebatóse en busca de sus tijeras, y al encontrarlas se cortó la trenza y, libre de su hechizo, huyó en busca del refugio seguro de la madre superiora, sin sentir más sobre sus pies los de la monja. (*LG*, 39–40)

In severing her connection with the natural vitality bred by the conjunction of her braid and the 'hombre-adormidera', the novice also relieves herself of the shadow of the paralysed nun. This awareness of the nun—that is, of her own death-in-life—has been summoned by the provocative presence of the 'hombre-adormidera'. Once she banishes these potentially liberating forces, she ceases to perceive her convent life as oppressive. Her recognition of the nature of this life springs from its collision with another, alien reality. In signalling this point, Asturias underlines the way in which the personality is never constituted in a void: all identity is identity *against* the articulation of another entity or a different way of being. As Asturias's immersion in Paris both enhances his awareness of his Spanish American identity and increases his dissatisfaction with that identity's substance and expression, so the novice must contend with a being who heightens her consciousness of her position while undermining it. By cutting off her braid, the novice flees the challenge of self-definition. Yet as the story's coda makes clear, her renunciation of the tensions raised by her confrontation with the 'hombre-adormidera' fails to dissolve the forces of witchcraft, animism and sensuality. The severed braid comes to life as a rattlesnake which kills the 'hombre-adormidera' and with him the enlightenment represented by the light of his candle. The 'hombre-adormidera', transmuted into a being with 'cascos de cabro, orejas de conejo y cara de murciélago', carries the braid down to hell with him while the novice 'soñaba entre sonrisas de ángeles' in her cell (*LG*, 40). By spurning the natural and supra-rational forces incarnated in her braid, she converts them into a source of destructive malevolence. Like 'Leyenda de la Tatuana', this story veers inexorably towards an outlook in which syncretism, doubleness, heterogeneity are portrayed as the inevitable human condition. Taken together, the stories demonstrate the impossibility of maintaining purity of identity. *Mestizaje*, both racial and cultural, comes to be seen as both un-avoidable and desirable. Asturias advances his own fraught condition as both a Guatemalan and a human norm.

The depiction of identity as a complex play of oppositions is introduced in the first of the five *leyendas*, 'Leyenda del Volcán'. Beginning as a myth of the origin of the world, the story quickly evolves into a disquisition on expatriation and duality. Asturias's inherent syncretism emerges in his infusion of Christian motifs into his Mayan myth of origins. The narrator recounts Mayan history in pseudo-Biblical diction: 'Seis hombres poblaron la Tierra de los Arboles' (*LG*, 31). He draws explicit parallels with Christian mythology: 'a los primeros hombres les fue dado comprender que no hay fruto malo' (*LG*, 32). This transcultural narrative tone, mingling two distinct cultural identities, infects not only the story's language, but the characters' perceptions of themselves. When his companions are mesmerized by the sight of their reflections in a river, the symbolically-named Nido tells them:

—¡Son nuestras máscaras, tras ellas se ocultan nuestras caras! ¡Son nuestros dobles, con ellos nos podemos disfrazar! ¡Son nuestra madre, nuestro padre, Monte en un Ave, que matamos para ganar la tierra! ¡Nuestro nahual! ¡Nuestro natal! (*LG*, 32–3)

This catalogue of the possible permutations presented by the model of duality displays the narrator's awareness of the variety of roles which may be played by paired tensions such as those announced in the book's double introduction. The Other may be a mask behind which to conceal one's true identity, a parent, a predecessor to be displaced, a protective *nahual* figure or a homeland. It is this final formulation of the dilemma of doubleness—the homeland as Other—which governs the story's development. When the eruption of the volcano annihilates all around him (his companions' disappearance is accompanied by that of 'sus dobles, en el agua' (*LG*, 34)), Nido finds himself heading into exile. A story which started out as a myth of origins ripe with dualities comes to depend for its resolution on the protagonist's efforts to overcome the curse of expatriation. In the wake of the destruction precipitated by the eruption of the volcano, the narrator waits to hear 'la voz de su corazón', but instead becomes aware of 'otra voz en su alma, el deseo de andar hacia un país desconocido' (*LG*, 35). The origins of exile, in this portrait, lie in duality. Nido's divided nature—the existence of two separate voices in his soul—provides the force which propels him towards a foreign land. The image implies that a nation characterized by division and lacking social integration will be forced to project its search for identity abroad. Yet Nido's pilgrimage also contains the solution to the problem of a divided identity. In trekking through the world ('Anduvo y anduvo'), Nido eventually reaches a place where bells among the clouds 'repetían su nombre' (*LG*, 35). A voice tells him to build a temple. The return to the homeland, therefore, implies a sense of purpose; it is not a neutral act, but entails participation in changing the country's landscape. Yet the 'dulce regreso de aquel país lejano' also exacts a price. Nido, who was young before the volcano's eruption, 'volvió viejo, no quedándole tiempo sino para fundar un pueblo de cien casitas alrededor de un templo' (*LG*, 35). The experience of wandering through unknown lands enables Nido to focus on what he must achieve in his country. Yet it also depletes him, integrating his two conflicting selves at the cost of sapping him of his youth.

Despite this personal cost, the process of integration itself is presented as relatively unproblematic. The later stories complicate this picture. The novice's confrontation with the 'hombre-adormidera' in 'Leyenda del Cadejo' makes clear that the constitution of cultural identity cannot be completed through the sanguine construction of a solitary temple; rather, it demands an ongoing definition of oneself *against* an alien being or cultural formation. This problematization of the issue of cultural identity reaches its climax in the final story, 'Leyenda del tesoro del lugar florido'. Here the dynamics of doubleness become permeated with questions of cultural power. Asturias demonstrates a growing awareness of the subordination bred by the dialectical struggles inherent in cultural *mestizaje*: the intermingling of two colliding cultures is never innocent; essential elements of the weaker culture will always be subjugated by the cultural dictates of the stronger.

'Leyenda del tesoro del lugar florido' develops this tension in the context of the central cultural collision in Guatemalan history: the Spanish conquest of the Maya. The story is set in a bustling Mayan settlement on the day it is sacked by the Conquistador Pedro de Alvarado. The first sentence foreshadows the city's imminent destruction: 'Se iba apagando el día entre las piedras húmedas de la ciudad' (*LG*, 52). The narrative voice, in this final, most sophisticated attempt to reconcile the tensions outlined in the two introductory sketches, exemplifies the condition of standing simultaneously inside and outside Mayan culture. The advancing conquistadors are perceived with an eye whose gaze recreates Mayan expectations: '¿Eran fantasmas o seres vivos? No se oían sus tambores, no sus clarines, no sus pasos, que arrebataba el silencio de la tierra' (*LG*, 56). Yet when Alvarado's men open fire, the narrative consciousness is able to identify their weapons: 'A los primeros disparos de los arcabuces' (*LG*, 57). Likewise, the narrator's description of the festival curtailed by the conquistadors' arrival focuses on exotic detail destined, as Smith argues in his analysis of Castellanos, 'merely to be re-appropriated, to reconfirm the "neutral" host community or target readership' (*Representing the Other*, 140). Describing the city's floating market, the narrator observes

Barcas de vendedores de frutas. Barcas de vendedores de vestidos y calzas. Barcas de vendedores de jadeítas, esmeraldas, perlas, polvo de oro, cálamos de pluma llenos de aguas aromáticas, brazaletes de caña blanca. Barcas de vendedores de miel, chile verde y en polvo, sal y copales preciosos. Barcas de vendedores de tintes y plumajería... (*LG*, 52–3)

Continuing in this vein for four more sentences, the description presents to the European gaze the marvellous external trappings of the Mayan universe. This romanticized portrait of a pre-lapsarian Mayan world furnishes both the implicit author's *ladino* psyche and his predominantly European readership with desired forms of imaginative sustenance. The divided *ladino* expatriate conjures a world of perfect wholeness; the disillusioned European reader contemplates a society innocent of the technologically instigated destruction of the First World War. The integration of the Mayan world is such, in this depiction, that human duality does not spring from alienation. When the masked warriors dance during the ceremony, the narrator reports that 'Las madres encontraban a sus hijos entre los guerreros, porque conocían sus máscaras' (*LG*, 54). Doubleness, here, does not possess the divisive resonances it later acquires. In the pre-conquest environment of 'Leyenda del volcán', Nido's glimpse of his image in the water precipitated a description of duality as an eternal human verity; here the pre-Columbian world is portrayed as innocent of duality as anything more complicated or trying than a mere extension of the self.

It is the conquest that splits the Guatemalan identity, ushering the alien Other into the self. The volcano, whose eruption in the opening story spawned destruction, provides an image of peace and stability: 'era anuncio de paz, de seguridad en el Lugar Florido' (*LG*, 53). The conquistadors' attack, however, shakes the volcano into violence. Once again, a seismic upheaval enables Asturias to create an ambience riven by destruction, duality and spiritual exile. But where the eruption in 'Leyenda del Volcán' occurred in the context of an implicitly unified pre-Columbian culture, in 'Leyenda del tesoro del lugar florido' it is the cataclysmic impact of the Spanish invasion which summons the volcano's destructive fury. Throughout the conquistadors' attack, the text signals the continued survival of the Mayan warriors through its repetition of the phrase: '¡Sonaban los clarines! ¡Sonaban los tambores!' (*LG*, 57, 58). As the conquistadors prepare to seize the treasure which the retreating Maya have abandoned, the volcano stages a pre-emptive eruption that obliterates the integrity of both cultures. The Mayan city's death is announced by the reversal of the battle motif: '¡Callaron los clarines! ¡Callaron los tambores!' (*LG*, 58). The conquistadors, barred from reaching the object of their quest, are left adrift amid the residue of the destruction they have wrought. The story ends:

Sobre las aguas flotaban los tizones como rubíes y los rayos del sol como diamantes y, chamuscados dentro de sus corazas, sin gobierno sus naves, flotaban a la deriva los de Pedro de Alvarado, viendo caer, petrificados de espanto, lívidos ante el insulto de los elementos, montañas sobre montañas, selvas sobre selvas, ríos y ríos en cascadas, rocas a puñados, llamas, cenizas, lava, arena, torrentes, todo lo que arrojaba el Volcán para formar otro volcán sobre el tesoro del Lugar Florido, abandonado por las tribus a sus pies, como un crepúsculo. (*LG*, 58)

Nature thwarts the European appropriation of the Maya's cultural treasures, reinforcing the text's identification of the Maya as a 'natural' people. The 'rubíes' and 'diamantes' perceived by the Spaniards are illusory and ungraspable. The final scene contains both a historical and a contemporary significance, re-enacting the pivotal moment of the Guatemalan past while also emphasizing that for the contemporary observer—Guatemalan bourgeois *ladino* or Parisian reader—the cherished wholeness represented by pre-Columbian Mayan culture remains irrevocably lost. The conquistadors, the ancestors of the modern *ladino*, are rebuked by nature and cut off from the chimerical treasure of integration; the Maya, on the other hand, have abandoned these gems. Both groups have become fissured, psychically incomplete beings. Yet their conditions are not equal. The final image of 'crepúsculo', reconfirming the judgement implicit in the story's opening sentence, makes clear that it is the Maya whose history—in its natural, autonomous form—has come to an end.

This image invests the volcanic upheaval which serves as the story's climax with some of the force of a declaration of allegiance. Throughout *Leyendas de Guatemala*, Asturias the Mayan prince of Paris works his way towards an acceptance of his own Parisian identification with a people he was brought up to disdain. The text's concession of irreparable cultural fragmentation serves, paradoxically, to unite Asturias's public and private selves more closely. The book's twin introductions—the first drawing the outsider into Guatemalan reality, the second concluding with the outsider-turned-insider recognizing his estrangement from Indian realities—trigger a creative expression of the ongoing, eternally unfinished *process* of the constitution of a distinctively Guatemalan cultural identity.

Leyendas de Guatemala marks the culmination of the development, traceable from his early journalism and apprentice fiction, through *El Alhajadito* and 'La barba provisional', of Asturias's gradual elaboration of a myth of the racially and culturally divided Guatemalan self which would prove viable within a Parisian context (in which his own status as an expatriate introduced an additional source of internal division). By forcing him to identify with the Maya he had constructed as Other in his law thesis, this environment enjoined Asturias to become his own Other; he assumed Mayan history as his own at the very moment when he was defining his bourgeois conception of Guatemalan nationality against the weight of European culture. Having been brought to doubt his Guatemalan 'alma nacional' as an entity fractured, partial, provisional and in constant flux, he none the less grew into the outstanding representative of Guatemalan nationhood in Europe. Never a European, he still managed to become Europe's emissary to the mountains and jungles of Guatemala. The fact that Europe conceived of Guatemalan identity primarily in terms of a romanticization of the Mayan past arising out of a specific set of post-1918 needs constrained Asturias to adopt a Mayan persona while at the same time according him a creative space in which to enlarge and complicate that definition. His Parisian apprentice work prepared the ground for his acceptance of the initially unpalatable French message that Guatemala *was* the Maya; it made possible his embrace of the Maya as the prime symbol of Guatemalan nationhood in *Hombres de maíz* and a number of the novels and plays that followed it.

Having written *Leyendas de Guatemala*, Asturias needed to test his dawning conception of personal and national identity against the reality of modern Guatemalan society. The result was the most enduring creative achievement of his Paris years, the urban novel (his only major work set in a city) which he completed shortly before his return to Guatemala in 1933: *El señor presidente*.

Notes to Chapter 5

1. Luis de Arrigoitia, 'Leyendas de Guatemala', in *Homenaje a Miguel Angel Asturias*, ed. Helmy F. Giacoman (New York: Las Américas Publishing Company, Inc., 1972), 48.
2. 'Para conocer lo que somos, como individuos y como pueblos, no tenemos otro recurso que salir de nosotros mismos y, ayudados por la memoria y la imaginación, proyectarnos en esas "ficciones" que hacen de lo que somos algo paradójicamente semejante y distinto de nosotros. La ficción es el hombre

"completo", en su verdad y en su mentira confundidas' (Vargas Llosa, *La señorita de Tacna*, (Barcelona: Seix Barral, 1981), 10).

3. Ramón J. Sender, 'Un poeta de Guatemala', in Asturias, *París 1924–1933*, 530.

4. 'As a genre, the broadly "critical" role, or critical typology of the preface, is characterized by a number of elements [...] it constitutes a program for reading: it sets out the perspective which the reader should bring to the text. In certain cases, it also rules out other possible perspectives. It has, therefore, both a programmatic and pre-emptive function' (Belinda Elizabeth Jack, *Negritude and Literary Criticism: The History and Theory of 'Negro-African' Literature in French* (Westport, Connecticut and London: Greenwood Press, 1996), 22).

5. Reprinted in Couffon, *Miguel Angel Asturias*, 32.

6. Gerald Martin, 'Génesis y trayectoria del texto', in Asturias, *Hombres de maíz*, 489 n.

7. Asturias, *Leyendas de Guatemala* (1930; Buenos Aires: Losada, 1957), 20. Henceforth *LG*.

8. Charles Minguet, 'Miguel Angel Asturias, ¿Creador de Conceptos Vanguardistas?' in *La Vanguardia Europea en el Contexto Latinoamericano*, ed. Harald Wentzlaff-Eggbert (Frankfurt: Vervuet Verlag, 1991), 408.

9. Rincón, 'Nociones surrealistas', 28, 34.

10. This reference represents Prieto's best attempt to document Asturias's reading. Prieto writes: 'Aragon recommends that filmmakers should "whip the public", a notion he no doubt borrows from Artaud's *Theater of Cruelty* (another author with whom Asturias was undoubtedly familiar; cf. Cheymol, *Années folles*, 179)' (*Archeology of Return*, 52). The reader is likely to infer that Cheymol provides evidence that Asturias had read Artaud's work. Yet Cheymol's only claim is that Asturias was probably familiar with Artaud's artistic theories and had almost certainly met Artaud. The citation reads: 'Asturias est convaincu qu'il faut en revenir au théâtre de masques, à un théâtre magique renouvelé par un retour aux sources: la mode des arts primitifs, à l'œuvre dans le cubisme, atteint aussi la scène. Le parallélisme de cette position avec celle d'Artaud est remarquable [...]. Cette coïncidence de dates rend étonnant le silence total d'Asturias au sujet d'Artaud, qu'il a pourtant sans doute rencontré à cette époque' (Cheymol, *Années folles*, 179). Asturias's failure to cite Artaud in his journalism may, in fact, be evidence that despite his 'familiarity' with the French author's ideas and his probable, if glancing, personal acquaintance with him, he had not read or contemplated his work, and knew of his ideas through hearsay or café conversations at which both he and Artaud may have been present. The citation from Cheymol falls well short of providing support for Prieto's claim.

11. Carlos Meneses, *Miguel Angel Asturias* (Madrid: Ediciones Jucar, 1975), 32.

12. Paul Julian Smith, *Representing the Other: 'Race', Text and Gender in Spanish and Spanish American Narrative* (Oxford: Clarendon Press, 1992), 139.

CHAPTER 6

❖

Light in the Shadow, Shadow in the Light: *El señor presidente*

The completion of Asturias's metamorphosis from bourgeois *ladino* to the 'Gran Lengua' who would write *Hombres de maíz* required an imaginative separation from the predominantly white milieu of the city and the consolidation of his identification with the Guatemalan countryside. In *El problema social del indio*, Asturias had written: 'La vida política del indio se reduce a saber que en la Capital hay un señor Presidente.'[1] In his first major novel, he charted his growing dis-illusionment with *ladino* norms by making the Indian's perspective his own. The symbolic and narrative movement, in *El señor presidente*, from city to countryside, from *ladino* to Mayan precepts, develops through a struggle between images of light and darkness. The striking literary techniques Asturias exploits to deploy these images resemble Surrealist procedures. Yet, as becomes evident on close examination, this resemblance is superficial. Asturias's innovations spring not from one of André Breton's manifestos, but from his own youthful enthusiasm for the work of Lautréamont and Remy de Gourmont; his grasp of Surrealist concepts remains hazy. Paris in the 1920s and 1930s encouraged Asturias to express himself as a distinctively Guatemalan writer, and to reassess his reading of nineteenth-century French literature. *El señor presidente* could not have been written anywhere other than in Paris, yet it would be a mistake to interpret the novel as a Spanish-language emanation of Bretonian Surrealism.

The novel's origins in Asturias's immersion in the French capital are beyond doubt. Georges Pillement, Asturias's friend and sometime translator, recalled:

El señor presidente transcurre en Ciudad de Guatemala, pero los apuntes que sirvieron a su redacción fueron redactados en una mesa del Dôme, en medio del murmullo de las conversaciones, mientras que los camareros, como prestidigitadores, hacían juegos malabares con las sillas y las consumiciones.[2] By force of contrast, Asturias's Parisian apprenticeship sharpened his awareness of the dictatorship under which he had grown up, engendering the images of interlocked light and shadow ('maldoblestar de la luz en la sombra, de la sombra en la luz')[3] announced in the novel's second sentence. As Cheymol has pointed out, *El señor presidente*, brought to Paris in embryonic form as the unpublished (and now lost) short story 'Los mendigos políticos' and carried back to Guatemala in 1933 as a novel in manuscript, constitutes the central document of Asturias's Parisian sojourn.

Dans les conversations des cafés de Montparnasse, Asturias, en racontant les anecdotes de son pays, en se remémorant le cadre concret et l'ambiance de son enfance assombrie par la dictature, prend conscience de la nécessité d'étoffer 'Les mendiants politiques' et d'en faire un roman. D'abord parlée, puis écrite (mi-parlée, mi-écrite), l'élaboration de *Monsieur le Président* couvre la totalité du séjour parisien de M. A. Asturias. (*Années folles*, 199)

From its origins to its deployment of detail, *El señor presidente* represents Asturias's most sustained summation of the impact of his encounter with Paris on his construction of his identity. Asturias's initial journalistic dispatches from Europe indicate that his arrival in the French capital induced a traumatized re-evaluation of his *ladino* heritage, exemplified in his series 'Realidad social guatemalteca' by his reference to the governing classes as 'los semicivilizados' (*París 1924–1933*, 26–30). The consequences of his growing contempt for his own social class shine through his account of the café conversations which provided the genesis of *El señor presidente*.

Llegado a Europa, nos reuníamos con amigos en los cafés de Montparnasse y en la charla de café empezó a surgir lo que podríamos llamar una rivalidad entre los venezolanos, los guatemaltecos, los mexicanos, que referíamos algunas anécdotas de nuestros respectivos dictadores, de don Porfirio Díaz, de Estrada Cabrera, del dictador de Venezuela, y cada quien hacía cuentos sobre el particular. Esta 'rivalidad' me fue haciendo a mí ir recordando indudablemente una gran cantidad de cosas que yo había oído contar en mi casa.[4]

Asturias's recollection of the conversations as a 'rivalry', in which Spanish Americans of different nationalities attempted to outdo one another's boasts about the horrors of their respective dictators, underlines the point that *El señor presidente* germinated in his appalled repudiation of the social reality of his native land. His account emphasizes the novel's origins in the awareness of Guatemalan 'backwardness' thrust upon him by his arrival in Paris. This awareness acted as a catalyst, enabling Asturias to 'remember' (and no doubt occasionally mis-remember and embellish) anecdotes and events from the Estrada Cabrera dictatorship. The forms in which he recalled these moments were conditioned by the context of Parisian café 'rivalry' in which his memories emerged: a sort of inverted snobbery of ghastliness among Spanish Americans whose reassessments of their respective homelands had been galvanized by their encounters with the integration of French society. The fact that this novel, rather than an *indigenista* work along the lines, say, of Jorge Icaza's *Huasipungo* (1934), constituted the central project of Asturias's Parisian years underlines the contrived, subordinate nature of his 'Mayan prince' façade. Behind this exotic mask, Asturias's psyche was irredeemably fissured. If *Leyendas de Guatemala* was essentially a fiction of the divided self, the cracks in Asturias's identity radiated along two principal axes: he was a Mayan in Paris and a *ladino* in Guatemala, a picturesque being from a backward country in the eyes of Europe and a remote, urbanized cosmopolitan in the view of his compatriots. *El señor presidente*, with its insistent clash of dualities, was the book Asturias had to write to anchor the identity which would serve as the basis for his neo-*indigenista* novels. Gerald Martin, in his summary of the novel's composition, emphasizes *El señor presidente*'s contemporaneity with the less sophisticated works of *indigenismo*.

El señor Presidente, then, was born in Guatemala as 'Los mendigos políticos' in 1922, rewritten nine times in Paris between 1923 and 1932 as *Tohil* (the Maya-Quiché god of fire), and completed, with substantial changes only to Chapter 12, 'Camila', and minor amendments to the Epilogue, on his return to Guatemala [...]. If we speak genetically, in terms of the creative process of a novel conceived as a cultural construct, then *El señor Presidente* must be restored to its true origin as a work largely written in the avant-garde Parisian 1920s and therefore contemporaneous with such 'Regionalist' novels as Gallegos's *Doña Bárbara* (1929) or Icaza's *Huasipungo* (1934).[5]

The novel's 1946 publication date, Martin argues, is an aberration occasioned by the oppressive conditions of the Ubico dictatorship ruling Guatemala at the time of Asturias's return. It should be ignored in any effort to place *El señor presidente* in historical context. Other commentators claim that Asturias continued revising the novel until shortly prior to its publication. Jimena Sáenz writes: 'La escribió por etapas en París y Guatemala entre 1922 y 1945' (*Genio y figura*, 109). Himelblau's more detailed account follows similar lines:

By the end of 1939, the first version of the novel was completed [...]. It was then decided to place it in a safe-deposit box in the Banco de Occidente [...]. After General Ubico's resignation on June 30, 1944, Asturias withdrew the manuscript and once more altered its content in 1945.[6]

Yet these alterations appear to have been minor. Pillement reports that 'Cuando tuvo que volver a Guatemala, Asturias acababa de terminar *El señor Presidente* y me dejó una copia dactilografiada encargándome la traducción' (Asturias, *París 1924–1933*, 745). Most of the available evidence indicates that Asturias wrote the bulk of the novel in Paris, probably during the final years of his stay.

El señor presidente must be read as a novel conceived in response to the author's early 1920s rejection of the intellectual and moral stagnation of his own class, yet written primarily by an Asturias who, subsequent to his 1928 visit to Guatemala, was at the peak of his interaction with French artistic and cultural life. The Asturias who completed the task of expanding 'Los mendigos políticos' into a novel was conscious of the *realities*—as opposed to the overpowering mythic essence—of French life. The Asturias of 1924–8 lived in a self-contained Spanish American world, which drew upon Paris as a point of reference and authority in endogenous Spanish American debates. Asturias's post-1928 articles, plagued by the conflict between the 'prepared' intellectual's duty to return and contribute the benefits of his training to the development of his *patria*, and the artist's need for the freedom and cultural stimulation offered by Europe, emanate from a different consciousness. This Asturias, as attested by his articles on Alfredo Wyld and Carlos Mérida, construes himself as a representative of a community of Spanish American artists resident in Paris. He belongs to a cultural enclave, an ethnic minority; like any minority spokesperson, he must master the cultural reference points both of his own community and of the surrounding majority.[7] In contrast to *Leyendas de Guatemala*, but like 'La barba provisional', *El señor presidente* possesses a subtext which brings it close to a form of immigrant writing.

At its most obvious level—the plane stemming from Asturias's student revolt against Estrada Cabrera and his verbal 'rivalry' on the subject of dictators with other Paris-based Spanish Americans—the novel serves as a denunciation of dictatorship. The dictator both seduced and corrupted, tantalized and thwarted, the *ladino* bourgeoisie to which Asturias belonged. While appealing to a modernizing ideology to which this class was sympathetic, dictators such as Estrada Cabrera ultimately stifled *ladino* professionals through alliances with foreign (mainly United States) capital with which these sectors were unable to compete. Yet the dictator's putatively integrative, nationalistic, modernizing policies, reinforced by the threat of violent coercion, created an environment in which most of the *ladino* bourgeoisie found collaboration—even at the expense of damage to their long-term economic interests—a less painful option than rebellion. The conservative Venezuelan social critic Carlos Rangel both explains this mentality and exemplifies its persistence when he argues:

En Latinoamérica los supercaudillos han sido además los verdaderos integradores de nuestras precarias nacionalidades, al lograr la hazaña de establecer una red de obligaciones interpersonales recíprocas sobre todo el territorio, crear por primera vez ejércitos modernos, profesionales y centralizados, en lugar de las montoneras cantonales o regionales, tender telégrafos que hicieron posible recibir información y dar órdenes rápidamente, y construir ferrocarriles por donde enviar tropas leales y bien armadas en días (en lugar de meses) del centro a los extremos de los países.[8]

For Asturias the dictatorship's claim to be a force of national integration had broken down in childhood with his family's internal exile in Salamá. His Parisian encounters with other expatriate Spanish Americans who despised their respective dictatorships absorbed him into a broader movement. Asturias joined ranks with the continent-wide revulsion at dictatorship that was provoking bourgeois intellectuals from many Spanish American nations to enlist the downtrodden into their struggle against obscurantism. In this sense, despite its Parisian birthplace and *avant-garde* trappings, *El señor presidente* remains in its conception a typical regionalist novel of its era: a true contemporary of the writings of Gallegos, Icaza or Ricardo Güiraldes. Beverley and Zimmerman summarize the dominant traits of the fiction of this period:

The vision that these novels project of a progressive and democratic national destiny built on the integration into national life of sectors of the population previously marginalized (e.g. the mestizo) was integral with [*sic*] the providential logic of their plots, which, as in the case of *Doña Bárbara*, tended to pit enlightened upper or middle-class heroes against representatives of oligarchic backwardness and anarchy. In this sense, they were literary allegories of the political premise of an antioligarchic alliance between the popular classes and a reform-oriented bourgeoisie (or sectors that aspire to this status), partly defined by its literary tastes.[9]

Miguel Cara de Angel's transformation, leading to his ostracism and destruction by the dictator, conforms to Beverley and Zimmerman's model. The sympathetic portrait of the villagers who assist the dissident General Canales in fleeing the country (to name only one significant scene of this type) incarnates the ideal of a bourgeois–peasant alliance described by Beverley and Zimmerman. But *El señor presidente*'s status as a novel of greater literary interest than its regionalist contemporaries stems from its off-kilter linguistic exuberance, its quirky imagery, fractured syntax and fragmented chronology. These features proceed not from Asturias's bourgeois revolt against the dictatorship but from his construction of his own cultural position, subsequent to his meeting with Desnos and his more thorough assimilation into French life, as a member of a community of writers who, though resident in Paris, expressed themselves in Spanish.[10] While the thematic and even symbolic conception of *El señor presidente* belongs to the modernizing bourgeois regionalism typical of Spanish American fiction of the late 1920s and early 1930s, the novel's literary constitution bespeaks a different phenomenon. Commenting on the literary vitality of the Spanish American enclave in Paris at this time, Cheymol reports that

[l]e nombre de journaux et revues consacrés spécialement à l'Amérique latine, et qui paraissaient à cette époque à Paris est assez surprenant. [...]

Le monde du journalisme latino-américain à Paris est donc constitué par l'ensemble des écrivains, des journalistes, des diplomates résidant à Paris et gravitant autour de ces organes de presse, mais aussi des intellectuels français qui mettaient leur talent, et leurs relations, au service de la cause latino-américaine. (*Années folles*, 29, 31)

The Spanish American community's links to the wider Parisian world through the activities of go-betweens such as Desnos, Valéry Larbaud and Georges Pillement helped to foster conditions in which writers such as Asturias perceived themselves as representatives of what might be characterized as a 'minor' literary culture. As Deleuze and Guattari posit: 'Une littérature mineure n'est pas celle d'une langue mineure, plutôt celle qu'une minorité fait dans une langue majeure. Mais le premier caractère est de toute façon que la langue y est affectée d'un fort coefficient de déterritorialisation'.[11]

Drawing on their study of the German of Prague at the time of Kafka, Deleuze and Guattari suggest two other defining characteristics of 'minor' literatures, the first of which is that 'tout y est politique' (Kafka, 30). Whether this is true in all such communities is questionable, but on the evidence of El señor presidente, Uslar Pietri's Las lanzas coloradas (1931) and Alejo Carpentier's ¡Ecué-Yamba-O! (1933), in the enclave culture in which Asturias worked personal preoccupations became politicized through their literary expression.

Deleuze and Guattari then argue that

tout prend une valeur collective [...] ce que l'écrivain tout seul dit constitue déjà une action commune, et ce qu'il dit ou fait est nécessairement politique [...]. Le champ politique a contaminé tout énoncé. Mais surtout, plus encore, parce que la conscience collective ou nationale est 'souvent inactive dans la vie extérieure et toujours en voie de désagrégation', c'est la littérature qui se trouve chargée de ce rôle et de cette fonction d'énonciation collective, et même révolutionnaire: c'est la littérature qui produit une solidarité active, malgré le scepticisme; et si l'écrivain est en marge ou à l'écart de sa communauté fragile, cette situation le met d'autant plus en mesure d'exprimer une autre communauté potentielle, de forger les moyens d'une autre conscience et d'une autre sensibilité. (Kafka, 31–2)

Deleuze and Guattari's contention that literature itself produces 'une solidarité active' on the part of the writer, while possibly sustainable in the case of Kafka, does not transfer harmoniously to the context of widespread opposition to a long-standing dictatorship in which Asturias was raised. Solidarity was also the inheritance of many expatriate Guatemalans who were not writers. But the description of the 'minor' writer's inextricably political vocation does illuminate Asturias's greater freedom in formal experimentation compared with his contemporaries resident in Spanish America. Gallegos and Icaza, immersed in the very stagnation they were denouncing, could not afford this luxury. Such indulgences as grotesque exaggeration, word-play and juggled time-sequences would have imperilled their earnest efforts to communicate vital social problems; assured of a political reaction to whatever he writes, Asturias can engage in aesthetic experimentation without relinquishing his political relevance. His innovative language originates, in large part, in his expatriation.

Asturias writes in a typically Guatemalan Spanish which is shaken into new shapes by deliberate syntactical ruptures, some of them reflecting the influence—either through borrowings from the techniques of Desnosian Surrealism or through linguistic structures adapted from French—of the author's long residence (and increasing immersion) in a French-speaking city. The combination of a Guatemalan 'alma nacional' enfeebled by dictatorship—and above all, in Asturias's eyes, by the dictatorship's subservience to US commercial interests—and the author's marginalization within Paris, breed the necessary preconditions for his reimagining of Guatemalan identity. Asturias's peripheral position within French life, and his growing hostility to the *ladino* values characteristic of 'familias distinguidas' such as those comprising most of the Guatemalan community of Paris, enables him, in other words, to undertake the daunting work of beginning to 'forger les moyens d'une autre conscience'.

This transformation of national mythology is possible, in part, because Asturias's position on the fringes of the Parisian cultural hierarchy reshapes his language. Deleuze and Guattari stress that in a minor literature, '*Le langage cesse d'être représentatif pour tendre vers ses extrêmes ou ses limites*' (*Kafka*, 42; original emphasis). Literary language, therefore, either reflects the impoverished vocabulary, influenced by that of the dominant language, generally employed by most speakers living in such situations, or evolves towards baroque excess. Turning to another 'minor' literature active in Paris during the 1920s—that of writers of English—one finds the work of Ernest Hemingway and James Joyce respectively occupying the extremes predicted by Deleuze and Guattari (although Hemingway's pared-down English seeks through implication to create a persuasive representation of reality, whereas, to return to Deleuze and Guattari's paradigm, Kafka's denuded German becomes a vehicle for constructing a non-representational imaginative world). Asturias, like Joyce and unlike Hemingway and Kafka, develops towards linguistic excess. His often jarring syntactical rearrangements demonstrate his penchant for inhabiting Guatemalan Spanish in the guise of a linguistic outsider (a French–Quiché hybrid) or, in Deleuze and Guattari's terms, his ability to 'faire de sa propre langue [...] un usage mineur. Etre *dans* sa propre langue comme un étranger' (*Kafka*, 48). It was as an outsider, almost as a foreigner, Cardoza y Aragón argues, that Asturias approached Guatemalan reality:

Este cosmopolita tan parroquial vio a nuestra tierra como pródigo hijo suyo y como extranjero sorprendido por su 'exotismo', por su mágica 'extravagancia' […]. En Asturias hubo, al unísono, esa capacidad inaugural de ser extranjero, de ser indio y de ser ladino. (*Asturias*, 16)

Asturias's toying with his means of self-expression (for example, his wordplay at café tables in the company of Carpentier and Uslar Pietri in the years after 1928) plays a crucial role in enabling him to develop his iconoclastic approach to the myths of Guatemalan social reality. His enshrinement of the Maya, a being despised by the *ladino* bourgeoisie, as the emblem of an essentially bourgeois Guatemalan nationalism is possible, in large part, because his inscription within the boundaries of a 'minor' Parisian literature elides social realities by making language paramount. Deleuze and Guattari write:

Une littérature majeure ou établie suit un vecteur qui va du contenu à l'expression: un contenu étant donné, dans une forme donnée, trouver, découvrir ou voir la forme d'expression qui lui convient. Ce qui se conçoit bien s'énonce […]. Mais une littérature mineure ou révolutionnaire commence par énoncer, et ne voit et ne conçoit qu'après […]. L'expression doit briser les formes, marquer les ruptures et les embranchements nouveaux. Une forme étant brisée, reconstruire le contenu qui sera nécessairement en rupture avec l'ordre des choses. Entraîner, devancer la matière. (*Kafka*, 51–2)

Viewed in these terms, Asturias's entry into the imaginative world of *El señor presidente* through the singsong introductory incantation, his smashing of linear logic and subsequent reconstitution of national mythology through a growing identification with the darkness of the Indian-dominated countryside appears as the expression of a minor literature in pursuit of the means to create an alternative consciousness. The novel's opening paragraph underscores the primacy, in the implicit author's perceptions, of pure language:

¡Alumbra, lumbre de alumbre, Luzbel de piedralumbre! Como zumbido de oídos persistía el rumor de las campanas a la oración, maldoblestar de la luz en la sombra, de la sombra en la luz. ¡Alumbra, lumbre de alumbre, Luzbel de piedralumbre, sobre la pobredumbre! ¡Alumbra, lumbre de alumbre, sobre la pobredumbre, Luzbel de piedralumbre! ¡Alumbra, alumbra, lumbre de alumbre… alumbre… alumbra…, alumbra, lumbre de alumbre…, alumbra, alumbre…! (*SP*, 37)

The novel begins with the intoning of a religious service, as it will end with the revolutionary student's mother praying over her rosary beads. The reader is presented with a linguistic façade which establishes a sonorous enunciatory pattern creating a linguistic context in which the text's 'contenu' (to echo Deleuze and Guattari's terminology) may be forged. The opening sentence serves as an invocation of the light which both illuminates and corrupts: '¡Alumbra, lumbre de alumbre, Luzbel de piedralumbre!' In his anxiety to bestow the brilliance of the City of Light on the Guatemalan darkness, the narrator accepts the risk of summoning up Lucifer. This double-edged vision of the consequences of seeking enlightenment foreshadows the fate of Cara de Angel and the repeated description, throughout the rest of the novel, of the favourite as 'bello y malo como Satán' (*SP*, 66 et seq.). The ambivalence with which the novel portrays mental and spiritual illumination reflects Asturias's awareness of the contradictory consequences of his own irradiation by the light of another continent. The movement from the opening scene's call to spill the light of progress over the blackness of Guatemalan backwardness and oppression to the positive view, by the novel's end, of the darkness of the countryside as a place of refuge, fecund with mythology, constitutes the work's central ideological development. As a result, both light and shadow develop into double-edged images. At different points in the book, each becomes affirmative; at other junctures, illumination debases the characters and darkness stifles them. Light and shadow, therefore, do not represent fixed polarities but mobile nodes whose oscillations draw along and tug into fresh patterns specific clusters of assumptions. The traditional interpretation of *El señor presidente* as a struggle between good and evil fails to capture this important dimension. An early article by Martin typifies the standard reading: 'As love purifies [Cara de Angel's] soul and the recognition of the President's true significance brings a kind of moral redemption, so light triumphs inside him […] and the darkness without moves to destroy him.'[12]

From the novel's opening incantation, illumination is both desired and feared. The call for light contains a recognition of illumination's Satanic potential. And it is illumination itself which, by contrast, bares the appalling poverty blighting the streets of Guatemala City. When the opening oration is repeated in the novel's third sentence, the clause 'sobre la pobredumbre' is appended to it like a stutter. It is in this sense that enunciation precedes vision: the rhythms of the chant, demanding an additional clause, result in poverty being mentioned for the first time. The movement from pure enunciation to a conception of social reality continues in the next sentence. The oration is repeated once more; but this time the mention of 'pobredumbre' has advanced to become the third of the sentence's four clauses. The increasing centrality of the fact of poverty breaks down the opening mantra, shattering its rhythms into a single repeated (though inflected) tone— 'alumbre..., alumbra..., alumbra, lumbre de alumbre..., alumbra, alumbre'—whose onomatopoeia echoes the funereal tolling of the church bell. Having broken out of the purely linguistic realm, the novel undertakes what Deleuze and Guattari refer to as the reconstruction of its content, starting from the fact of poverty. The next paragraph begins the work of sketching the surface contrast of Guatemalan shadow and Parisian light which the remainder of the novel will attempt to resolve. In unvarnished language, it establishes the novel's vision of Guatemalan society through the image of beggars lost in darkness: 'Los pordioseros se arrastraban por las cocinas del mercado, perdidos en la sombra de la Catedral helada'; the city itself, the reader learns, 'se iba quedando atrás íngrima y sola' (*SP*, 37). The use of the adverb 'atrás' in this context implies a point of comparison, the existence of another world by contrast with whose advance Guatemalan society appears to be slipping backwards. It is in this way that Paris makes its first implicit appearance in the text.

   The reproach France poses to Guatemala weighs most heavily in the realm of culture. Among the range of cries uttered by the beggars on the church steps, 'el grito del idiota era el más triste. Partía el cielo. Era un grito largo, sonsacado, sin acento humano' (*SP*, 38). This initial image of Guatemalan society as an idiot—an idiot who goes on to strike out blindly at his oppressor in the form of the undercover agent Parrales Sonriente, setting in train the violent events that consume the remainder of the novel—is quickly countered by the beggar known as Patahueca. In the novel's first line of dialogue, Patahueca reacts to 'los gritos y los saltos del idiota' by shouting: '¡Viva Francia!' (*SP*, 38). His response to dictatorship echoes that of Asturias during his student days. In an article published in the March 1920 issue of *El Estudiante*, Asturias interrupted a lengthy fulmination against Estrada Cabrera in order to address the dictator directly, largely in block capitals: 'MANUEL: ¿No recuerdas lo que dijo el pensador más grande de la Francia? "NO SE ARROJAN PIEDRAS SINO AL ARBOL DE ORO"'.[13] This appeal to French cultural hegemony did not, in all likelihood, play a decisive role in overthrowing Estrada Cabrera. Asturias, his relationship with French culture now more intricate and mature, recognizes the impotence of such idealistic invocations. (He places his faith instead in nature acting, as so often in his fiction, in concert with the will of the Maya. A political prisoner later in the novel predicts that 'ya no tarda un terremoto en acabar con todo' (*SP*, 231)—an allusion to the earthquake which Asturias saw as having been instrumental in bringing down Estrada Cabrera.)

The beggars, having been arrested *en masse* in the wake of the murder of Parrales Sonriente, cross paths in prison with the priest and the revolutionary student. In the setting of a prison cell, Patahueca's defiance becomes (as his name implies) hollow:

—¡Viva Francia!—gritó *Patahueca* al entrar.
—Estoy preso...—franqueóse el sacristán.
—¡Viva Francia!
—....por un delito que cometí por pura equivocación.... (*SP*, 44)

As the priest's interjections make clear, mere words in praise of France will not alleviate the pain of unjust imprisonment. Despite his ideals, Patahueca capitulates without a struggle to the monstrous Auditor de Guerra, agreeing to swear, against the evidence of his own eyes, that General Canales and the lawyer Carvajal, rather than the idiot, murdered Parrales Sonriente. Only the blind, deformed Mosco refuses to comply—a refusal which costs him his life. Displaying the polyvalence of the novel's deployment of images of light and shadow, the arrest and interrogation scenes associate light with the secret police. It is their capture of the tools of power and modernity— symbolic of the dictatorship's hijacking of the rhetoric of progress— which enable them to draw the pall of darkness over the country. Though portrayed as cannibalistic, they remain in possession of the limited, strictly material fruits of progress. The beggars, by contrast,

lagrimeaban como animales con moquillo, atormentados por la oscuridad, que sentían que no se les iba a despegar más de los ojos [...]. Las caras de los antropófagos, iluminadas como faroles, avanzaban por las tinieblas, los cachetes como nalgas, los bigotes como babas de chocolate. (*SP*, 43)

The description recalls Asturias's early division of Guatemalan society into 'los semicivilizados' and 'la masa negra'. The latter term, apart from its unfortunate racial connotations, refers to the slumbering darkness of oppression in which the majority of Guatemalans live. As the arrest scene illustrates, the forces of order, in spite of their propagation of injustice and corruption, have cast the population into darkness by capturing the light. This appropriation is symbolized in the chapter's final paragraph by the application of the word 'lumbre', a key term in the novel's opening call for illumination, to the eyes of death exhibited by the horses bearing the Auditor de Guerra to his meeting with the President. The Auditor travels 'en un carricoche tirado por dos caballos flacos, que llevaban de lumbre en los faroles los ojos de la muerte' (*SP*, 47). In the perverted order enforced by the President, light brings death, progress is linked to more effective oppression. The association of light with positivist-style efficiency in carrying out the chores of dictatorship returns in the scene where Cara de Angel hits upon his ploy for persuading the secret policeman Vásquez to assist him in kidnapping Camila (whom at this point he is planning to rape): 'El favorito sintió que le llovía luz en los ojos' (*SP*, 71). Enlightenment, Asturias insists, contains no moral governor: in a society lacking the integrating impulse provided by a sense of its own interests and self-worth (in other words, lacking an 'alma nacional') the insights of the illuminated, rather than aiding the culture's development, will facilitate dictatorship.

These contradictions receive their most complex embodiment in the character of Miguel Cara de Angel. Cara de Angel is the pivotal figure in the novel's metatextual depiction of the cultural process engendering its own composition. Like Asturias himself, Cara de Angel is a cultural hybrid, a being constituted of elements of both light and shadow. Through him, Asturias assesses the price paid by the *ladino* bourgeoisie for its cultural alienation and identification with Europe, which render it easy prey for dictators such as the President. Cara de Angel's odyssey dramatizes Asturias's own wrestling with the mental shackles of his cultural training. The favourite's quest, once touched by the love of the darker, more 'natural' Camila, to disengage himself from the President's thrall, parallels Asturias's efforts, throughout his Parisian apprenticeship, to generate an independent creative identity encompassing a durable, ethnically inclusive conception of Guatemalan nationhood. Writing as both the representative of a 'minor' Parisian literature and a disaffected member of the *ladino* bourgeoisie anxious to co-opt the underprivileged classes into his struggle, Asturias constructs in Cara de Angel an *alter ego* who reflects the cultural alienation and political corruption endemic to his class. It is worth recalling that 1928, in all likelihood a crucial year in the composition of *El señor presidente*, marks the final mention in Asturias's journalism of the *afrancesado* Gómez Carrillo—a harshly critical reference to the older Guatemalan's role as an apologist for Estrada Cabrera. As Martin observes, the precedent of Gómez Carillo and his ilk was clearly on Asturias's mind as he wrote of Miguel Cara de Angel.

Given the similarity to the author's own name and [...] the novel's genesis in self-analysis, it would be surprising if [Cara de Angel] were not also a form of metaphorical self-criticism and a comment on those intellectuals and artists (like Darío, Chocano and Gómez Carrillo), and in general the parasitical middle sectors from which Asturias himself came, who supported Estrada Cabrera. (Swanson, *Landmarks*, 57)

In fact, the tensions incarnated by Miguel Cara de Angel reverberate well beyond 'metaphorical self-criticism'. As the arrest scene alluded to above demonstrates, light in the novel can symbolize the cruel implementation of positivist doctrine as well as the possibility of enlightenment; shadow, especially in the novel's later stages, can represent the cultural authenticity of the nurturing autochthonous darkness in addition to the black night of dictatorship. Cara de Angel, repeatedly described in terms of the violent meeting of light and shadow, enfolds all of these multiple strands. The sole character whose social position changes as a result of a development in his mentality, Cara de Angel reacts to his liaison with Camila as Asturias himself reacted to his encounter with Paris: he attempts to draw himself closer to the roots of his culture and society. The shock of his love for Camila converts (yet fails at core to transform) Cara de Angel, as Georges Raynaud's 'Vous êtes maya' converted Asturias, inducing him to recast his *ladino* nationalism in a Mayan form without changing its essence. Both figures abruptly alter their identification with the power structures of Guatemalan society. Cara de Angel's love for Camila, therefore, occupies a role analogous to that played by the mythologization of the Mayan past in Asturias's own life. It is hardly surprising that she is described as being darker, more Indian in her facial features and more intuitively in touch with the forces of the natural world than is Cara de Angel. The introductory description of Cara de Angel presents him as being torn between European and Guatemalan shadings. His unearthly beauty reflects his positioning of himself above and outside the sordid everyday world of Guatemalan reality. He is first described through the eyes of the wood-cutter: 'El que le hablaba era un ángel: tez dorado mármol, cabellos rubios, boca pequeña y aire de mujer en violento contraste con la negrura de sus ojos varoniles. Vestía de gris. Su traje, a la luz del crepúsculo, se veía como una nube' (*SP*, 56–7). Cara de Angel's beauty emanates from an identity whose contours remain unresolved. Both blond and dark-eyed, womanly and 'varonil', he dresses in a way that extends the contradictions expressed by his appearance. His physiognomy displays the interleafing of darkness and light; his choice of grey clothing deliberately sustains this ambiguity. By describing his suit as resembling a cloud, the narrator alludes to Cara de Angel's career of duplicity. Suave and cultivated on the surface, he remains the agent of a thuggish dictatorship. His sordid compromise epitomizes that of the *ladino* bourgeoisie as a whole. Subsequent scenes make it clear that it is this class's corruption and betrayal of its supposed allegiance to 'civilized' (implicitly European) values that buttresses the President's grip on power. General Canales's house, for example, contains a portrait of the President 'con ferrocarriles en los hombros, como charreteras, y un angelito dejándole caer en la cabeza una corona de laurel' (*SP*, 69). The transaction could not be clearer: the President has earned his figurative epaulettes by providing the bourgeoisie with material advances such as railways; they, in return, in the angelic personage of Miguel Cara de Angel, have crowned him. The image helps to explain the President's role as a minor character in the novel. If he remains little more than a pair of dark glasses and a black suit (representing the resolute extreme of which Cara de Angel's grey clothing serves as a modulation), it is because his personality and history are irrelevant. The President is a creation of the bourgeoisie's collaboration with foreign imperialism, the point of convergence of disparate forces rather than an autonomous actor. The bourgeoisie flatters him (and itself) that his regime stands for the implantation of cultured norms in a barbaric land. The price paid for maintaining this stance is that hypocrisy is never far away. Cara de Angel appears at his most unctuous when telling the President that some have said he should not govern this country. To the President's angry demand to know who has uttered this calumny, Cara de Angel responds by deftly inverting the phrase's apparent meaning:

> —¡Yo, el primero, Señor Presidente, entre los muchos que profesamos la creencia de que un hombre como usted debería gobernar un pueblo como Francia, o la libre Suiza, o la industriosa Bélgica o la maravillosa Dinamarca!... Pero Francia..., Francia sobre todo... ¡Usted sería el hombre ideal para guiar los destinos del gran pueblo de Gambetta y Víctor Hugo! (*SP*, 67)

Cara de Angel's choice of icons highlights the dictatorship's theft of the legitimizing authority of progressive French ideals. His slippery inversion of the meaning of his original statement demonstrates the debasement of language (and hence of culture) inherent to the postures the bourgeoisie must adopt in order to sustain its support for the dictatorship. Yet the fact that Cara de Angel has allowed himself to voice the potentially treacherous (since honest) initial statement illustrates his subconscious awareness of the truth: the scene sketches Cara de Angel's potential for change, foreshadowing his rebellion. The ironic invocation of France as the ultimate touchstone of cultural attainment lampoons the pretensions of the dictatorship and its supporters. The question raised by the scene is not of the aptness of applying European-influenced models to Guatemala, but of whether the President can claim to be the authentic embodiment of these models. It is within this context of the overarching dominance of the Europeanized *ladino* that the novel's later turn towards the culture of rural Guatemala takes place.

Cara de Angel leaves his meeting with the President 'con media cara cubierta en la bufanda negra. (Era bello y malo como Satán.)' (*SP*, 68). His status as a divided being is clear: the image repeats in the chapter's final paragraph, when Cara de Angel 'partió a toda prisa con la bufanda negra sobre la cara pálida' (*SP*, 73). His union with Camila begins to weld the two halves of his identity into a more harmonious whole. Cara de Angel, a white man with blond hair and pale skin, has had his being split by exposure to the moral darkness of dictatorship reflected in his eyes. Camila breaks down his sterile dichotomy between light and shadow by enabling him to develop an alternative definition of darkness as the source of a potentially affirmative connection with the cultural core of his homeland. The illumination invoked by the novel's images of light, therefore, regains its positive connotations. The vital Chapter XII, which according to Martin is the part of the manuscript Asturias rewrote most significantly between 1933 and 1946, establishes Camila's ties with a natural, racially darker universe than that with which Cara de Angel has hitherto been acquainted. Describing her appearance, the narrator writes of 'el pelo en llamas negras alborotado, la cara trigueña lustrosa de manteca de cacao para despercudirse, náufragos los ojos verdes, oblicuos y jalados para atrás. La pura China Canales, como la apodaban en el colegio' (*SP*, 107). The shape of Camila's eyes and her schoolgirl nickname suggest a mixed racial heritage, despite her middle-class background. The complex image of her 'cara trigueña lustrosa de manteca de cacao para despercudirse' resonates with contradictory messages. The adjective 'lustrosa' lends a positive connotation to Camila's darkness, while the invocation of 'manteca de cacao' affiliates her with the natural world. Yet Camila's bonds to dark, instinctual forces are impugned by the image's extension: the cacao-butter, the reader learns, is of the sort that might be used to cleanse her face of stains. The narrator's desire to generate an affirmative picture of a woman of partly Mayan ancestry collides in this description with a reflexive need to depict a conventional (hence white) bourgeois romantic heroine. Behind the ambivalence of this description lies Asturias's struggle to accept the redemptive potential of a dark-skinned woman in the life of a blond, light-skinned man. Asturias's use of the word 'trigueña'—which, in addition to its adjectival meaning, carries connotations of racial categorization—is especially striking. As was noted earlier, Guatemalan Spanish divides racial origin into 'indio' or 'ladino'. The use of 'trigueño'—a designation common in countries such as Venezuela and Colombia, where racial classification depends on a more varied spectrum of possibilities—represents an attempt on the narrator's part to enlarge the repertoire of racial categories available to him. The term recurs in the description of the rising tide of Camila's sensual awakening: 'Y sin oler lo que se besa, el beso no sabe a nada. Su carne salobre y trigueña como la arena, y las piñuelas y los membrillos, la enseñaron a besar con las ventanas de la nariz abiertas, ansiosas, anhelantes' (*SP*, 111). The linkage between Camila's 'trigueña' flesh and her identification with uncorrupted Guatemalan nature has been tightened in this passage. The texture and pigmentation of her skin make her 'como la arena' of her country's beaches. The equivalence comes within a hair of equating Camila with the Guatemalan earth itself. (In this way she prefigures the earth-mother figure María Tecún, the object of Goyo Yic's quest in *Hombres de maíz*.) Camila's affinities with nature, here likening her to cypress nuts and quince trees, lead her to kiss in a frank manner that stands in stark opposition to the hypocrisy and deception which enmeshes Cara de Angel's every gesture.

Yet like Cara de Angel, Camila is a product of the bourgeoisie. Her freedom from *ladino* strictures stems not from innate characteristics, but from experience. This point is crucial to Asturias's ideology of transculturation. The central thematic movement of *El señor presidente* is predicated on an assumption that the individual, and particularly the artist, possesses the capacity to develop or resuscitate atrophied, repressed or dormant cultural allegiances. Angel Rama writes of the transculturation process:

Nace de una doble comprobación: registra en su cultura presente—ya transculturada—un conjunto de valores idiosincráticos que puede reencontrar si se remonta hasta fechas remotas dentro de su historia; corrobora simultáneamente en su seno la existencia de una energía creadora que con desenvoltura actúa tanto sobre su herencia particular como sobre las incidencias provenientes del exterior y en esa capacidad para una elaboración original, aun en las difíciles situaciones a que ha sido sometida históricamente, encuentra una prueba de la existencia de una sociedad específica, viva, creadora, distinta, la cual alienta, más que en las ciudades estrechamente asociadas a las pulsiones universales, en las capas recónditas de las regiones internas.[14]

Both Asturias's project of instilling a Mayan 'alma nacional' as the unifying symbol of a splintered Guatemalan identity and his own claim to legitimacy as a representative 'Maya' within Parisian literary circles depend upon an assumption that individuals possess the capacity for fundamental change in their outlooks, responses, preconceptions and intimate identifications.

In *El señor presidente*, the values destined to compose this 'alma nacional' reside, as Rama posits, in the world outside the cities. The novel's iconoclasts—Camila Canales, General Canales and Cara de Angel—enlarge their respective visions through a growing iden-tification with the traditional cultures and natural forces present in the Guatemalan countryside. This interaction, directed towards the consolidation of a firm 'alma nacional', expresses a change in national consciousness through the change wrought by events on a group of individuals. As Beverley and Zimmerman argue:

Asturias's ideological project was based on his notion of a core Mayan/ladino identity for the Guatemalan people; his artistic problem was the forging of a literary mode able to both express and embody the transculturation process that the achievement of such an identity required. (*Literature and Politics*, 209–10)

Given Guatemala's harsh racial dichotomies, the term 'Mayan/ladino' might appear at first glance to be an oxymoron. In fact, it expresses the nearly inconceivable leap of consciousness demanded by the transculturation process on which Asturias has embarked. The trajectory of *El señor presidente* sketches this process through the union of Cara de Angel and Camila Canales. To adopt Beverley and

Zimmerman's terms, it expresses the transculturation process but does not *embody* it as fully as, say, *Hombres de maíz*. The earlier novel's form narrates a break with traditional *ladino* false consciousness in a mode which, despite its experimentation, continues to adhere to many of the literary conventions (such as the use, despite juggled chronology, of a standard Western conception of time) associated with a bourgeois *ladino* vision of reality. Zimmerman, in a later work, writes:

in this urban, ladino dictator novel, the world of the Indians only emerges gradually and indirectly, as if like the 'return of the repressed'. Of course it is the only partial emergence of this theme which is one of the modes by which European consciousness has overlaid Latin American realities, one of the modes by which the president's power constructs and maintains itself.[15]

Camila's rupture with *ladino* constraints, preparing her to become the catalyst for Cara de Angel's own transformation, is engendered by her exposure to the natural force of the ocean. The atmosphere of Camila's childhood is devout and emotionally embalmed: 'Ser la nena. Ir con [sus tíos y tías] a la parada. Ir con ellos a todas partes. A misa de doce, al Cerro de Carmen' (*SP*, 107). Her life, subordinated to the routines of her widowed father, revolves around the photograph album containing pictures of her late mother and other relatives. The album dominates the family's social life to such an extent that the narrator remarks that 'Un amigo escapaba a veces del álbum de retratos y se detenía a conversar con el general' (*SP*, 108). The dedication beneath one of the photographs—'Remember 1898' (*SP*, 108)—makes ironic reference to the year of Estrada Cabrera's ascent to power (which was also the year of the outbreak of the Spanish-American War: the beginning of the US imperialist thrust into the Caribbean Basin of which dictators such as Estrada Cabrera became one salient result).[16] The caption's inclusion in the cherished family album underlines the point that it is precisely this sort of repressed, unquestioning behaviour on the part of the bourgeoisie that maintains the dictatorship's grip on power. The fact that the words are in English serves to emphasize the cultural consequences of such subservience. Camila's world, symbolized by the reification of reality in her father's album of portraits, is reactionary in the sense that it is rooted in an attempt to impose total stasis, to stem the flow of time. Camila's first glimpse of the sea overturns this ideology by introducing her to a universe whose contours are in perpetual flux.

La inmensidad en movimiento. Ella en movimiento. Todo lo que en ella estaba inmóvil, en movimiento. Jugaron palabras de sorpresa en sus labios al ver el mar por primera vez, mas al preguntarle sus tíos qué le parecía el espectáculo, dijo con aire de huera importancia: '¡Me lo sabía de memoria en fotografía! [...]' (*SP*, 109)

Camila's dissimulation of the extent to which she has been moved by the sight of the sea demonstrates both the hold of the bourgeois hypocrisy to which she has been raised, and her recognition that the consciousness nudged into existence by this sight is one which lies beyond the cosseted understanding of her uncles and aunts. As she continues to gaze upon the ocean, the vision's subversive effect on her conception of a reality pinned down in photograph albums becomes evident:

Todo en movimiento. Nada estable. Retratos y retratos confundiéndose, revolviéndose, saltando en pedazos para formar una visión fugaz a cada instante, en un estado que no era sólido, ni líquido, ni gaseoso, sino el estado en que la vida está en el mar. El estado luminoso. En las vistas y en la mar. (*SP*, 110)

The sea's constant motion represents the symbolic dissolution of the family portraits. The fleeting visions which she substitutes for the photographs constitute 'un estado luminoso'. This authentic illumination, untainted by bourgeois pretensions or dictatorial brutality, is inextricably linked to the darker essences of nature by the subsequent description of Camila's 'trigueña' skin as being 'como la arena'. Her enlightenment entails the renunciation of positivist doctrines for something richer yet more uncertain. The rift between Camila's candid approach to reality and her family's ingrained hypocrisy becomes an unbridgeable chasm when, after her father's flight, her uncles refuse to acknowledge or shelter her. These scenes play a vital role in inducing Cara de Angel to transcend his own cynicism. Camila's predicament provokes him into criticism of behaviour resembling his own, isolating him from the structures of power and eventually sealing his union with Camila (and hence condemning him to death). Moments before leaving the presidential palace to visit Camila's uncle, Cara de Angel's response to a dispute between two powerful officials is to think: 'en aquel conflicto de autoridades lo mejor era lavarse las manos' (*SP*, 130). Yet his idealization of Camila's purity is such that when Juan Canales energetically denounces his brother's 'crime', the other man's opportunistic words inspire in him a feeling of disgust: 'Cara de

Angel, muy lejos de lo que don Juan pensaba, lo observaba en silencio, preguntándose hasta dónde aquel hombre cobarde y repugnante era algo de Camila' (*SP*, 132). His effort to pass off Camila on her uncles having been thwarted, Cara de Angel finds himself both literally and figuratively stuck with her. His growing respect for her sincerity finally causes him to confess that he lied to her in leading her to believe that Juan and Judith Canales were willing to take her in. 'Mentía por ternura', he tells her, 'por querer ahorrarle hasta el último momento el dolor que ahora va a sufrir', and as his explanation of his lie stutters to a close, the narrator notes that 'Las calles alumbradas se ven más solas' (*SP*, 154). The union of Camila and Cara de Angel begins the process, within the novel's patterns of imagery, of re-claiming the light from the forces of oppression (and simultaneously of separating them from *ladino* assumptions). It is their alliance— a bond forged between a light-skinned man working within the government's power structures and a darker-skinned woman ostracized by those structures—which renders enlightenment affirmative. No longer associated with positivist efficiency in enforcing oppression, the images of light now come to represent the possibility of transculturation: of re-imagining Guatemalan identity through cross-cultural alliances that will restore the nation to a more authentic rapport with its own origins and national interest. The depressing tragic import of this novel, and the reason why Asturias's subsequent fiction needed to evolve away from the city into the highlands and the banana plantations, is that the cowardice, insularity and hypocrisy of the urban bourgeoisie causes this class to crush such unions. The *ladino's* fear of change limits the repertoire and potential outcomes of dramatic situations emerging from this sort of revolt; the untainted countryside offers greater hope and more varied possibilities for reshaping conventional cultural formations.

When Cara de Angel and Camila go together to visit Juan Canales's house, Camila's uncle recoils in horror. As he reports to his brother on the phone: 'Pues figúrate... Ella y el tipo, sí... Ya lo creo, ya lo creo... ¡Nooo, no le abrimos' (*SP*, 159). The bourgeoisie locks out the potentially creative, liberating union of shadow and light. In so doing, it drives these disenchanted but not necessarily inherently compatible figures into one another's arms. Prior to being turned away at her uncle's door, Camila thinks of Cara de Angel as 'aquel hombre cuyos ojos negros despedían fosforencias diabólicas... aquel individuo repugnante a pesar de ser bello como un ángel' (*SP*, 156).

She feels happy to be separated from him. But after their rejection, she finds herself prolonging their friendship. When he bids her farewell, her response reflects her assumption that they will remain in touch: '—¡Hasta luego!—dijo sin saber por qué; él ya no tenía qué hacer allí' (*SP*, 160). Cara de Angel, while less immediately eager to maintain contact with Camila, discovers that their encounter has bared the flimsiness of his conception of his identity. The mounting feelings of need drawing the couple together are consistently expressed in terms of Cara de Angel's awareness of the inadequacy of his self-definition. At first this takes the form of an ill-formulated sense of emptiness at no longer playing the role of the President's henchman. 'Y al sobreponerme a mí mismo para librar a Camila de mis intenciones, dejé una parte de mi ser sin relleno y por eso me siento vacío, intranquilo, colérico, enfermo, dado a la trampa' (*SP*, 173). A few pages later, Cara de Angel pinpoints the source of his unease in his own cultivated amorphousness. The evasive manoeuvres that have allowed him to thrive in a climate of terror fail him when he tries to define himself against another human being. The challenge posed by Camila's forthright self-possession and openness to forces that he has banished from his consciousness throws him back on the fact that years of hypocrisy have eroded any firm sense of his own core being. He lies in his bed

despierto a una azulosa combustión angélica. Y poco a poco, ya dormido, flotando bajo su propio pensamiento, sin cuerpo, sin forma, como un aire tibio, móvil al soplo de su propia respiración. […]
    Sólo Camila persistía en aquel hundirse de su cuerpo en el anulamiento, alta, dulce y cruel como una cruz de camposanto. […]
    El Sueño, señor que surca los mares oscuros de la realidad, le recogió en una de sus muchas barcas. (*SP*, 176)

Cara de Angel's manicured self-image dissolves into a bluish 'combustión angélica'; he is depicted floating, without body or form. In a telling inversion, the traditional attributes of angels have become a kind of malaise. The terms in which this malaise is described propel him towards Camila; both the use of the verb 'hundirse' and the description of his breathing as 'móvil' recall the scene relating her visit to the ocean. Camila's integrated sense of self attracts Cara de Angel but also threatens him. The one solid entity occupying his imagination, she is none the less associated with the image of a cemetery cross, foreshadowing the fact that his marriage to her will lead to his death. The dreams bearing him towards an acceptance of his need for her are likened to 'mares oscuros', evoking both Camila's moment of liberation from her own *ladino* repression and the autochthonous darkness which she represents in the constitution of Cara de Angel's revised identity. When he suffers from nightmares at the thought of 'la sombra que le separa de Camila', his anguish coalesces into a repeated image of 'cinco hombres de vidrio opaco [que salen] a cortarle el paso' (*SP*, 211–12). In counterpoint to this vision of dehumanization, lack of self-definition and estrangement from natural essences, Camila is associated, in the continuing motif of intermingled menace and naturalness, with a 'cementerio oloroso a membrillo, a mango, a pera y melocotón' (*SP*, 212).

In the novel's final section, the recapturing of images of light for the forces of humanistic illumination ushers in a proliferation of metaphors and similes connecting the dictatorship to darkness and shadow. While a parallel notion of a fertile, affirmative darkness takes root as the novel progresses, the binary tension between the City of Light (Paris and its cultural subsidiaries) and the City of Shadow (Guatemala and its dictatorship) becomes accentuated during the final hundred pages. This pattern is projected onto the descriptions of Camila and Cara de Angel's marriage contained in Part Three; yet it does not grow out of their union. The chapter that introduces this structure into the text is, significantly, dedicated to the description of General Canales's flight out of the country. The consciousness whose perceptions make this pattern of imagery cohere, in other words, is that of the exile. (The chapter is entitled 'Camino al destierro'.) On his trek to the border Canales meets an Indian who gives him a detailed account (in an accent transcribed with condescending *costumbrista* exhaustiveness) of the injustices endured by the rural population. The knowledge of his country that Canales carries abroad with him hence becomes more complete and multifaceted than that he possessed as a pillar of urban *ladino* society. The text depicts expatriation as an experience promoting the individual's accession to a broader understanding of national problems. Like Asturias himself, General Canales discovers the suppressed human riches of the rural world as a result of fleeing the country. In this scene, as in his later meeting in the village with the dispossessed peasant women who assist him in crossing the border, Canales embodies both the superiority of the expatriate's understanding of national realities and the pain of exile:

Le dolía su país como si se le hubiera podrido la sangre. Le dolía afuera y en la médula, en la raíz del pelo, bajo las uñas, entre los dientes. ¿Cuál era la realidad? No haber pensado nunca con su cabeza, haber pensado siempre con el quepis. Ser militar para mantener en el mando a una casta de ladrones, explotadores y vendepatrias endiosados es mucho más triste, por infame, que morirse de hambre en el ostracismo. A santo de qué nos exigen a los militares lealtad a regímenes desleales con el ideal, con la tierra y con la raza. (*SP*, 218–19)

The passage betrays a slippage from an evocation of exile to narrative intervention propounding an explicitly nationalist ideology. The linkage emphasizes the fact that the contours of the implicit author's nationalism have been moulded by the experience of expatriation. The diatribe announces what the narrative consciousness decries ('vendepatrias') and what it has come to value ('el ideal… la tierra… la raza'). The figure of the 'desterrado' is portrayed as treading an unmarked path cutting a course between foreign illumination and the shadowed, repressed world of Guatemala: 'Adelante se perdían las huellas de un tigre. Sombra. Luz. Sombra. Luz' (*SP*, 219). The transformative power of exile is reiterated in the scene where Canales, guided by the smuggler, dodges between slumbering alligators in order to cross the border: 'Sus sombras los perseguían como lagartos. Los lagartos como sus sombras' (*SP*, 225). The imagery associates the nation which the men are fleeing with a shadow that threatens, literally, to swallow them. But the text also recognizes the presence of another order, wild and unpredictable yet intimately bound to the country's rural core, for which nature acts as authentic self-expression. Despite his newly declared allegiance to his 'raza', this is a universe into which the *ladino* Canales has not yet integrated: 'Canales volvía la cabeza a todos lados, perdido en medio de aquella naturaleza fatídica, inabordable y destructora como el alma de su raza' (*SP*, 225). The world inhabited by rural people is seen as potentially destructive (presumably of *ladino* certainties), but destructive in a way that accurately expresses the people's 'alma'—and, to extend the metaphor to Asturias's own activities, in a way that offers a paradigm which may be used as the foundation for the construction of a viable 'alma nacional'. The formulation of this 'alma nacional', however, requires the illumination provided by the world beyond Guatemala. When, in the final sentence of Part Two, Canales looks back at his homeland from across the border, his vision of perilous shadow and unpredictable nature is turned on its head: 'Sobre la esmeralda del campo, sobre las montañas del bosque tupido que los pájaros convertían en cajas de música, y sobre las selvas pasaban las nubes con forma de lagarto llevando en los lomos tesoros de luz' (*SP*, 226).

Viewed from without, the Guatemalan natural world becomes an object of beauty and a source of promise. The clouds, an image earlier associated with Cara de Angel's ambivalence and hypocrisy, are converted by the experience of exile into the repository of 'tesoros de luz'. The fact that these storehouses of illumination have adopted the form of 'lagartos' underscores the inherent value and potential richness latent in even the most threatening aspects of rural Guatemalan life. This chapter, tapping in to the broader perspective of the exile, establishes an overarching symbolic pattern to which Cara de Angel and Camila, trapped inside the Guatemalan darkness, do not have access. It also serves as the denouement to the quest for self-definition triggered by their relationship. Canales's exile's consciousness represents the paramount constitution of Guatemalan identity offered by the text. The integration of the rural, Mayan world into a European-based *ladino* nationalism, constructed from within the optic of expatriate experience, dictates that the search for the Guatemalan self must inevitably conclude outside the country's borders.

This chapter represents the culmination of the process set in motion by the incantatory chant with which the novel opens. As Deleuze and Guattari write, in the context of 'minor' literature, 'l'expression doit entraîner le contenu' (*Kafka*, 106). The opening call for light stumbles over the presence of poverty. The humiliation pent up in this consciousness expresses itself through the violence of Parrales Sonriente's murder, whose consequences radiate out into an anguished inventory of national society. The survey of Guatemalan reality transmutes inexorably into both a denunciation of dictatorship and, at a connotative level, a metatextual description of the constitution of the conception of Guatemalan identity that has allowed the book to be written.

The installation, through the account of Canales's exile, of an expatriate consciousness as the novel's dominant narrative intelligence, reinforces the patterns of shadow and light. Cara de Angel's dark eyes, for example, come to be seen as even more sinister than in the first two parts of the novel. Twice in Part Three, the darkness of his eyes, staining his pale face, is likened to 'terciopelo' (*SP*, 252, 290), an image that associates him not only with glibness and corruption but also with deadly menace. Rodríguez explains: 'En Centroamérica, la "terciopelo" es un tipo de serpiente, de color negro, conocida y temida por la letalidad de su veneno'.[17]

In the novel's final section, the pervasive blackness which envelops the country becomes inextricably linked with death. Guatemala slumbers beneath the shadow of dictatorship; the dark, natural world beyond the city offers the hope of rebirth; but in order to be in a position to develop these hopes one must first flee the country. The opening chapter of Part Three, entitled 'Habla en la sombra', consists of the dialogue of a group of prisoners, isolated from each other by the impenetrable darkness of their dungeon, struggling to communicate with one another. The image stands for the country as a whole. In the words of the 'second voice', 'A ratos me imagino que la ciudad entera se ha quedado en tinieblas como nosotros, presa entre altísimas murallas, con las calles en el fango muerto de todos los inviernos' (SP, 227).

The chapter concludes with an exhortation to '¡...sigan hablando!' (SP, 232). Having incorporated the concept of the unity of the 'raza' into its ideology during its detour through the countryside—a movement analogous to Asturias's repositioning of himself as a 'Maya' within Paris—the text now portrays the chaos and injustice of Guatemalan society as consequences of a false consciousness which denies that unity. When the lawyer Carvajal is executed by firing squad, his widow thinks:

No era posible que lo fusilaran hombres así, gente con el mismo color de piel, con el mismo acento de voz, con la misma manera de ver, de oír, de acostarse, de levantarse, de amar, de lavarse la cara, de comer, de reír, de andar, con las mismas creencias y las mismas dudas. (SP, 249)

But the unity which Caravajal's widow invokes is not axiomatic. Since it depends upon the unity of a mixed race, of which the dominant component (ethnically, though not economically) belongs to an animist culture, the consciousness of an integrated 'alma nacional' must be nurtured through a heightened awareness of the rural environment and the natural forces from which this darker element springs. Cara de Angel and Camila are inducted into this consciousness in the chapter entitled 'Luz para ciegos'. Emblematic of the novel's retreat to the countryside, this chapter depicts a rebirth into light—but a light emanating from dark natural sources—for the beleaguered (and, in Camila's case, recuperating) couple. Their initiation into a more authentic, rooted conception of their own beings extends their perceptions of reality while at the same time heightening their awareness of the inherent precariousness of an identity based on the union of two different races. Stumbling across the yard on her cane, Camila feels that '[h]abía muerto sin dejar de existir, como en un sueño, revivía juntando lo que en realidad era ella con lo que estaba soñando' (*SP*, 266). Her incorporation, while in a state resembling that of the 'recién nacida', of a dimension beyond lived experience into her self-image evokes the process Asturias himself was undergoing in coming to terms with the Indian as an integral component of his own creative identity. Similarly, Cara de Angel's vestigial doubts about the marriage echo social concerns as loudly as personal ones. Given the novel's association of him with *ladino* whiteness and of Camila with the darker natural world, Cara de Angel's feeling of apartness from Camila epitomizes the Guatemalan bourgeoisie's unresolved tensions concerning its own origin in miscegenation: 'Se sentía separado de Camila por una falta que ninguno de los dos había cometido, por un matrimonio para el que ninguno de los dos había dejado su consentimiento' (*SP*, 267–8). This unease arises as the consequence of Cara de Angel's effort to extend his awareness beyond the comfortable, hypocritical boundaries of *ladino* convention. The natural world in which they immerse themselves remains foreign to their alienated consciousnesses. The narrator evokes this world in terms of shadow, of a darkness that liberates by traducing urban norms. The reader is told: 'Las sombras de los árboles manchaban las camisas blancas' of the merchants; the alligators of the 'Camino al destierro' chapter, shrunken to newts, are evoked as 'lagartijas relumbrantes, en la penumbra, que se iba haciendo oscura miel de talco a medida que penetraban en el bosque' (*SP*, 268). Yet as they enter the baths which represent their renewal through immersion in natural essences, the narrative emphasizes the couple's fundamental separateness. The caretaker who looks after the baths leads them to 'dos aposentillos divididos por una pared. Cada cual ocupó el suyo' (*SP*, 269). The paradox that emerges in this passage is that, although different, Camila and Cara de Angel—like the Maya and the *ladino*—are accustomed to inhabiting the same territory: 'lejos uno del otro, se encontraban extraños' (*SP*, 269). The experience of their immersion in nature enables them to convert mere proximity into union. Cara de Angel relinquishes the ideology that accords primacy to the presumption of 'civilization' when he thinks:

'¡Ser hombre, cuando mejor sería ser árbol, nube, libélula, burbuja o burrión!' (*SP*, 269). The narrator ceases to focus on the couple's separation from one another in their respective bathing cubicles, the description shifting its emphasis to their common experience of immersion in the same waters:

El agua saltaba con ellos como animal contento. [...] Penetraba la atmósfera el olor del suquinay, la presencia ausente de los volcanes, la humedad de las pancitas de las ranas, el aliento de los terneros que mamaban praderas transformadas en líquido blanco, la frescura de las cascadas que nacían riendo, el vuelo inquieto de las moscas verdes. Los envolvía un velo impalpable de haches mudas, el canto de un guardabarranca y el revoloteo de un shara. (*SP*, 269–70)

The natural lushness enveloping them produces an atmosphere in which sexual desire creates a bond 'sellando el tácito acuerdo que entre los dos faltaba' (*SP*, 271). The passage acts both as a description of the circumstances of the early stages of a particular marriage and, at an allegorical level, as a mapping-out of the transculturation process which the text proposes as the solution to Guatemalan backwardness.

This process derives its validity from its fidelity to the nation's *mestizo* essence, its 'alma nacional' expressed as an emanation of the natural world. Camila and Cara de Angel, the reader learns, repeatedly tell each other: 'Si el azar no nos hubiera juntado...' (*SP*, 272). The phrase's significance resonates beyond the limits of their own relationship to conjure up the pivotal moment of Guatemalan history: the collision of Spanish and Mayan worlds described in 'El tesoro del lugar florido'. Subsequent imagery sustains this theme. When Camila and Cara de Angel make love, they are described as being 'en feliz concierto con los árboles recién inflados de aire vegetal verde y con los pedacitos de carne envueltos en plumas de colores que volaban más ligero que el eco' (*SP*, 272). The couple's association with images of greenery reinforces their alliance with the natural world. These images also contain nods in the direction of the Mayan past, in the metonymical reference to birds as 'plumas de colores' making flights 'más ligero que el eco'. The passage describing their bathing offers a similar allusion to echoes of the Mayan rituals of the nation's past in its mention of 'la presencia ausente de los volcanes'. The apparent paradox of this phrase refers both to the volcanoes' extinction and, given Asturias's use of the volcanic eruption in 'El tesoro del lugar florido', to the persistence of the Mayan heritage. The merging of the residue of the indigenous past with the expressions of natural forces has been presaged earlier in the novel by descriptions of Camila's eyes, which while Mayan in shape are green in colour.

As a result of their more integrated, authentic sense of themselves, Camila and Cara de Angel no longer fit in at the President's party; they feel 'como en casa ajena' (*SP*, 272). In political terms, Cara de Angel loses his influence by becoming the renegade Canales's son-in-law; at a symbolic level, this affiliation converts him into the agent, within the Guatemalan shadow, of Canales's exile's enlightenment. The illumination offered by Guatemalan 'progress', as the description of 'la luz muerta de las calles' (*SP*, 273) makes clear, can only suppress the life-affirming forces Camila and Cara de Angel have discovered. They cannot overcome the dictatorship's theft of the light; possessed of a firm sense of themselves, they none the less lack the requisite consciousness to parlay their insights into actions. Their liberation remains partial and ultimately impotent, stunted by the impoverishing dictatorship under which it has taken place. A concerted effort to overthrow the dictator requires the illumination provided by the world beyond Guatemala. It is General Canales, who has viewed the country from without, who mounts a military campaign against the President. His death from poisoning is attended by the victory of unrelenting blackness: 'Los fuegos de los "vivacs" se fueron apagando y todo fue una gran masa oscura, una solíngrima tiniebla' (*SP*, 280–1).

Canales's ironic polar opposite emerges in the form of the gigantic, drunken gringo Mr Gengis, an imperialist supporter of the President, who, owing to his long immersion in the Guatemalan darkness, betrays 'ademanes y gestos de negro a pesar de ser blanco' (*SP*, 283). Mr Gengis urges Cara de Angel to save himself by pledging eternal allegiance to the President. The interview during which Cara de Angel attempts to do this is framed by two unusual scenes which break the flow of the narrative. The first, a lengthy document supporting the President's re-election, bombastically proclaims the President's kinship with (and even superiority to) European culture; the second, occurring after the President has ordered Cara de Angel to travel to Washington on his behalf, consists of a vision of primitive sacrifice that overwhelms Cara de Angel's consciousness, equating the President with Tohil, the Quiché god of fire.

The government pronouncement reasserts the President's prerogative to define and give meaning to the ideology of progress. In a parody of the novel itself, the declaration opens with the key word 'alumbrar': 'Pronunciar el nombre del Señor Presidente de la República, es alumbrar [...] los inapreciables beneficios del Progreso' (*SP*, 285). In an oblique, unintentionally satirical form, the document articulates the dictator's perversion of Enlightenment ideals:

> La Democracia acabó con los Emperadores y los Reyes en la vieja y fatigada Europa, mas, preciso reconocer es, y lo reconocemos, que trasplantada a América sufre el injerto cuasi divino del Superhombre y da contextura a una nueva forma de gobierno: la Superdemocracia. (*SP*, 287)

This hymn of praise skirts inadvertent condemnation of the system it purports to laud. In striving to portray the President's perpetual re-election as an improved form of democracy, the document draws an unwitting parallel between his 'Superdemocracia' and the emperors and kings whose reigns democracy brought to an end in Europe. The clumsy language, exposing meanings the President's supporters wish to conceal, enables Asturias to ridicule the dictatorship's assumption of the role of bearer of the European cultural heritage. Yet when the declaration states that 'trasplantada a América sufre el injerto cuasi divino del Superhombre', the implications resonate beyond mere satire of a low-brow dictatorship's intellectual presumption. At the level of ironic social critique, the passage alleges the inappropriateness of wholesale transplantation of European models into American soil; but beneath this level of meaning the ambivalent use of the verb 'sufre' hints that it is vaunted European cultural norms which are cruelly debased by American experience, not the reverse. Asturias's satire criticizes the dictator as harshly for his perversion of the shining ideals of Europe as for the misery he has inflicted on his people. The hierarchy of values propelling this criticism emphasizes the point of origin of the novel's attack on the dictatorship within an ideologically cohesive, European-oriented *ladino* class.

This aspect of the satirical presentation of the President's pronouncement raises again the question of the bonds linking the *ladino* awakening into a fuller consciousness of national realities to the Maya whose majority role in national society has been repressed and forgotten. Rodríguez, interpreting the portrait of the Maya as static throughout the novel, writes that

> La contradicción que se observa entre la presencia del indio en la sociedad guatemalteca y la tendencia de Asturias a desdibujarle y negarle su valor humano en la narración corresponde a una contradicción objetiva que se da

en el seno de la sociedad chapina y *El Señor Presidente* no hace más que
hacerse eco de ella. (*La problemática*, 131)

Yet, as has been argued above, Cara de Angel's awareness of the rural,
Mayan world does grow through his marriage to Camila. Canales's
flight into exile serves to posit this universe, albeit firmly subordinated
within the boundaries of a romanticizing *ladino* nationalist ideology, as
a counterweight to the President's perverted version of 'progress'. As
he receives the President's orders to undertake the mission which he
correctly suspects will lead to his death, Cara de Angel's mind is
gripped by the reverie that represents the culmination of his welling
liminal awareness of Mayan culture. His mental turmoil summons
up all the colours which have served as components in the novel's
mobile patterns of imagery: 'Por una ventana abierta de par en par
entre sus cejas negras distinguía una fogata encendida junto a cipresales
de carbón verdoso y tapias de humo blanco, en medio de un
patio borrado por la noche' (*SP*, 291). The image of fire—light
in its Promethean form, supplying progress while threatening
enslavement—juxtaposed with 'cipresales de carbón verdoso y tapias
de humo blanco' (representing the natural and rural worlds
respectively) encapsulates the novel's unifying tensions. The 'patio
borrado por la noche' on which these opposing forces meet,
reiterating the images of blackness associated with the nation
throughout Part Three, symbolizes the Guatemalan background
against which the struggle unfolds. Viewed from beneath Cara de
Angel's 'cejas negras', these primary elements of the novel's symbolic
structure—illumination, nature, greenness, whiteness, the all-
enveloping night—coalesce into a hallucination in which a Mayan
ceremony acts out the origins of the Guatemalan people's vul-
nerability to the appeal represented by a dictatorship such as that of
the President. Cara de Angel envisions the crowd 'reclamando a Tohil,
Dador del Fuego, que les devolviera el ocote encendido de la luz'
(*SP*, 291; original emphasis). In order to regain the torch whose loss
they lament—a versatile image evoking both *ladino* shame at inhabiting a 'backward' country and Mayan melancholy at the
obliteration of past grandeur—the people are willing to accept a
worse-than-Faustian pact. The price Tohil demands for restoring the
flame is that the people agree to hunt each other down like animals.

'Y estos hombres, ¡qué! ¿cazarán hombres?', preguntó Tohil [...] ¡Como tú
lo pides—respondieron las tribus—, con tal que nos devuelvas el fuego, tú,

el *Dador del Fuego* […]. ¡Con tal que no se nos siga muriendo la vida, aunque nos degollemos todos para que siga viviendo la muerte!' '¡Estoy contento!', dijo Tohil […]. '¡Estoy contento! Sobre hombres cazadores de hombres puedo asentar mi gobierno. No habrá ni verdadera muerte ni verdadera vida'. (*SP*, 292)

Guatemala has bought a twisted sort of progress at the cost of ceding the moral content of civilized societies: in return for a few sparks of knowledge—or an ideology pretending to transmit such knowledge[18]—the people have agreed to slaughter each other in the manner exemplified by the firing squad that executes Carvajal (and, a few pages later, by Farfán who, owing his life to Cara de Angel, proceeds to arrest, imprison and torture his saviour). Cara de Angel's vision, employing Mayan imagery to express dilemmas of bourgeois *ladino* nationalism (in this case, the roots of the dictatorship which by allying the oligarchy with foreign capital stifles the aspirations of the professional classes) foreshadows Asturias's subsequent fiction. Most notably among the later novels, *Hombres de maíz* and *Mulata de tal* start from the point at which Cara de Angel's psyche arrives in the final chapter of *El señor presidente* in which he retains his physical freedom. The Indian has become the source of an interpretative code: the pure being whose shrouded rituals act out the veiled truths swathed by the hypocrisy of *ladino* convention. At the same time, the Mayan reality is one whose nuances Cara de Angel—and Asturias behind him—will never fully grasp. As Rodríguez contends:

Tohil simplemente no formaba parte de su herencia cultural, la de los españoles o ladinos. Por eso se paraliza, a pesar de la furia que lo posee. El mundo de Cara de Angel ha sido el racional, el europeo. Irónicamente, la parodia de Descartes hecha por Miguel, 'primero pienso con la cabeza del Señor Presidente, luego existo', […] subraya lo poco que su educación europea le sirve a la hora de tomar decisiones vitales en un ambiente regido por fuerzas irracionales. (*La problemática*, 47–8)

Despite her acute reading of the feelings of alienation gripping Cara de Angel at this juncture, Rodríguez's interpretation overestimates the extent to which the Guatemalan environment, as portrayed by Asturias, is 'regido por fuerzas irracionales'. The President is not a creation of Mayan sorcery, but of the present *ladino* bourgeoisie's betrayal of the national interest.[19] The narrative invokes the image of Tohil as an allegorical expression of this treachery. Asturias's own essay on the novel, 'El "Señor Presidente" como mito', reiterates this intention: 'En el capítulo XXXVII asistimos al baile de Tohil. Tohil, la divinidad indígena maya-quiché que exigía sacrificios humanos. ¿Qué otra cosa exigía el Señor Presidente? Sacrificios humanos'.[20] The use of Indian imagery to articulate liberal nationalist concerns is of pioneering significance. Beverley and Zimmerman, for example, write of 'the tendency in Guatemalan literature from Asturias on to allegorize the state of nature as a political force against the depredations of an imperialist "civilization"' (*Literature and Politics*, 168). This allegory-making, however, is situated within a *ladino* perception of national reality. Asturias's ultimate decision to abandon his provisional title, *Tohil* (indicative of how the Maya might refer to the President in Quiché) for *El señor presidente* (which, as he had observed in *El problema social del indio*, was how the Maya referred to the President when speaking Spanish) underlines the novel's assumption of an assimilating, *mestizo*izing national norm.

The mission to Washington, which leads to Cara de Angel's doom, teases him with the possibility of escape. During the last night that he spends with Camila, Cara de Angel 'no se atrevía a apagar la luz, ni a cerrar los ojos, ni a decir palabra. Estaban tan cerca en la claridad [...]. Y luego en la oscuridad era como estar lejos' (*SP*, 294–5). Light offers them the possibility of greater self-realization and intimacy; the darkness can only divide and destroy them. The pattern of imagery— foreign light versus Guatemalan shadow—remains consistent and condemnatory throughout the novel's final chapters. Cara de Angel's perception that the only feasible route to the future passes by way of foreign illumination is partly responsible for his compliance with the President's orders; he hopes that he will be able to smuggle Camila out of the country at a later date. As he approaches the port, he begins to assume the exile's nostalgia towards his homeland:

Aquella tierra de asidua primavera era su tierra, su ternura, su madre, y por mucho que resucitara al ir dejando atrás aquellas aldeas, siempre estaría muerto entre los vivos, eclipsado entre los hombres de los otros países por la presencia invisible de sus árboles en cruz y de sus piedras para tumbas. (*SP*, 297)

This passage, according Cara de Angel access to insights for which he does not yet possess an experiential basis, discloses the novel's thematic roots in the Spanish American exile community in Paris. Cara de Angel envisages himself, the emissary of a land of death where trees become crosses and stones become tombs, as 'muerto entre los vivos', rather than as basking in the light of civilization (as Asturias portrayed himself doing in his first enthusiastic articles from Paris). Cara de Angel, then, adopts the mentality of the long-term exile, not that of the young man going abroad for the first time.[21]

In tandem with his relatively subtle presentation of the changes in Cara de Angel's and Camila's respective positions within Guatemalan society, Asturias employs direct authorial intervention stemming from an older, nineteenth-century realist mode of writing. When Cara de Angel saves Farfán's life, for example, the narrator writes: 'Al marcharse el mayor, Cara de Angel se tocó para saber si era el mismo que a tantos había empujado hacia la muerte, el que ahora, ante el azul infrangible de la mañana, empujaba a un hombre hacia la vida' (SP, 207).

A similar patchwork approach, mingling nineteenth-century devices with avant-garde innovations, emerges at the level of the novel's techniques for generating imagery. Some critics read Asturias's quest for striking images and startling linguistic juxtapositions as a virtually unadulterated emanation of Surrealism. Gerald Martin, the most enthusiastic proponent of this view, contends that 'The President exemplifies more clearly than any other novel the crucial link between European Surrealism and Latin American Magic Realism. It is, indeed, the first fully-fledged Surrealist novel in Latin America' (Journeys Through the Labyrinth, 149). At the opposite extreme, Carlos Rincón claims that the methods employed by Asturias in El señor presidente 'nada tienen que ver con el surrealismo' ('Nocciones Surrealistas', 35). Uslar Pietri cuts a middle course, arguing that what has been interpreted as Asturias's Surrealism is simply naturalistic description of the atmosphere of extreme insecurity imposed by the dictatorship under which the author grew up:

La atmósfera de pasión, delación y venganzas secretas en la que vive el joven Asturias llega a crear una sobrerrealidad en la que los seres y las cosas dejan de ser lo que debían ser para convertirse en fantasmas o apariencias de lo que súbitamente pueden llegar a ser. Todo es transitorio, falso y cambiante. (Fantasmas de dos mundos, 18–19)

This position, however, leaves open the question of the process by which Asturias developed his literary techniques. Angel Rama goes part of the way towards resolving the dilemma by emphasizing that even when immersed in pure linguistic play, Asturias's ultimate allegiance remained to a society rather than to a conception of language. Bearing in mind Deleuze and Guattari's point that in a 'minor' literature the writer 'commence par énoncer, et ne voit et ne conçoit qu'après' (*Kafka*, 51), it is none the less clear that Asturias's overriding concern was to invent imaginatively, through his immersion in language, a recognizable Guatemalan reality capable of hosting a viable 'alma nacional'. Rama writes:

Miguel Angel Asturias ha declarado que sus primeros libros (*Leyendas de Guatemala, El señor presidente*) manejan los recursos de la 'escritura automática' que fue el gozoso descubrimiento de los surrealistas en los años veinte [...]. La lectura de ambos libros no corrobora enteramente el aserto: la voluntad del estilo poético que allí se manifiesta, las buscadas asociaciones de significantes para crear una melopea sonora, resultan más cercanas a las experiencias con la 'jitanjáfora' que practicaba Mariano Brull que a los productos franceses de la 'escritura automática' donde se construían significados irracionales. E incluso cuando se abordan estas desconexiones del sentido es perceptible la apelación a coartadas realistas que permiten una justificación realista. (*La novela*, 323–4)

Asturias acknowledged his familiarity with the 'jitanjáfora' and recognized this form of wordplay as a distinctive product of the Spanish American avant-garde. It is significant that in response to a question from López Alvarez about Surrealism, Asturias digressed at length into a discussion of the 'jitanjáfora':

Ya la palabra 'jitanjáfora' se había inventado en América. [...] Es una onomatopeya que quiere decir y no quiere decir nada.
   [...] No obstante su calidad de embajador, Alfonso Reyes se reunía con nosotros en los cafés de Montparnasse y nos presentaba 'jitanjáforas' muy bellas.
   Participó también en estos juegos Arturo Uslar Pietri, el cual ha publicado treinta y cinco años después un libro de poemas en Venezuela en el que encontramos muchas 'jitanjáforas'. (*Conversaciones*, 84–5)

But Asturias's innovations in language and imagery in *El señor presidente* extend beyond the realm of wordplay. His ultimate appeal, as Rama argues, continues to be to 'coartadas realistas'; but this realism is often presented through techniques whose predilection for violent distortion of both language and the personal characteristics of individuals does resemble certain effects created by Surrealism. As Campion writes:

Many of the scenes, images and verbal structures of *El señor Presidente* partake of the surrealist spirit. The galleries of grotesques, the smashing together of juxtaposed images, words and syllables, the dream sequences and cinematic 'jump cuts' all fall within the surrealist vocabulary.[22]

The relatively late date of Asturias's awareness of Surrealism, the lack of persuasive evidence of extensive Surrealist reading on his part at this time and the fact that most of his knowledge of Surrealism was probably gleaned aurally through his conversations with Robert Desnos makes the reading of *El señor presidente* as a Surrealist by-product, sustained by critics such as Campion and Martin, difficult to uphold. If, as Kristeva writes, 'tout texte est absorption et transformation d'un autre texte' (*Sémeiotiké*, 85), then such telling influences must be assimilated through the author's reading of a written text; a café sermon on Surrealist aesthetics would not have sufficed to alter Asturias's style. While 'jitanjáfora' may account for the wordplay in *El señor presidente*, it does not supply a literary aesthetic capable of providing a basis for systematic distortions of reality such as those that occur in the 'Ojo de vidrio' chapter, upon which Campion bases his 'Surrealist' reading. The disembodied eye that symbolizes Genaro Rodas's guilty conscience by floating persistently through his hands then virtually swallowing him ('el ojo creció en la sombra con tanta rapidez que en un segundo abarcó las paredes, el piso, el techo, las casas, su vida, su hijo...' (*SP*, 89)) might conceivably originate in Asturias's reading of Freud, but in order to explain the literary embodiment of such symbols one needs to look beyond either Surrealism or psychoanalysis to the writers whom Asturias is known to have read during his formative years as a student in Guatemala and the early years of his sojourn in Paris.

Two late nineteenth-century French writers stand out among Asturias's early influences. The first of these, as Carlos Rincón posits, was the author of

un libro llegado a Guatemala en 1920 en un único ejemplar. Asturias y sus compañeros se lo habrían arrebatado de las manos. Se trata del mismo texto cuya lectura está en los orígenes del intento surrealista de desarrollar determinados procedimientos automáticos del dadaísmo como vía para superar el estatus de la autonomía del arte uniéndolo a la vida: *Les chants de Maldoror*. ('Nociones Surrealistas', 52–3)

Though he had read few Surrealist texts, Asturias was setting out from the same literary point of departure as that from which the Surrealists had embarked. Furthermore, as a writer raised in Spanish America who forged his career of aesthetic rebellion in Europe,

Lautréamont provided a compelling symbol of the kind of literary trajectory which might be available to writers such as Asturias. A Frenchman out of place in France, expressing his alienation through violent, scatological imagery, Lautréamont legitimated the marginal position within French letters: his standing, unlike that of, say, Zola or Flaubert (unshakeably central figures however controversial) was one to which a Spanish American outsider might realistically aspire. It proved that a validated status for outsiders existed within French literary culture. At the same time, Lautréamont's odyssey from Montevideo to Paris confirmed the essential rightness of the physical displacement which Asturias and most young Spanish American literary intellectuals of his generation longed to undertake. In an article written nearly fifty years after his discovery of Lautréamont, Asturias's youthful enthusiasm remains palpable:

Lautréamont entró a nuestras vidas—hablo de los que decidimos dedicarnos a la literatura en 1920—después de la primera guerra […]. ¿Qué fue para los entonces veinteañeros lectores ya 'infectados' de Verlaine, Baudelaire y Rimbaud aquel pedazo de infierno que se nos ponía en las manos? Desde luego fue un mensaje de rebelión total. No lo leíamos, lo gritábamos, hubiéramos querido convertirlo en látigo para sacarnos nosotros mismos del templo de la rutina y el ripio de los modernistas, de nuestros modernistas. […]
   Los *cantos de maldoror* se desdoblan en columnas, en legiones de palabras de protesta, de denuncia y de testimonio. No literatura para nada. Literatura para algo más que escribir por escribir, para denunciar las dictaduras hispanoamericanas, la explotación de los peones miserables en 'tierras opulentas', el entreguismo al capital extranjero, la condición del indio, cada vez más esclavo. Todo este mundo de protesta estaba en nuestros pechos, y afloró, cuando nos pusimos en contacto de la vida, golpeados por el rayo maldoriano que nos alumbró y deslumbró. Lautréamont nos revelaba el nuevo valor de las palabras. (*Fábula de fábulas*, 82–4)

The illumination provided by Lautréamont, Asturias maintains, enabled him to fuse aesthetic innovation, breaking out of the cul de sac of 'nuestros modernistas', with a writing of sheer revolt against 'las dictaduras hispanoamericanas' such as that of Estrada Cabrera. *El señor presidente* provides ample evidence of this harnessing of Romantic disenchantment and aesthetic renovation to political ends. Asturias's pivotal rewriting of *Les Chants de Maldoror* is marked by his politicization of the notion of revolt. Lautréamont presents his repellent, scatological, often sexually shocking imagery as the outpouring of unbridled misanthropy:

Ma poésie ne consistera qu'à attaquer, par tous les moyens, l'homme, cette bête fauve, et le Créateur, qui n'aurait pas dû engendrer une pareille vermine. Les volumes s'entasseront sur les volumes, jusqu'à la fin de ma vie, et, cependant, l'on n'y verra que cette seule idée toujours présente à ma conscience.[23]

In *El señor presidente* the attack is narrower and more focused. The calculated repulsiveness of certain scenes and motifs—Pelele's falling asleep in a heap of refuse and being gnawed by vultures while still alive, Fedina Rodas's night in a prison cell in the company of the corpse of her baby son, the repeated background descriptions of dogs urinating and vomiting (e.g. 'Un perro vomitaba en la reja del Sagrario' (*SP*, 74))—collaborate to generate a portrait of life under the President's rule as a perversion of human norms. In this way, Asturias turns the spirit and devices of Lautréamont's writing to his own ends, just as the Surrealists developed a more aesthetically oriented species of rebellion from their reading of *Maldoror*. It is a mistake, therefore, to see *El señor presidente* as the product of Surrealism, when in fact both derived from a common ancestor. The impact of Lautréamont's writing on the form of Asturias's fiction is critical. Where the Surrealists despised the novel, Asturias was striving to develop fresh novelistic forms; it is significant that the lone Surrealist work which Asturias clearly read and paid homage to, Desnos's *La liberté ou l'amour!*, represents one of Surrealism's closest approaches to the novel.[24] This crucial aspect of his literary apprenticeship was one in which Surrealism could offer little help. Lautréamont, however, played an important role in Asturias's quest, not only in providing him with an aesthetic of disenchantment to fuel his experiments in *El señor presidente*, but also, at the level of structure, in his later work: *Hombres de maíz*, like *Les Chants de Maldoror*, consists of six loosely linked panels fitted together to create an overarching novelistic effect.

The price Asturias paid for acquiring his literary ideology of rebellion by way of Lautréamont is underlined by his acceptance, however qualified by quotation marks, of the European construction of nations such as Guatemala as 'tierras opulentas'. The narrator of *El señor presidente* often appeals to preconceived notions of exoticism embedded in the consciousness of an implied European reader. As in some of Asturias's earlier journalism and fiction, these evocations depend on Orientalist constructions of alien cultures that gather the traits of all 'backward' nations under the rubric of Far Eastern exoticism. The narrator describes the city's poorest districts as being scarred by 'una miseria sucia con restos de abandono oriental' (*SP*, 86). The account of Fedina Rodas's night sheltering the body of her baby son explains that 'Era suya la alegría de las mujeres que se enterraban con sus amantes en el Oriente sagrado' (*SP*, 178). This internalization of a particular Parisian view of the Other dwelling beyond the perimeter of European civilization, engendered by Romanticism and persisting into the works of early twentieth-century writers such as the Surrealists and André Malraux, lies behind the narrator's occasional separation from his material. In some passages the narrator speaks directly to the presumed European reader: 'Las noches de abril son en el trópico las viudas de los días cálidos de marzo' (*SP*, 100).

The other late nineteenth-century French writer instrumental in forging Asturias's conception of automatic writing and influencing his elaboration of literary techniques, often resembling those of Surrealism, designed to liberate the impulses and desires lying latent in the mind, was Remy de Gourmont. While Asturias's journalism ignores the Surrealists, Gourmont is referred to with reverence. Writing of a 1925 tour of an unidentified Paris library, Asturias lists the two highlights of his visit as being the manuscript of Victor Hugo's *Les Misérables* and

un manuscrito de Remy de Gourmont, el inimitable. A través de sus páginas creí que llegaba a nosotros, al recinto de la biblioteca, aquella su espiritualidad de enfermo y exquisito, de rey de los encajes más finos que en literatura galante y sexual se han hecho. Sobre el papel, un papel cualquiera, las letras señalaron infinitos anhelos, desconocidos momentos de la emoción sexual, afinada, exprimida, purificada a través de su vida dolorosa y terrible. (*París 1924–1933*, 34)

An article published in 1926 is inspired by Asturias's reading of Gourmont's decadent novel, *Sixtine* (*París 1924–1933*, 91); a piece from 1929 alludes to 'uno de los admirables cuentos de Remy de Gourmont' (*París 1924–1933*, 390). But as the article about the library visit indicates, Asturias's acquaintance with Gourmont's work predated his arrival in Paris. As editor of the influential journal *Le Mercure de France*, which served as probably the most important single source of information on European artistic developments for young Spanish American intellectuals, Gourmont played a pivotal role in Rubén Darío's formulation of *modernismo*. In October 1897,

Gourmont introduced a regular column in the *Mercure de France* called 'Lettres Latino-Américaines'.[25] This section ensured *Le Mercure de France*'s status as 'la revista francesa más leída y comentada en todos los núcleos cultos de las ciudades, grandes o no, de América latina' (*París 1924–1933*, 749). Gourmont's reputation in French literary circles waned quickly after his death in 1915. His influence on Spanish American writers—and their gratitude to Gourmont for his assiduous publicizing of Spanish American writing in France—proved more enduring.[26] During a memorial service for Gourmont held in Coutances in 1922, Baldomero Sanín-Cano, editor of *La Nación* of Buenos Aires, made a speech in which he said:

Aucun écrivain contemporain n'exerça sur l'intelligence américaine d'origine latine la douce, la bienfaisante, la très grande et la très profonde influence de Remy de Gourmont. Les grandes idées de l'époque nous parvinrent reflétées par le cristal vénitien de cette haute intelligence. Nous apprîmes par lui à connaître non seulement les formes de l'art nouveau dont commençait à rêver la jeunesse française mais également ce qu'il y avait d'original et digne d'attention dans l'art et la littérature des autres pays européens. [...] Nous tirâmes des forces vives pour créer l'œuvre nécessaire de notre rénovation.[27]

The literary innovations paraded by *El señor presidente* form part of the 'forces vives' drawn from Gourmont to fuel the renewal of Spanish American writing. While Gourmont made his greatest immediate impact on *modernismo*, his neo-symbolist theories, incorporating an awareness of new approaches to psychology, laid the groundwork for the creed of automatic writing and the revelatory nature of dreams expressed in different ways by both Asturias and Surrealism. In an essay first published in July 1900, Gourmont wrote:

L'état subconscient est l'état de cérébration automatique, en pleine liberté, l'activité intellectuelle évoluant à la limite de la conscience, un peu au-dessous, hors de ses atteintes [...].

La seule quête du mot dans le vaste et profond réservoir de la mémoire verbale est un acte qui échappe si bien à la volonté que, souvent, le mot qui venait s'enfuit au moment où la conscience allait l'apercevoir et le saisir. On sait combien il est difficile de trouver volontairement le mot dont on a besoin et on sait aussi avec quelle aisance et quelle rapidité tels écrivains évoquent, dans la fièvre de l'écriture, les mots les plus insolites, ou les plus beaux.[28]

This passage contains the kernel of André Breton's definition of Surrealism: 'Dictée de la pensée, en l'absence de tout contrôle exercé

par la raison, en dehors de toute préoccupation esthétique ou morale'
(*Manifestes du Surréalisme*, 40). Surrealism set the 'automatic' forces
of the non-conscious mind to the task of a ruthlessly individualist
liberation. Jacqueline Chénieux-Gendron argues that despite this
seemingly atomistic focus, Surrealism did contain the implicit promise
of a broader social morality: 'L'unification intérieure, la redécouverte
de ses forces subconscientes, va de pair avec la perception des liens
qui relient l'individu au cosmos' (*Le Surréalisme*, 38). But in formu-
lating his interpretation of these concepts, Asturias, drenched in
politics since early childhood, required a theory permitting tighter
links between the unfathomable inner world of the individual and the
concrete domain of society than those posited by most of the
Surrealists. Asturias's accomplice in this reworking appears to have
been Freud. (It is significant that where both Gourmont and the
Surrealists employ a Jungian vocabulary, speaking of the 'subconscious' mind, Asturias follows Freud in preferring the
'unconscious'.) During his 1928 speaking tour of Guatemala, Asturias
described the 'inconsciente' as 'esta región del espíritu donde están
encerradas las llaves de nuestra actividad mental, sentimental y
material' (*París 1924–1933*, 257). The third term in Asturias's list of
activities explains his divergence from the path leading from
Gourmont to Surrealism: the material world continues to provide the
core of his intellectual concern. His synopsis of the importance of
dreams illustrates the gulf separating him from Surrealism. In one of
the key texts of Surrealism, Louis Aragon wrote: 'Rêves, rêves, rêves,
tout n'est que rêve où le vent erre, et les chiens aboyeurs sortent
sur les chemins'.[29] In contrast to this ethereal universe, Asturias's
depiction of the possibilities of dreams occurs within the context of
a tangible reality directed towards concerns which are pragmatic,
functional, even policy-oriented. Invoking Freud, Asturias tells his
audience that

todo deseo no satisfecho ni confesado se *refulla*, se refunde, quiere decir [...]
en el inconsciente. Los sueños los explica por medio de estos deseos
inconfesados o insatisfechos que si perdimos de la memoria, del inconsciente,
no; así también explica las obsesiones, las locuras, los crímenes. (*París
1924–1933*, 257)

The speedy digression into the social realm ('los crímenes') is
succeeded by a prescription which Asturias hopes will convert his
audience into better citizens. He calls upon them to 'construir vuestra

vida mental y afectiva a base de sinceridad y lo que toca al inconsciente es parte de lo que podía llamarse la higiene del deseo' (*París
1924–1933*, 257). The talk ends with a two-sentence paragraph
combining a call to 'engrandecer nuestra patria' with advice to utilize
an awareness of the unconscious to 'controlar vuestros deseos' (*París
1924–1933*, 258). For Asturias, the ideology of individual liberation
sketched by Gourmont develops into recommendations for reinforcing the foundations of Guatemalan nationalism; his embrace of
doctrines of decadent artistic rebellion exists in an unceasing dynamic
tension with his nationalist urges to improve the *patria*.

An important point of overlap between Asturias's concerns and those
of Gourmont lies in their respective pursuits of the construction of
affirmative images of eccentric cultural identities. One of Gourmont's
major works, *Le Latin mystique* (1892), analyses and defends the
'incorrect' Latin of medieval mystic poets. Gourmont is fascinated by
the paradoxical position of these Christian poets writing in Latin.
Straddling two worlds, the Christian and the pagan, they destroy classical
Latin style to evoke a 'barbarian' consciousness. According to
Gourmont it was at

[l]'époque précise où on la délaisse que la langue latine commence à offrir çà
et là les séductions de la décomposition stylistique, à s'exprimer non plus en
un immutable jargon de rhéteur, mais selon le tempérament personnel
d'orientaux ou de barbares étrangers à la discipline romaine,—jusqu'à ce
que la victoire définitive des idiomes populaires la relègue au musée
des instruments oratoires. Définitive, cette victoire, mais combien tardive:
longtemps les deux langues, la mère et la fille, vécurent côte à côte dans les
pays romans, parlées l'une et l'autre par de différents clients.[30]

Striking parallels arise between the cultural position of writers of
mystic Latin poems and Asturias's status and aims during his years in
Paris: his efforts to express his cultural 'temperament' by infusing
'immutable' Real Academia literary Spanish with Guatemalan
modismos and Maya-Quiché borrowings; his growing awareness,
during his Parisian sojourn, of having grown up in a society in which
two languages lived side by side, spoken by 'différents clients'; his self-
construction, within the Parisian context, as a pillaging Oriental or
Barbarian—a role both lauded and delimited by European Orientalist
ideology and European hunger, during the 1920s, for the liberation
promised by artistic currents originating in 'primitive' societies.

All of these tensions are worked through, to a point of preliminary resolution, in *El señor presidente*. The novel's movement from the corrupt order of the opening, in which the President and his minions have seized the light, to Cara de Angel's discovery, through his marriage into the Canales family, of the authentic illumination provided by the native cultures and natural essences surviving outside the city, to the President's stifling of the potential epitomized by their union, describes a transfer of allegiance from the city to the country. This shift serves as an allegorical representation of the process through which Asturias consolidated his reshaping of his own identity during his years in Paris. The novel denounces the urban landscape as irredeemably perverted, re-positioning in the countryside the moral values associated with political resistance, human decency and cultural self-confidence. Camila's affiliation with the dark, natural world, the rebirth of Cara de Angel and Camila in the spring water, Canales's flight back into the primitive rural society, the selfless assistance he receives there and the revolutionary action which, having seen Guatemala from the outside, he is able to launch across the border, all culminate in the novel's two final chapters.

One prominent strand of criticism interprets *El señor presidente* as a novel about stagnation whose lack of forward momentum incarnates its theme. Martin argues: 'Cara de Angel is in a sense a static figure, as all the characters are' ('How to Read It', 231). In a similar vein, Carlos Navarro writes: 'El lector experimenta la misma sensación que los personajes: nada transcurre. Las personas, los hechos, los lugares se repiten y son siempre los mismos.'[31] Yet the novel charts a perceptible evolution, an undeniable if ultimately fatal broadening of Cara de Angel's consciousness and significant transformations in the outlooks of both Camila Canales and her father. The imagery of the closing pages captures this motion. Twice in the chapter describing Cara de Angel's death in prison, the narrator repeats the phrase: 'Ya la luz se iba, aquella luz que se estaba yendo desde que venía' (*SP*, 311, 314). The point here is not Cara de Angel's impotence to effect change, but the pivotal event of his exposure to the 'luz' which has illumined his mental outlook. His prison dreams include memories of an Austrian pastoral landscape—a deft recapitulation of the novel's nationalist symbolism of European civilization embodied in rural purity, rather than drafted into the service of a brutal positivism—that he has glimpsed in a magazine called *La Ilustración* (*SP*, 313), a transparent reference to Enlightenment-inspired ideals. While the revolutionary student, wedded to the city, returns from prison to his mother's house 'al final de una calle sin salida' (*SP*, 319), Cara de Angel leaves behind him the legacy of a transferral of allegiance to the countryside. His son, also named Miguel, 'creció en el campo, fue hombre del campo, y Camila no volvió a poner los pies en la ciudad' (*SP*, 310). The statement confirms Asturias's constitution of his own literary identity as an 'hombre del campo' (or 'hombre de maíz', as his next novel would construe this allegiance). In situating himself in this landscape, Asturias was definitively relinquishing one possible source of Guatemalan identity—that of the urban, Europeanized *ladino*—in favour of the other, concealed face of Guatemalan reality. This tension, as Carlos Fuentes has pointed out, pervades the literature of many Spanish American societies:

Habitamos, simultáneamente, un país legal y un país real, ocultado por la fachada del primero. La otra nación, más allá de los espacios urbanos, el mundo arcaico, paciente, poblado por quienes aún no alcanzan la modernidad, sino que continúan sufriendo sus explotaciones, estaba allí para comentar, con ironía a veces, con rabia otras, sobre nuestro limitado progreso, en las ficciones míticas de Miguel Angel Asturias, en el encuentro con la naturaleza primigenia del venezolano Romulo Gallegos, en las construcciones barrocas del cubano Alejo Carpentier y en los desnudos mitos rurales del mexicano Juan Rulfo.[32]

Fuentes depicts Asturias, Gallegos, Carpentier and Rulfo, in their differing ways, as belonging to a cycle whose romanticization of the 'vasto espacio natural del Nuevo Mundo' closed when García Márquez, in *Cien años de soledad*, 'logra combinar el asombro de los primeros descubridores con la ironía de los últimos: nosotros mismos' (*SP*, 19). Asturias continues in large measure to discover his own rural society through the guise of a besotted European. Within the European context, however, he presented himself as the 'Gran Lengua' of the Maya, and the Maya, in turn, as the emblem of a reinforced Guatemalan nationhood. The outcome of this sort of strategy, as Todorov makes clear in his discussion of Hernán Cortés, is assimilation of the Indian into the European's quest for identity.

Cortés se glisse dans sa peau [celle de l'Indien], mais de façon métamorphique, et non plus littérale [...]. Il s'assure ainsi la compréhension de la langue, la connaissance de la politique [...], il maîtrise même l'émission des messages dans un code approprié: voilà qu'il se fait passer pour Quetzalcoatl revenu sur terre. Mais, ce faisant, il ne s'est jamais départi de son sentiment de supériorité; c'est même le contraire, sa capacité de comprendre l'autre la confirme. Vient alors le deuxième temps, au cours duquel il ne se contente pas de réaffirmer sa propre identité (qu'il n'a jamais vraiment quittée), mais il procède à l'assimilation des Indiens à son propre monde.[33]

Asturias, paradoxically, undertook the first phase of the process described by Todorov—that of entering into the Indian's culture—in Europe. The 'deuxième temps' of assimilation is realized in his writing. *El señor presidente* charts his evolution in response to Georges Raynaud's charge: 'Vous êtes maya'; *Hombres de maíz* and *Mulata de tal* complete the work of assimilating Indian imagery and identity into a *ladino* nationalist project. By forging his Indian link in Europe, Asturias constituted himself as a European in Guatemalan eyes while he was constituting himself as a Maya beneath the European gaze. The result of this contradictory movement was to alienate him from the world with which he had allied himself. Though representing Guatemala more thoroughly and effectively than any other international figure prior to the emergence of Rigoberta Menchú, Asturias approached the country, by the end of his Parisian sojourn, in the role of a displaced European adventurer whose ultimate allegiance was to the culture of France. As he was preparing to leave Paris in 1933, he wrote a telling farewell letter to his friend Jean Balard in which he depicted himself not as a Spanish American returning home, but as a European setting off to seek out the exotic world beyond Europe's borders: 'Je ne toucherai pas Marseille, ma route est celle de Rimbaud le Voyou, mais je reviendrai bien vite et spirituellement, je suis avec vous tous.'[34]

Asturias's equation of his journey with Rimbaud's departure for exile in Ethiopia foreshadowed an ironic parallel between their respective careers: both lapsed into creative sterility once they left France. Asturias, so prolific during his Parisian apprenticeship, would write only a handful of poems during his twelve years in Guatemala. His next Paris would be Buenos Aires, where he arrived in 1948, and where his creativity and literary career once again began to flourish.

In writing *El señor presidente*, Asturias confirmed his alienation from white, urban Guatemala. Yet in consolidating his identification with the countryside, he inevitably constructed himself in the role of the Europeanized outsider whose quest for his own transcultured roots fed upon the voyeuristic pursuit of exoticism. In so doing, Asturias fell prey to what Deleuze and Guattari categorize as one of the 'Dangers de la lutte minoritaire: se reterritorialiser, refaire des photos, refaire du pouvoir et de la loi, refaire aussi de la "grande littérature"'

(*Kafka*, 154). In his search for a viable 'alma nacional'—a form of 'reterritorialization' which, to evoke the image of General Canales's portrait album, risks 'retaking photographs'—Asturias erected the scaffolding of a new ideological hegemony over the traditional cultures of Guatemala at the same time that he was agitating for literary liberation of those cultures. These two impulses, poised in a tenuous balance, would generate the narrative universe of his subsequent novels.

Notes to Chapter 6

1. Asturias, *El problema social del indio y otros textos*, ed. Claude Couffon (Paris: Centre de Recherches de l'Institut d'Etudes Hispaniques, 1971), 60.
2. Georges Pillement, 'El París que Asturias ha visto y vivido', in Asturias, *París 1924–1933*, 747.
3. Asturias, *El señor presidente* (1946; Buenos Aires: Losada, 1991), 37. Henceforth *SP*.
4. Hugo Cerezo Dardón and Ricardo Estrada, Salvador Aguado-Andreut, Guillermo Putzeys, and Francisco Albizúrez (eds.), *Coloquio con Miguel Angel Asturias* (Guatemala: Editorial Universitaria Guatemala, 1968), 5.
5. Gerald Martin, 'Miguel Angel Asturias: *El señor presidente*', in *Landmarks in Latin American Fiction* , ed. Philip Swanson (London and New York: Routledge, 1990), 57.
6. Jack Himelblau, ' *El señor presidente*: Antecedents, Sources, and Reality', *Hispanic Review* 41/1 (Winter 1973), 49.
7. One important, possibly vital factor generating Asturias's modified perception of himself as a participant in French society lay in his liaison, from 1929, with Andrée Brossut. See Cardoza y Aragón, *Miguel Angel Asturias*, 176.
8. Carlos Rangel, *Del Buen Salvaje al Buen Revolucionario* (Caracas: Monte Avila, 1977), 304.
9. John Beverley and Marc Zimmerman, *Literature and Politics in the Central American Revolutions* (Austin: University of Texas Press, 1990), 20.
10. This literary community, in turn, represented a larger (and substantial) community of mainly middle- and upper-class Spanish Americans living in Paris. Marta Pilón, describing the ambience of Asturias's Parisian years, reports: 'La colonia guatemalteca residente en París era entonces grande, vivían cerca de 60 familias distinguidas' (*Miguel Angel Asturias: semblanza para el estudio de su vida y obra con una selección de poemas y prosas* (Guatemala: Cultural Centroamericana, 1968), 31).
11. Gilles Deleuze and Félix Guattari, *Kafka, pour une littérature mineure* (Paris: Editions de Minuit, 1975), 29.
12. Gerald Martin, ' *El señor Presidente* and How to Read It', *Bulletin of Hispanic Studies* 47/3 (July 1970), 231. Jean Franco offers a similar interpretation: 'The fight is the eternal fight between good and evil' (*The Modern Culture of Latin America* (London: Pall Mall Press, 1967), 230). James W. Brown, in discussing the novel's dialectical oppositions, speaks of 'the ultimate polarity: good and evil'

('A Topology of Dread—Spatial Oppositions in *El señor Presidente*', *Romanische Forschungen*, 98/3–4 (1986), 342). Dorita Nouhaud claims that 'Visage d'Ange est en effet "beau et méchant comme Satan"', insoutenable dichotomie que l'amour corrige, restituant un cœur au visage d'ange' ('M. le Président, fils présumé de Tirano Banderas et Juan Manuel Rosas, "un cadavre exquis"', in *Co-Textes No. 7: Miguel Angel Asturias*, ed. Jean-Marie Saint-Lu (Montpellier: Presses de l'Imprimerie de Recherche–Université Paul-Valéry, 1984), 60).

13. Cited by Himelblau, '*El señor presidente*', 45. I have been unable to identify the source from which Asturias was citing.

14. Angel Rama, *La novela en América Latina: Panoramas 1920–1980* (Bogotá: Procultura/Instituto Colombiano de Cultura, 1982), 209–10.

15. Marc Zimmerman, *Literature and Resistance in Guatemala: Textual Modes and Cultural Politics from* El Señor Presidente *to* Rigoberta Menchú (Athens, Ohio: Ohio University Center for International Studies, 1995), i. 133.

16. 'It was Theodore Roosevelt who embodied the self-righteous attitude of the USA towards its Latin American neighbours at the turn of the century [...]. This attitude led to intervention by US troops in several Central American and Caribbean countries, the overthrow of governments deemed hostile to US interests, and the installation of puppet dictators likely to be friendly to US investors'. Williamson, *The Penguin History of Latin America* (Harmondsworth: Penguin, 1992), 323–4.

17. Teresita Rodríguez, *La problemática de la identidad en* El Señor Presidente *de Miguel Angel Asturias* (Amsterdam-Atlanta: Rodopi, 1989), 85.

18. Critics who have failed to distinguish between ersatz and 'authentic' images of light in the novel have been confused by this scene. Rogmann's structural analysis, which interprets light and dark as rigidly analogous to good and evil, stumbles over the vision of Tohil: 'Man kann sich fragen, ob der Vergleich des Präsidenten mit Tohil angebracht ist. Tohil übergab seinem Stamm das Feuer, überliess es anderen Stämmen aber nur gegen Menschopfer. Der Präsident scheint dem eigenen Volk nichts zu geben, und doch verlangt er von diesem ganzen Volk Opfer' (Horst Rogmann, *Narrative Strukturen und »magischer Realismus« in den ersten Romanen von Miguel Angel Asturias* (Frankfurt: Verlag Peter Lang, 1978), 177). What the President has given his people is an ideology of material progress shorn of most of the human benefits such progress purports to bring; it is the willingness of the people (or the powerful portion of the people represented by the urban bourgeoisie) to accept this chimera of progress that maintains the President in power.

19. Dorita Nouhaud pushes this overestimation of the power wielded by the Indian even further, claiming that Asturias's provisional title for the novel, *Tohil*, should be accorded a validity equal to that of *El señor presidente*, 'le président sanguinaire n'étant que l'incarnation romanesque des "forces ancestrales" qui à travers la religion régissaient le monde américain, avant la conquête espagnole' ('M. le Président', 63). This approach projects the public persona of Asturias's later years onto the text, overlooking both the work's sustained critique of *ladino* norms and the Indian's marginalized role throughout the novel.

20. Asturias, *América, fábula de fábulas* (Caracas: Monte Avila Editores, 1972), 137.

21. For an examination of Cara de Angel's thwarted flight from the homeland as a paradigm of 20th-cent. Spanish American expatriate writing, see Stephen

Henighan, 'The Trapped Bachelor: Doubles and Escape, from Paris to the Post-Boom', *Bulletin of Hispanic Studies* [Glasgow] 65/2 (1998), 221–35.

22. Daniel Campion, 'Eye of Glass, Eye of Truth: Surrealism in *El señor Presidente*', *Hispanic Journal* 3/1 (Autumn 1981), 123.

23. Le Comte de Lautréamont, *Les Chants de Maldoror. Poésies I et Poésies II* (1868; Paris: Flammarion, 1990), 143.

24. 'Pour le groupe surréaliste, tel qu'il s'exprime dans le texte théorique du *Manifeste*, le modèle romanesque est le genre à fuir par excellence, celui où la copie du réel, le vraisemblable psychologique, ont force de loi' (Marie-Claire Dumas, *Robert Desnos, ou l'exploration des limites* (Paris: Klinksieck, 1980), 370). No evidence exists that Asturias read the other full-fledged novel to emerge from Surrealism during this period, André Breton's *Nadja* (1928).

25. Karl-D. Uitti, 'Remy de Gourmont et le monde hispanique', *Romanische Forschungen* 72/1–2 (1960): for Gourmont's influence on Darío, see pp. 64–6; for 'Lettres Latino-Américaines', see p. 68.

26. The absorption of Gourmont's unrelentingly élitist aesthetic could prove dangerous to Spanish American writers who construed themselves as being engaged in 'acquiring the light' of Parisian culture, encouraging flight from Spanish-American realities into the *preciosismo* that plagued some of Darío's work. The narrator of *Sixtine* expresses Gourmont's aesthetic in uncompromising terms: 'Zola et d'autres peuvent continuer de cataloguer leurs animaux inférieurs, nous n'y prenons nul interêt: ce sont d'informes créatures en train d'acquérir la lumière, des intelligences chrysalidées: peu nous importe la qualité des soûleries dont ils se gorgent et les prurits qui font craquer la virginité de leurs filles. Ce qui n'est pas intellectuel nous est étranger' (Gourmont, *Sixtine* (1890; Paris: Union Générale d'Editions, 1982), 279).

27. Cited by Karl-D. Uitti, *La Passion littéraire de Remy de Gourmont* (Paris: Presses Universitaires de France, 1962), 289.

28. Remy de Gourmont, *La Culture des idées* (Paris: Mercure de France, 1910), 45–7.

29. Louis Aragon, *Une Vague de rêves* (1924; Paris: Seghers, 1990), 21.

30. Remy de Gourmont, *Le Latin mystique* (Paris: Mercure de France, 1892), 12.

31. Carlos Navarro, 'La hipotiposis del miedo en *El señor Presidente*', in Helmy F. Giacoman, *Homenaje a Miguel Angel Asturias* (New York: Las Américas Publishing Company, Inc., 1972), 166.

32. Carlos Fuentes, *Valiente mundo nuevo: Épica, utopía y mito en la novela hispanoamericana* (Madrid: Narrativa Mondadori, 1990), 19.

33. Tzvetan Todorov, *La Conquête de l'Amérique: la question de l'autre* (Paris: Seuil, 1982), 252.

34. Cited by Blanca Asturias, 'Miguel Angel Asturias dans sa vie et son travail', *Europe* 553–4 (May–June 1975), 21.

CONCLUSION

The tension between the liberating impulses of literary innovation and the more conservative forces brought to bear by the search for a national tradition were experienced by other writers of Asturias's generation. Writing of literary debates in Buenos Aires, Beatriz Sarlo observes:

En la coyuntura estética de los años veinte, los ideologemas nacionalistas son producidos por los escritores de la renovación que los procesan desde la perspectiva de 'lo nuevo'. Borges discute muchas veces cuál es el criollismo aceptable y el inaceptable, de qué modo uno, inclinado al color local, es tributario del pasado, mientras que otro, al rechazar las marcas conocidas de localismo, es una invención formal-estética portadora de 'lo nuevo'.[1]

The question is highly relevant to *Hombres de maíz* (1949) since this, the first and most successful of Asturias's neo-*indigenista* novels, was probably at least partly written by the time Asturias returned to Guatemala in 1933 (most of the remainder was written in Buenos Aires in 1948–9). René Prieto reports that 'Parts I, III and VI of the novel existed wholly or in part by 1935'.[2] It is telling that Asturias wrote virtually no fiction during the twelve years (1933–44 and parts of 1946–7) of his adult life that he lived in Guatemala. His creativity returned when he settled in Buenos Aires, the capital of a country whose Native American population had been exterminated during the nineteenth century, where distance from the Mayan people and the tropics once again enabled him to filter Guatemalan reality through the optic of the marvellous. Having constituted his cultural identity outside his homeland, Asturias was able to tap into his Guatemalan cultural resources only at a distance, in Paris and then in Buenos Aires, the 'Paris of South America'.

Discussing the development of Spanish American fiction between the late 1940s and the early 1960s, the Brazilian critic Irlemar Chiampi astutely argues that 'Pode-se dizer sem risco de exagero, que a renovação da linguagem ficcional hispanoamericana tem como eixo a problematização da perspectiva narrativa e a conseqüente crítica do própio ato de contar'.[3] Chiampi's insight throws light on *Hombres de maíz*, while helping to explain the relative stagnation into which Asturias's fiction lapsed after this high-water mark. The three major novels published during this period by Asturias's contemporary Alejo Carpentier—*El reino de este mundo* (1949), *Los pasos perdidos* (1953) and *El siglo de las luces* (1962)—chart an odyssey from the distanced posture necessary to produce what Carpentier initially referred to as 'lo real maravilloso',[4] to an increasing engagement with Spanish American history and society viewed 'from within'. Carpentier's stance sacrificed the marvellous, rejecting key components of his earlier self-definition within the Parisian context, to achieve a strengthening verisimilitude and cultural rootedness.[5] Asturias, banned from returning to his country after the 1954 military coup, wafted during the same period from the early magic realist invocations of an animist tradition in *Hombres de maíz* to the wooden dogma of *La trilogía bananera* (1950–60). His dependence on maintaining a distance from Guatemalan reality in order to promote the country, within an implicitly Parisian frame, as the land of Mayan wonders eventually dulled into a kind of mechanism. On 3 March 1956, responding to his French translator Jean Camp's doubts that the play *Soluna* (1955) would work on stage ('je vois qu'elle est plus faite pour le livre que pour la scène'), Asturias wrote in his faulty French:

Je crois que ce que pourrait intéresser a un directeur de thetre d'avant-garde, dans ma comédie, c'est ce qu'elle a de magie indigene, et la possibilité de faire une belle présentation, inspirant les masques et habillements des personnes dans les scultures et codexs mayas.[6]

Even at this late stage of his career, Asturias continued to regard the primitive and the picturesque as his passport into French artistic circles. The twofold distancing imposed by political exile and the creative identity he had forged in Paris, prevented him from undertaking the transformation of narrative perspective which Chiampi presents as crucial to Carpentier and other writers of this generation.

If *Hombres de maíz* is an avant-garde national epic, conceived in the Parisian climate where Asturias expressed his bourgeois nationalism through Mayan metaphors and completed in Buenos Aires beneath the sway of similar assumptions, then its status as an ethnographic document of Mayan culture is in doubt. Yet it was in this light that Asturias himself preferred to present the novel:

En *Hombres de maíz*, como en *Mulata de tal*, he tratado de encerrarme en lo puramente indoamericano, en lo indígena y en lo americano [...] buscando dentro de la hermosa lengua española aquella que exprese mejor el sentir y el pensar de las gentes de mi raza [...]. A efecto de que, usando mi español, yo exprese lo que el indígena quiere, y ésta es una de las formas de la literatura mestiza. Es por eso que he tratado en estos libros [...] de revivir todos los mitos, de revivir todas las creencias, de recrear todas las leyendas, buscando siempre y recordando siempre lo que al pueblo oí. (López Alvarez, *Conversaciones*, 163)

Asturias's surprising characterization of the Indians as belonging to 'mi raza' indicates the extent to which his conception of his role as the author of *Hombres de maíz* remains couched in his Parisian identity as a 'Maya'. At the same time, he recognizes that in assuming the prerogative of expressing 'lo que el indígena quiere' he is writing 'literatura mestiza'. The implications of this assumption may be harsher than Asturias is willing to concede: in deciding 'lo que el indígena quiere', he is incorporating the Indian into his own ideological framework. The 'literatura mestiza' of which he speaks is a literature in which Indians act out *mestizo* preoccupations. Gordon Brotherston captures the continuity between the traits attributed to Indians by Asturias in *El problema social del indio* and his dramatization of Gaspar Ilóm in *Hombres de maíz*:

The manner in which Ilóm is bound by his beliefs-superstitions as a primitive agriculturist; the amazing stimulation that a pull of alcohol gives him; the rough way he makes love to his wife; the impassive, almost ceremonial deliberation with which he picks off the *ladinos*, as if they were so many sacrificial victims: all these traits are meticulously described as characteristics of Indians in Asturias's thesis, though as evidence for a different overall argument.[7]

It is hardly surprising that Asturias's vision of the Maya remained static. He almost certainly received little exposure to Mayan people during his residence in Guatemala from 1933 to 1944 (he was living in Guatemala City, at that time largely a *ladino* preserve). Indigenous peoples, for him, continued to mean those he had encountered as a child, primarily during his three years in Salamá. (Martin reports that in later childhood Asturias met 'arrieros y campesinos'[8] on the patio of his father's import business in Guatemala City; it is unclear to what extent these people maintained a Mayan culture.) A crucial fact about Asturias's encounter with Guatemala's indigenous peoples, almost invariably overlooked, is that the meeting did not take place in the North-West Highlands, where most of the country's Native population is concentrated and where Mayan people form an oppressed but indomitable majority. Asturias's discovery of the Maya occurred in the ranching district of Baja Verapaz, east of the capital— one of the few regions of the country where indigenous Guatemalans are a minority. He encountered the Maya, therefore, in a situation conducive to his imagining them as an unthreatening, potentially malleable component in a nationalist pageant. The essential fact about the Maya for Asturias is that they are a people who have lost control of their land. In this they resemble the impotent Guatemalan bourgeoisie, its suzerainty over the national territory gutted by years of bad deals with foreign capital made on its behalf by despots subservient to Washington. The equation of dispossessed Maya with the dispossession of Guatemala as a national entity, though submerged, is the ruling assumption of *Hombres de maíz*.

In writing *El señor presidente*, Asturias shifted his identification from the urban *ladino* milieu to that of the autochthonous darkness of the countryside. He had become the 'Gran Lengua', his Guatemalan-ness channelled through indigenous culture. Thus, in *Hombres de maíz*, Asturias resorts to copious evocation of a 'local' culture as the most effective means of generating a national allegory. The slippage from 'Mayan' to 'Guatemalan', observed by a number of critics, begins with the characters' language. Luis Cardoza y Aragón writes:

Los indios para hablar como Asturias escribe habrían menester de vasta cultura. No es una lengua de los indios: es un esforzado lenguaje de barriadas desválidas; el coctel es más bien de mestizos 'homéricos'. El pintoresquismo (en lo que sea) no lo entiendo como enraizamiento específico: lo entiendo como forma de alarde nacionalista. (*Miguel Angel Asturias*, 90)

One of Asturias's achievements in *Hombres de maíz* is to pave the road to the Boom's development of a literary language capable of rendering national realities with immediacy; a language mimetic of autochthonous speech, yet crisp, poetic and free of the tedious transcriptions of *costumbrismo*. As Rama writes: 'El gran salto que, en materia lingüística, en esta línea de la utilización del habla espontánea y popular, se ha producido [...] es aquel por el cual el escritor ha ingresado al mismo lenguaje de sus personajes' (*La novela*, 62–3). When Asturias uses a word like 'mesmo' in his narrative (*HM*, 25), he is validating a non-standard Spanish, opening the way to the freer, more untrammelled language of, for example, Mario Vargas Llosa's *La casa verde* (1965) or José Donoso's *El lugar sin limités* (1966). Vargas Llosa writes: 'Asturias emplea un vocabulario maniáticamente "local", pero este lenguaje no es descriptivista, no está elegido para retratar un habla viva, sino por razones poéticas y plásticas, incluso herméticas'.[9] Notwithstanding the disagreement between Rama and Vargas Llosa over the spontaneity of poeticized local diction, there is little doubt that Asturias's language is both carefully manicured and broadly mimetic of rural *ladino* speech. But this is not the creation of a writer immersed in Mayan concerns. As Martin Lienhard emphasizes, the motivating force behind the creation of this language is ladino nationalism:

El mundo de esta novela, considerado en general por los lectores como 'maya', es en realidad un mundo imaginario o mítico, no por tener que ver con alguna mitología maya en el sentido que dan los etnólogos a esta palabra, sino por constituir mediante la escritura, a partir de elementos dispersos y heterogéneos, un mito literario *ladino*, guatemalteco, tendencialmente nacional. ('La legitimación', 118–19)

In a later article, Lienhard refines his analysis, bringing it to bear on the language spoken by Asturias's indigenous characters:

Los personajes caracterizados como 'indígenas' [...] no se distinguen siempre claramente, en términos de lenguaje, de los 'ladinos'. El propio 'héroe mítico' Gaspar Ilóm, al dirigirse a su esposa, se expresa en un 'español guatemalteco' inverosímil en el contexto socio-cultural arcaico del comienzo de la novela: "Ve, Piojosa, diacún rato va a empezar la bulla" [...]. El hecho de atribuir a los personajes indígenas, aún cuando dialogan entre iguales, un sociolecto hispánico, tiende sin duda alguna a borrar su especificidad: los indios, al parecer, se han vuelto definitivamente "guatemaltecos".[10]

Yet, as Homi K. Bhabha has observed, the practice of domination makes a language hybrid.[11] The price of Asturias's enlistment of Mayan realities into the assertion of Guatemalan nationhood is that he must write in a literary language which, though *ladino*, remains studded with words of Mayan derivation; his language *ladino*izes his characters at the risk of alienating *ladino* (and foreign) readers.[12]

Hombres de maíz, though completed elsewhere, represents the final instalment in Asturias's Parisian *obra*. The novel's *ladino* nationalism falls into relief when the book is contrasted with Asturias's late travel book, *Rumania: su nueva imagen* (1964), in which, as in *Hombres de maíz*, modernization is seen to destroy forests and an ancestral rural culture. The novel situates the Guatemalan 'alma nacional' within the trees themselves, which the Maya regard as holy, while the rapacious *maiceros* slash and burn them: 'De entrada se llevaron los maiceros por delante con sus quemas y sus hachas en selvas abuelas de la sombra, doscientas mil jóvenes ceibas de mil años' (*HM*, 24). The novel's opening scene, where Gaspar Ilóm decides that he must go to war to defend the land, establishes the Maya's interpenetration with nature: 'Lo que hablaba el Gaspar ya viejo, era monte. Lo que pensaba era monte recordado, no era pelo nuevo. De las orejas le salía el pensamiento a oír el ganado que le pasaba encima' (*HM*, 8). In *Rumania*, by contrast, Asturias launches into a fervid description of the destruction of woods and wildlife along the Bristriţa River in the wake of the construction of a dam:

Estaban levantando aquella gigantesca mole de hierro y cemento. Más hombres. Cada vez más hombres. Era necesario. No podía detenerse la fundición.

Y más cemento y más hierro, y más piedra triturada. Camiones, trenes de camiones con el zumbar de sus motores, zumbido de grandes insectos, comparados con el ruido de roedores y el cañeono incesante de la dinamita.

Los árboles caían como borrachos, al faltarles el piso que huía bajo sus raíces, al remover las montañas. Otros eran traídos, para formar con ellos barreras momentáneas. Madera. Madera y más madera para los encoframientos.[13]

These trees, it is clear, do not have souls. They are simply wood. A similar contradiction of Asturias's animist ideology arises in his indulgent description of the peasants whose land disappears beneath the water backed up by the dam:

Hora por hora subía el nivel. No tan rápidamente, como los constructores hubieran querido. Sí, demasiado para los ojos de los viejos campesinos que miraban desaparecer terrenos que sus pies hollaron, donde sus ganados pastaron, por dónde subían y bajaban caminos de montañas. Los árboles del fondo ahogados, en el agua agitando sus ramas, como brazos. Allí quedarían sepultados. Decían adiós.

Un lago, sí, un lago.

Sólo un poeta pudo hacer esto. ¿Un poeta? Pues lo es, según confesión propia del ingeniero que planeó y dirigió estas obras. (*Rumania*, 146)

Asturias presents the points of view of both peasants and builders, but opts firmly for that of the engineers. The peasants are presented as 'viejos'. Their attachment to the land is depicted as understandable yet outmoded. Neither land nor trees are invested with spiritual significance; the trees drowned beneath the flood are portrayed as waving goodbye to the peasants before being decently 'sepultados'. Where the 'ganado' passing through Gaspar Ilóm's head aroused his consciousness of his lost land, here the cattle possess no significance beyond that of having occupied the flooded pasture. The breakdown of Asturias's stated ideology is startling. The contradiction between his descriptions of the irruption of modernization into the rural world in Guatemala and in Romania respectively appears to stem from his perception that the Romanian poet-engineers are carrying out the national will of an autonomous people, while in *Hombres de maíz* the *maiceros* are agents of foreign capital.[14] The Romanians, in Asturias's depiction, have achieved the fulfilment which a series of political catastrophes—from the dictatorships of Estrada Cabrera and Ubico during the first half of the century, to the 1954 military coup and the savage, intermittent civil war that raged in Guatemala from the early 1960s to the late 1990s—denied to the bourgeois *ladinos* of Asturias's generation: they are bringing to fruition their nation's 'alma nacional'. Their liberation affords them the twofold gratification of self-realization in both professional and artistic spheres.

Asturias's final novels, the two-volume autobiographical sequence consisting of *Viernes de Dolores* (1972) and its projected successor *Dos veces bastardo* (left incomplete and unpublished at his death), delve into the origins of his generation's ideology, limitations and failings. The burden of belonging to the *ladino* class of the Guatemalan nation weighs heavily upon the youthful characters. On the final page of *Viernes de Dolores*, the protagonist Ricardo, like Asturias himself, discovers that his father has delivered him from facing the consequences of his deepening dissidence from the laws of his society by buying him a steamer ticket to Liverpool. Ricardo resolves to renounce his recently earned law degree, then wonders whether it is possible for him to shed this defining qualification of the bourgeois *ladino* (*Viernes de Dolores*, 312–3). This doubt, appearing in the final scene of Asturias's last completed novel, illustrates both the roots and the tenacity of the cultural identity Asturias constructed for himself during his years in Paris. In his art, as in his life, Asturias's role as the guardian of the Guatemalan 'alma nacional' remained inescapable.

Notes to Conclusion

1. Beatriz Sarlo, *Una modernidad periférica: Buenos Aires 1920 y 1930* (Buenos Aires: Nueva Visión, 1988), 98.
2. Prieto, *Archeology of Return*, 91. One section of what became *Hombres de maíz* was published as early as 1933 in *Le Phare de Neuilly* as 'Le sorcier aux mains noires'. See Asturias, *Hombres de maíz* (1949; Nanterre: Centre de Recherches Latino-Américaines, 1992), 418–22. Henceforth *HM*.
3. Irlemar Chiampi, *O Realismo Maravilhoso: Forma e Ideologia no Romance Hispano-Americano* (São Paulo: Editora Perspectiva, 1980), 72.
4. Alejo Carpentier, 'Prólogo', *El reino de este mundo* (1949; Mexico, D.F.: Compañía General de Ediciones, 1973), 7–17.
5. For a discussion of the significance of Carpentier's battle with his Parisian legacy to the later development of Spanish American fiction, see Stephen Henighan, 'The Pope's Errant Son: Breton and Alejo Carpentier', in *André Breton: The Power of Language*, ed. Ramona D. Fotiade (Exeter: Elm Bank Press, 2000).
6. Le Fonds Asturias, Bibliothèque nationale, Paris. Correspondance: Dossier Jean Camp.
7. Gordon Brotherston, *The Emergence of the Latin American Novel* (Cambridge: Cambridge University Press, 1977), 30.
8. Gerald Martin, 'Cronología', in Asturias, *HM*, 461.
9. Vargas Llosa, 'Una nueva lectura de *Hombres de maíz*', in Asturias, *HM*, 652.
10. Martin Lienhard, 'Antes y después de *Hombres de maíz*: La literatura ladina y el mundo indígena en el área maya', in Asturias, *HM*, 581.
11. Bhabha writes that 'the word of divine authority is deeply flawed by the assertion of the indigenous sign, and in the very practice of domination the language of the master becomes hybrid' (*The Location of Culture* (London and New York: Routledge, 1994), 33).
12. This *ladino* portrait of the Maya remains the favoured lens through which to mediate European perceptions of Mayan culture. Elisabeth Burgos, the editor of Rigoberta Menchú's memoirs, heads many chapters with quotes from *Hombres de maíz*. Thus the significance of the words of the Quiché radical Menchú (who does not mention Asturias and displays no awareness, at this early stage of her career, of Asturias's work or existence) is pre-programmed and pre-defined by the liberal *ladino* Asturias's conception of Mayan culture. See Elisabeth Burgos (ed.), *Me llamo Rigoberta Menchú y así me nació la conciencia* (Barcelona: Argos Vergara, 1983).
13. Asturias, *Rumania: su nueva imagen* (Xalapa: Universidad Veracruzana, 1964), 146.
14. For a discussion of Asturias's relationship with Romania and his uses of Romanian imagery at different stages of his career, see Stephen Henighan, 'Lands of Corn: Guatemalan-Romanian Analogies in the Work of Miguel Angel Asturias', *Romance Studies* 29 (Spring 1997), 85–96.

BIBLIOGRAPHY

I: Works by Miguel Angel Asturias

A. Books

El alhajadito (Buenos Aires: Editorial Goyanarte, 1961).

América, fábula de fábulas, y otros ensayos (Caracas: Monte Avila Editores, 1972).

El árbol de la cruz, ed. Aline Jacquart and Amos Segala (Nanterre: Centre de Recherches Latino-Américaines, 1993).

La arquitectura de la vida nueva (Guatemala: Editores Goubaud & Cia., 1928).

Clarivigilia primaveral (Buenos Aires: Editorial Losada, 1965).

El espejo de lida sal (Mexico: Siglo Veintiuno Editores, 1967).

Hombres de maíz, ed. Gerald Martin (1949; Nanterre: Centre de Recherches Latino-Américaines, 1992).

Latinoamérica y otros ensayos (Madrid: Guadiana de Publicaciones, 1968).

Leyendas de Guatemala (1930; Buenos Aires: Editorial Losada, 1957).

Maladrón (Buenos Aires: Editorial Losada, 1969).

Mulata de tal (Buenos Aires: Editorial Losada, 1963).

La novela latinoamericana testimonio de una época (Stockholm: The Nobel Foundation, 1968).

Novelas y cuentos de juventud, ed. Claude Couffon (Paris: Centre de Recherches de l'Institut d'Etudes Hispaniques, 1971).

Los ojos de los enterrados (1960; Madrid: Alianza Editorial, 1982).

El Papa verde (1954; Barcelona: Salvat Editores, 1971).

París 1924–1933. Periodismo y creación literaria, ed. Amos Segala (Nanterre: Centre de Recherches Latino-Américaines, 1988).

El problema social del indio y otros textos, ed. Claude Couffon (Paris: Centre de Recherches de l'Institut d'Etudes Hispaniques, 1971).

Rumania: su nueva imagen (Xalapa: Universidad Veracruzana, 1964).

El señor presidente (1946; Buenos Aires: Editorial Losada, 1948).

Soluna (Buenos Aires: Ediciones Losange, 1955).

Tres de cuatro soles (Paris-Mexico, D.F.: Editions Klinksieck/Fondo de Cultura Económica, 1977).

Viento fuerte (Buenos Aires: Editorial Losada, 1950).

Viernes de dolores (Buenos Aires: Editorial Losada, 1972).

Week-End en Guatemala (Buenos Aires: Editorial Goyanarte, 1956).
(with Pablo Neruda) *Comiendo en Hungría* (Barcelona: Editorial Lumen, 1969).

B. Uncollected articles

'Préface à la poésie de Léopold Sedar Senghor', *Europe* 553–4 (May–June 1975), 40–5.

C. Notebooks and letters

Le Fonds Asturias. Bibliothèque nationale, Paris.

D. Translation

(with J. M. González de Mendoza) *Los Dioses, los Héroes y los Hombres de Guatemala Antigua, o El libro del consejo, Popol-Vuh, de los indios Quichés. Traducción de la versión francesa del Profesor Georges Raynaud* (Paris: Editorial París-America, 1927).

II: Primary Sources: French Literature

APOLLINAIRE, GUILLAUME, *Les onze mille verges* (1907; Paris: Editions J'ai Lu, 1973).
ARAGON, LOUIS, *Le Paysan de Paris* (Paris: Gallimard, 1926).
—— *Une Vague de Rêves* (1924; Paris: Editions Seghers, 1990).
BRETON, ANDRÉ, *Manifestes du Surréalisme* (Paris: Jean-Jacques Pauvert, 1962).
—— *Nadja* (1928; Paris: Gallimard, 1963).
—— *Œuvres complètes, Volume I* (Paris: NRF/ Gallimard, 1988).
—— *Les Pas perdus* (1924; Paris: NRF/ Gallimard, 1969).
COMTE, AUGUSTE, *Politique d'Auguste Comte*, ed. Pierre Arnaud (Paris: Armand Colin, 1965).
DESNOS, ROBERT, *Cinema* (Paris: Gallimard, 1966).
—— *Destinée Arbitraire* (Paris: Gallimard, 1975).
—— *La liberté ou l'amour! suivi de Deuil pour Deuil* (Paris: Gallimard, 1962).
—— *Nouvelles Hébrides et autres textes, 1922–1930* (Paris: Gallimard, 1978).
ELUARD, PAUL, *Anthologie Eluard*, ed. Clive Scott (London: Methuen, 1983).
GOURMONT, REMY DE, *La Culture des Idées* (Paris: Mercure de France, 1910).
—— *Le Latin mystique* (Paris: Mercure de France, 1892).
—— *Le Problème du Style* (Paris: Mercure de France, 1902).
—— *Sixtine. Roman de la vie cérébrale* (1890; Paris: Union Générale d'Editions, 1982).

LAUTRÉAMONT, LE COMTE DE, *Les Chants de Maldoror. Poésies I et II* (1868; Paris: Flammarion, 1990).

LE BON, GUSTAVE, *Les Lois psychologiques de l'évolution des peuples* (Paris: Félix Alcan, Editeur, 1894).

MALRAUX, ANDRÉ, *La Voie royale* (1930; Paris: Grasset, 1969).

III: Critical Works and Other Secondary Sources

A. Books

ALBIZÚREZ PALMA, FRANCISCO, *La novela de Asturias* (Guatemala: Editorial Universitaria, 1975).

ARIAS, ARTURO, *Ideología, literatura y sociedad durante la revolución guatemalteca 1944–1954* (La Habana: Casa de las Américas, 1979).

AUDOIN, PHILIPPE, *Les Surréalistes* (Paris: Editions du Seuil, 1973).

AUER-RAMANISA, BEBY, *Miguel Angel Asturias et la révolution guatemaltèque: étude socio-politique de trois romans* (Paris: Editions anthropos, 1981).

BARRERA VÁSQUEZ, ALFREDO, and RENDÓN, SILVIA (eds.), *El Libro de los Libros de Chilam Balam* (Mexico: Fondo de Cultura Económica, 1948).

BELLINI, GIUSEPPE, *La narrativa di Miguel Angel Asturias* (Milano: Istituto Editoriale Cisalpino, 1966).

BETHELL, LESLIE (ed.), *The Cambridge History of Latin America,* Vol. V: *c.1870 to 1930* (Cambridge: Cambridge University Press, 1986).

BEVERLEY, JOHN, and ZIMMERMAN, MARC, *Literature and Politics in the Central American Revolutions* (Austin: University of Texas Press, 1990).

BHABHA, HOMI K., *The Location of Culture* (London and New York: Routledge, 1994).

BLOOM, HAROLD, *The Anxiety of Influence: A Theory of Poetry* (London: Oxford University Press, 1973).

BOWIE, MALCOLM, *Lacan* (Cambridge, Mass.: Harvard University Press, 1991).

BROTHERSTON, GORDON, *The Emergence of the Latin American Novel* (Cambridge: Cambridge University Press, 1977).

BURGOS, ELISABETH (ed.), *Me llamo Rigoberta Menchú y así me nació la conciencia* (Barcelona: Argos Vergara, 1983).

CALLAN, RICHARD J, *Miguel Angel Asturias* (New York: Twayne Publishers, 1970).

CARDOZA Y ARAGÓN, LUIS, *Miguel Angel Asturias: casi novela* (Mexico, D.F.: Ediciones Era, 1991).

—— *El Río: Novelas de caballería* (Mexico: Fondo de Cultura Económica, 1986).

CARPENTIER, ALEJO, *Crónicas,* 2 vols. (La Habana: Editorial Arte y Literatura, 1976).

—— *Ecue-Yamba-O* (1933; Barcelona: Editorial Bruguera, 1979).

—— *La novela latinoamericana en vísperas de un nuevo siglo* (Mexico, D.F.: Siglo Veintiuno Editores, 1981).

—— *El recurso del método* (1974; Mexico, D.F.: Siglo Veintiuno Editores, 1988).

—— *El reino de este mundo* (1949; Mexico, D.F.: Compañía General de Ediciones, 1973).

—— *Tientos, diferencias y otros ensayos* (Barcelona: Plaza y Janés Editores, 1984).

CARRERA, MARIO ALBERTO, *¿Cómo era Miguel Angel Asturias?* (Guatemala: Universidad de San Carlos, 1975).

CASTELPOGGI, ATILIO JORGE, *Miguel Angel Asturias* (Buenos Aires: Editorial La Mandrágora, 1961).

CEREZO DARDÓN, HUGO and ESTRADA, RICARDO, AGUADO-ANDREUT, SALVADOR, PUTZEYS, GUILLERMO and ALBIZÚREZ, FRANCISCO, *Coloquio con Miguel Angel Asturias* (Guatemala: Editorial Universitaria Guatemala, 1968).

CHÉNIEUX-GENDRON, JACQUELINE, *Le Surréalisme* (Paris: Presses Universitaires de France, 1984).

CHEYMOL, MARC, *Miguel Angel Asturias dans le Paris des années folles* (Grenoble: Presses Universitaires de Grenoble, 1987).

CHIAMPI, IRLEMAR, *O Realismo Maravilhoso: Forma e Ideologia no Romance Hispano-Americano* (São Paulo: Editora Perspectiva, 1980).

COUFFON, CLAUDE, *Miguel Angel Asturias* (Paris: Editions Seghers, 1970).

DELEUZE, GILLES, and GUATTARI, FÉLIX, *Kafka, pour une littérature mineure* (Paris: Les Editions de Minuit, 1975).

DUMAS, MARIE-CLAIRE, *Robert Desnos, ou l'exploration des limites* (Paris: Librairie Klincksieck, 1980).

FOTIADE, RAMONA D. (ed.), *André Breton: The Power of Language* (Exeter: Elm Bank Press, 2000).

FRANCO, JEAN, *An Introduction to Spanish-American Literature* (Cambridge: Cambridge University Press, 1969).

—— *The Modern Culture of Latin America: Society and the Artist* (London: Pall Mall Press, 1967).

FUENTES, CARLOS, *La nueva novela hispanoamericana* (Mexico: Joaquín Mortiz, 1969).

—— *Valiente mundo nuevo: épica, utopía y mito en la novela hispanoamericana* (Madrid: Narrativa Mondadori, 1990).

GALLEGOS, RÓMULO, *Doña Bárbara* (1929; Madrid: Espasa-Calpe, 1975).

GIACOMAN, HELMY F. (ed.), *Homenaje a Miguel Angel Asturias* (New York: Las Américas Publishing Company, Inc., 1972).

GÓMEZ CARRILLO, ENRIQUE, *Treinta Años de mi vida*, 3 vols. (Buenos Aires: Casa Vaccaro, 1921).

GONZÁLEZ, ANÍBAL, *Journalism and the Development of Spanish American Narrative* (Cambridge: Cambridge University Press, 1993).

GUIBERT, RITA, *Seven Voices: Seven Latin American Writers Talk* (New York: Alfred A. Knopf, 1972).

GUIOL-BENASSAYA, ELYETTE, *La Presse face au Surréalisme de 1925 à 1938* (Paris: Editions du Centre National de la Recherche Scientifique, 1982).

HARSS, LUIS, *Los nuestros* (Buenos Aires: Editorial Sudamericana, 1973).

HEMINGWAY, ERNEST, *A Moveable Feast* (London: Jonathan Cape, 1964).

——— *The Sun Also Rises* (1926; London: Arrow Books, 1994).

HENRÍQUEZ UREÑA, MAX, *Breve historia del modernismo* (Mexico: Fondo de Cultura Económica, 1954).

HOARE, QUINTON, and NOWELL SMITH, GEOFFREY (eds.), *Selections from the Prison Notebooks of Antonio Gramsci* (London: Lawrence and Wishart, 1971).

ICAZA, JORGE, *Huasipungo* (1934; Buenos Aires: Editorial Losada, 1953).

JACK, BELINDA ELIZABETH, *Negritude and Literary Criticism: The History and Theory of 'Negro-African' Literature in French* (Westport, Conn. and London: Greenwood Press, 1996).

KING, JOHN (ed.), *Modern Latin American Fiction: A Survey* (London: Faber and Faber, 1987).

KRISTEVA, JULIA, *Sémeiotiké. Recherches pour une sémanalyse* (Paris: Editions du Seuil, 1978).

LACAN, JACQUES, *Ecrits I* and *Ecrits II* (Paris: Editions du Seuil, 1966).

LEÓN HILL, ELADIA, *Miguel Angel Asturias: Lo ancestral en su obra literaria* (New York: Eliseo Torres & Sons, 1972).

LÓPEZ ALVAREZ, LUIS, *Conversaciones con Miguel Angel Asturias* (Madrid: Editorial Magisterio Español, 1974).

LORAND DE OLAZAGASTI, ADELAIDA, *El indio en la narrativa guatemalteca* (San Juan: Editorial Universitaria–Universidad de Puerto Rico, 1968).

LORENZ, GÜNTER W., *Miguel Angel Asturias: Porträt und Poesie* (Bonn: Luchterhand, 1968).

MARTIN, GERALD, *Journeys through the Labyrinth: Latin American Fiction in the Twentieth Century* (London–New York: Verso, 1989).

MENESES, CARLOS, *Miguel Angel Asturias* (Madrid: Ediciones Júcar, 1975).

MENTON, SEYMOUR, *Historia crítica de la novela guatemalteca* (Guatemala: Editorial Universitaria, 1960).

MOLLOY, SYLVIA, *La Diffusion de la littérature hispano-américaine en France au XXe siècle* (Paris: Presses Universitaires de France, 1972).

MUÑOZ, BRAULIO, *Sons of the Wind: The Search for Identity in Spanish American Indian Literature* (New Brunswick, N. J.: Rutgers University Press, 1982).

NADEAU, MAURICE, *Histoire du Surréalisme* (Paris: Editions du Seuil, 1945).

—— *Histoire du Surréalisme II: Documents Surréalistes* (Paris: Editions du Seuil, 1948).

NOUHAUD, DORITA, *Miguel Angel Asturias, l'écriture antérieure* (Paris: L'Harmattan, 1991).

PATOUT, PAULETTE (ed.), *Correspondance Valéry Larbaud/Alfonso Reyes, 1923–1952* (Paris: Librairie Marcel Didier, 1972).

—— *Alfonso Reyes et la France* (Paris: Klincksieck, 1978).

PÉREZ-BRIGNOLI, HECTOR, *A Brief History of Central America* (Berkeley: University of California Press, 1989).

PILÓN, MARTA, *Miguel Angel Asturias: Semblanza para el estudio de su vida y obra con una selección de poemas y prosas* (Guatemala: Cultura Centroamericana, 1968).

PINILLOS IGLESIAS, MARÍA DE LAS NIEVES (ed.), *Manuel Ugarte* (Madrid: Ediciones de Cultura Hispánica, 1989).

PRIETO, RENÉ, *Miguel Angel Asturias's Archeology of Return* (Cambridge: Cambridge University Press, 1993).

RAMA, ANGEL, *La novela en América Latina: Panoramas, 1920–1980* (Bogotá: Procultura/Instituto Colombiano de Cultura, 1982).

RANGEL, CARLOS, *Del buen salvaje al buen revolucionario* (Caracas: Monte Avila Editores, 1977).

RECINOS, ADRIAN (ed.), *Popol Vuh: Las antiguas historias del Quiché* (San José: Editorial Universitaria Centroamericana, 1977).

RODRÍGUEZ, TERESITA, *La problemática de la identidad en* El Señor Presidente *de Miguel Angel Asturias* (Amsterdam–Atlanta: Editions Rodophi, 1989).

ROGMANN, HORST, *Narrative Strukturen und »magischer Realismus« in den ersten Romanen von Miguel Angel Asturias* (Frankfurt: Verlag Peter Lang, 1978).

ROYANO GUTIÉRREZ, LOURDES, *Las novelas de Miguel Angel Asturias desde la teoría de la recepción* (Valladolid: Secretario de Publicaciones/Universidad de Valladolid, 1993).

RUY SÁNCHEZ, ALBERTO, *Una introducción a Octavio Paz* (Mexico, D.F.: Editorial Joaquín Mortiz, 1990).

SÁENZ, JIMENA, *Genio y figura de Miguel Angel Asturias* (Buenos Aires: Editorial Universitaria de Buenos Aires, 1974).

SAID, EDWARD W., *Culture and Imperialism* (London: Chatto & Windus, 1993).

—— *Orientalism* (London: Routledge & Kegan Paul, 1978).

SAINT-LU, JEAN-MARIE (ed.), *Co-Textes No. 7: Miguel Angel Asturias* (Montpellier: Presses de l'Imprimerie de Recherche—Université Paul-Valéry, 1984).

SARLO, BEATRIZ, *Una modernidad periférica: Buenos Aires 1920 y 1930* (Buenos Aires: Ediciones Nueva Visión, 1988).

SCHLESINGER, STEPHEN, and KINZER, STEPHEN, *Bitter Fruit: The Untold Story of the American Coup in Guatemala* (Garden City, New York: Doubleday, 1982).

SMITH, PAUL JULIAN, *Representing the Other: 'Race', Text and Gender in Spanish and Spanish American Narrative* (Oxford: Clarendon Press, 1992).

SOUPAULT, PHILIPPE, *Mémoires de l'Oubli, 1914–1923* (Paris: Lachenal & Ritter, 1981).

—— *Mémoires de l'Oubli, 1923–1926* (Paris: Lachenal & Ritter, 1986).

SWANSON, PHILIP (ed.), *Landmarks in Modern Latin American Fiction* (London and New York: Routledge, 1990).

TODOROV, TZVETAN, *La Conquête de l'Amérique: La question de l'autre* (Paris: Editions du Seuil, 1982).

UGARTE, MANUEL, *Escritores Iberoamericanos de 1900* (Santiago de Chile: Ediciones Orbe, 1943).

—— *El porvenir de la América Latina* (Valencia: F. Sempere y Compañía, 1910).

UITTI, KARL-D., *La Passion littéraire de Remy de Gourmont* (Paris: Presses Universitaires de France, 1962).

USLAR PIETRI, ARTURO, *Fantasmas de dos mundos* (Barcelona: Seix Barral, 1979).

—— *Las lanzas coloradas y cuentos selectos* (Caracas: Biblioteca Ayacucho, 1979).

VALLE-INCLÁN, RAMÓN DEL, *Tirano Banderas: Novela de tierra caliente* (1937; Madrid: Espasa-Calpe, 1965).

VARGAS LLOSA, MARIO, *El pez en el agua* (Barcelona: Seix Barral, 1993).

—— *La señorita de Tacna* (Barcelona: Seix Barral, 1981).

VASCONCELOS, JOSÉ, *Obras Completas, II* (Mexico: Libreros Mexicanos Unidos, 1958).

VERDUGO, IBER, *El carácter de la literatura hispanoamericana y la novelística de Miguel Angel Asturias* (Guatemala: Editorial Universitaria, 1968).

WENTZLAFF-EGGBERT, HARALD (ed.), *La vanguardia europea en el contexto latinoamericano* (Frankfurt: Vervuet Verlag, 1991).

WILLIAMSON, EDWIN, *The Penguin History of Latin America* (Harmondsworth: Penguin, 1992).

WRIGHT, RONALD, *Time Among the Maya: Travels in Belize, Guatemala, and Mexico* (Markham, Ontario: Penguin Books Canada, 1989).

ZIMMERMAN, MARC, *Literature and Resistance in Guatemala: Textual Modes and Cultural Politics from* El Señor Presidente *to* Rigoberta Menchú, 2 vols. (Athens, Ohio: Ohio University Center for International Studies, 1995).

B. Articles

M.D.A., 'Rodrigo Asturias: "No Debemos Pasarnos las Facturas"', *Cambio* 16 (3 Nov. 1997), 49.

ASTURIAS, BLANCA, 'Miguel Angel Asturias dans sa vie et son travail', *Europe* 553–4 (May–June 1975), 11–25.

BATAILLON, MICHEL, 'Miguel Angel Asturias et Bartolomé de las Casas', *Europe* 473 (Sept. 1968), 6–10.

BELLINI, GIUSEPPE, 'Dimensión mítica en la narrativa de Miguel Angel Asturias', *Studi di Letteratura Ispano-Americana* 22 (1991), 35–44.

BROWN, JAMES W., 'A Topology of Dread—Spatial Oppositions in *El Señor Presidente*', *Romanische Forschungen* 98/3–4 (1986), 341–52.

CAMPION, DANIEL, 'Eye of Glass, Eye of Truth: Surrealism in *El Señor Presidente*', *Hispanic Journal* 3/1 (Autumn 1981), 123–35.

DÍAZ ROZZOTTO, JAIME, 'Asturias et la vérité poétique', *Europe* 553–4 (May–June 1975), 78–89.

GUTIÉRREZ MOUAT, RICARDO, 'La letra y el letrado en *El Señor Presidente*, de Asturias', *Revista Iberoamericana* 53/140 (July–Sept. 1987), 643–50.

HENIGHAN, STEPHEN, 'Asturias's *Arquitectura*: A Novelist's First Construction', *Journal of Hispanic Research* 2–3 (Summer 1994), 385–92.

——— 'Lands of Corn: Guatemalan-Romanian Analogies in the Work of M. A. Asturias', *Romance Studies* 29 (1997), 85–96.

HIMELBLAU, JACK, 'Chronologic Deployment of Fictional Events in M. A. Asturias's *El Señor Presidente*', *Hispanic Journal* 11/1 (Spring 1990), 7–28.

——— 'Love, Self and Cosmos in the Early Works of Miguel Angel Asturias', *Kentucky Romance Quarterly* 18/3 (1971), 243–64.

——— '*El Señor Presidente*: Antecedents, Sources, and Reality', *Hispanic Review* 41/1 (Winter 1973), 43–78.

——— 'The Sociopolitical Views of Miguel Angel Asturias: 1920–1930', *Hispanofilia* 20/3 (May 1977), 61–80.

LIENHARD, MARTIN, 'La legitimación indígena en dos novelas centro-americanas', *Cuadernos Hispanoamericanos* 414 (Dec. 1984), 110–20.

LUNDKVIST, ARTUR, 'De Miguel Angel Asturias', *Europe* 553–4 (May–June 1975), 8.

MARTIN, GERALD, 'Emir Rodríguez Monegal y "Los dos Asturias"', *Revista Iberoamericana* 69 (Sept.–Dec. 1969), 505–16.

——— '*El Señor Presidente* and How to Read It', *Bulletin of Hispanic Studies* 47/3 (July 1970), 223–43.

POTTIER, BERNARD, 'Asturias et la France: une coïncidence spirituelle', *Europe* 553–4 (May–June 1975), 9.

RINCÓN, CARLOS, 'Nociones surrealistas, concepción del lenguaje y función ideológico-literaria del *realismo mágico* en Miguel Angel Asturias', *Escritura: Teoría y Crítica Literarias* 3/5–6 (Jan.–Dec. 1978), 25–62.

RODRÍGUEZ MONEGAL, EMIR, 'Los dos Asturias', *Revista Iberoamericana*. 67

(Jan.–Apr. 1969), 13–20.
—— 'Emir Rodríguez Monegal contesta a Gerald Martin', *Revista Ibero-americana* 69 (Sept.–Dec. 1969), 517–19.

ROGMANN, HORST, 'Miguel Angel Asturias, dios maya', *Escritura: Teoría y Crítica Literarias* 3/5–6 (Jan.–Dec. 1978), 11–24.

SENGHOR, LÉOPOLD SEDAR, 'Asturias et le Métis', *Europe* 553–4 (May–June 1975), 46–54.

UITTI, KARL-D., 'Remy de Gourmont et le monde hispanique', *Romanische Forschungen* 72/1–2 (1960), 51–88.

VÁSQUEZ, CARMEN, 'Miguel Angel Asturias et Robert Desnos: une amitié méconnue', *Revue de Littérature Comparée* 222 (Apr.–June 1982), 195–204.

VERDEVOYE, PAUL, 'Miguel Angel Asturias et le "nouveau roman" hispanoaméricain', *Europe* 473 (Sept. 1968), 10–15.

INDEX